Justin Hill was born in the Bahamas in 1971, grew up in England and went to university at Durham. He worked in China with VSO and is currently teaching in Eritrea, Africa's newest nation state. He has contributed articles on China to the *Guardian Weekly* and the *China Review.*

A Bend in the Yellow River

JUSTIN HILL

PHŒNIX

The publishers would like to thank
Mr Yip Wai Yee for his contribution to the Work

A Phoenix Paperback
First published in Great Britain by Phoenix House in 1997
This paperback edition published in 1998 by Phoenix,
a division of Orion Books Ltd,
Orion House, 5 Upper St Martin's Lane,
London WC2H 9EA

A CIP catalogue record for this book
is available from the British Library.

ISBN: 0 75380 114 0

Printed and bound in Great Britain by
The Guernsey Press Co Ltd,
Guernsey, Channel Islands.

In memory of my father,
Reg Jerome Hill,
30 September 1942–2 November 1994

CONTENTS

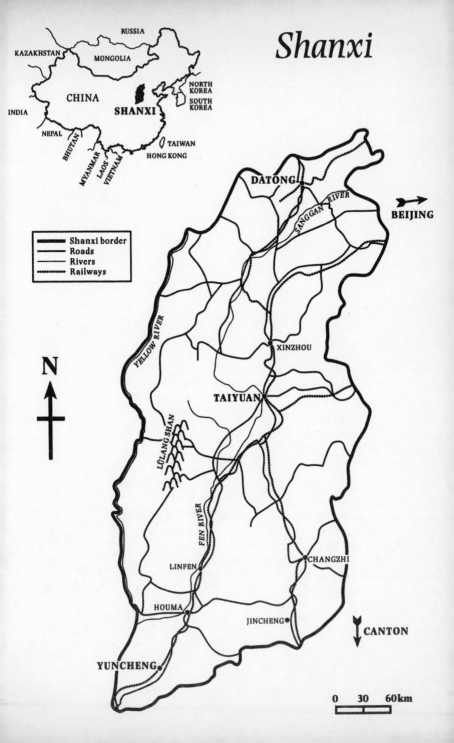

20 February 1993

Of all the places in China it seemed strange that we should end up here – at the eastern edge of Yuncheng, a small town where the people have narrow horizons between mountains and chimney stacks.

The first time Mario, my colleague, and I were driven up the long straight main road, Hedong Donglu, to our new home was after a sixteen-hour train journey inland from Beijing. Our train had rambled through sleepy stations and past peasants on terraced hillsides before arriving without warning at Yuncheng. There was a sudden scramble to get off the train with piles of luggage, then our soon-to-be colleagues seized our bags and raced across the platform to a waiting minibus. It was all we could do to follow them. After endless hours of watching the Chinese countryside roll by, frame by frame in the square of our cabin window, the sudden speed was bewildering. I had just about caught my breath back when we started out of town along Hedong Donglu.

I remember how different it was from the China of my imagination. The road was lined with squat concrete boxes, their lifeless grey walls brightened up with Chinese characters and gaudy adverts, vivid in the harsh sunlight. Each box seemed to contain a food or hardware store whose contents – sacks of rice and flour, rush mats, plastic bowls and stools, earthenware pots and aluminium kitchen utensils – had all spilt out over the pavement.

In the gutter peasants squatted selling their crops. Tomatoes, cucumbers, sweet potatoes and thick green clumps of coriander were sold from the backs of rickshaws or from sackcloth spread over the road. Here and there pool tables were lined up on the dusty pavement and men in white vests were potting the balls. As a backdrop were the dismal blocks of four-storey flats with plastic sheeting tacked over the windows. Over it all spread an enamel-blue sky.

Our minibus chugged along to the end of the road, which came to an abrupt halt at our feet. It was as if the builders had just clocked off for lunch. The tarmac crumbled away, and the fields of wheat began. Beyond the piles of rubbish the road continued in the form of an earthen path to the villages beyond. We turned sharply into a yard and with a screech of brakes came to a halt inches away from a small boy, willy out, peeing in a puddle. We had arrived.

CHAPTER ONE

Back to the Cradle

In the early mornings, when the old go through their *taiqi* routines – boxing, sword and spear – in beautiful slow motion, the sun rises up sullen and red over the heads of peasants, cycling into town along the mud track that becomes Hedong Donglu with their reed panniers full of produce to sell. Eggs carefully packed with straw, strings of garlic, cabbages and spring onions. Food shacks are set up, and their families of tables and chairs are spread along the pavement. There soyabean soup is served to the children and young couples – still rubbing sleep from their eyes and slurping loudly. Up and down the street people do plodding exercises as they beat out the early morning chill.

As the sun rises, housewives come into town with blue and red plastic baskets, out to buy fresh for the day's lunch. All shouting to each other across the street and arguing over prices. Country girls in faded padded cotton jackets come to look at the bright factory-made clothes, too expensive for them to buy, while city girls cycle past on mountain bikes from Shanghai, wearing frilly clothes in day-glo yellows, pinks and greens. Men sit comparing their motorbikes, or squat under a tree playing chess. As the sun grows hotter the old people come out of their courtyard houses to sit by the road with their walking sticks. Ancient women hobbling on their bound feet and old men with wispy white beards smoking their fags: basking like lizards in the sun, till it sets again at the opposite end of Hedong Donglu, silhouetting the post office tower and the new Communist Party offices, when they hobble back to their burrows.

Neither Guillin, with its mythical peaks, nor Hangzhou's delicate temples and lakes are more truly Chinese than Yuncheng, and this short stretch of Hedong Donglu.

In those first days as I cycled into town past the bicycle repair man – a small man with a bald head like burnished copper, huddling under a thatched awning and looking for punctures by dipping tyres in a bowl of dirty water – then the scale of it all hit me. I had travelled across the world to China, and had landed here, into this street and into the lives of these people.

On our first afternoon in Yuncheng we were summoned to an exclusive side room in the teachers' canteen for our customary welcoming banquet. All the notables of the college were there and we were given hasty introductions to the people we had met at the station. They were the Dean, Wu XiaoShan – hello – and the President's Office men, Mr Cao, Mr Zhang, and Mr Lu – hello! The President's Office, as we were soon to find out, was the administrative heartbeat of the college. It was hard to know what exactly they did – they always claimed to be terribly busy, but seemed to spend large amounts of time absent or asleep. But when we really needed their help they seldom let us down.

Dean Wu was a fifty-five-year-old man with a never-ending cigarette stub in between his yellowed fingers. He had spent two years in England just before the Cultural Revolution, when he had been recalled to China. He still remembered his old landlady's address in Sheffield.

'Mr and Mrs Williamson,' he told us. 'They had a house at 113 Everet Street. My landlady was very kind to me. They had a little son, and I used to play with him. You know he taught me much English. Surely! I was playing with a toy and he said to me, "Can I have it please?" – "*Can* I have it *please?*" In Chinese we would say, "Give it to me." He taught me all about English manners. He was a very good teacher. Surely!'

Mr Cao was a much younger man, from a different generation

to Dean Wu. Dean Wu was responsible for our teaching in the college, and Mr Cao – our *Waiban* – was responsible for everything else. Every foreigner working or studying in China has a Waiban – a 'Foreign Persons Officer' and Cao – as ours, was our official keeper – accountable for all we did in our time in China. Mr Lu was his boss, a man with a big smile who didn't speak a word of English. He beamed at me as we shook hands, and didn't let go, so that we were locked together smiling and nodding for some time. Mr Zhang was a tall well-educated man, with impeccable manners. When he spoke, to tell an anecdote or a fragment of Chinese history, then everyone listened, and remained silent until Dean Wu had finished translating for us.

At the banquet they were all quick to tell us what made Yuncheng such a special place.

'Yuncheng is in the bend of the Yellow River, the cradle of Chinese civilization,' Dean Wu began, as more and more dishes arrived and I struggled to find room to taste each of the local delicacies as they were put in front of me by the chef, who beamed with pleasure at having two foreigners to serve.

'In ancient times this area was known as *"Hedong"* which means "East of the River",' Mr Zhang continued. 'It was here that the Yellow Emperor fought his enemies and taught our Chinese people to sow and reap wheat. He was the first to make bronze money, and taught us how to raise silkworms. This is the ground from which China sprang into the world.'

I nodded, not sure what reaction was required, but no answer seemed necessary. Just my attention.

'Have you heard of Guan Yu?'

I turned back to Dean Wu.

'Guan Yu of the Three Kingdoms period?' he asked.

My answer 'no' would confuse him. Not wanting to start off on a sour note, and as they were all expecting me to say 'yes', I bluffed. 'Oh, *that* Guan Yu.'

'Yes!' Wu clapped. 'He was born in Yuncheng. At a village just outside here.'

Zhang began, and Wu stopped talking and politely waited, then translated. 'Before Liberation he was as revered as Confucius. Everywhere there was a temple to Confucius, there was

5

a temple to Guan Yu as well. Many Taiwanese and Japanese come to visit his birthplace. He was a very famous general in Chinese history, and so became the Chinese War God.'

Throughout the meal I was bombarded with facts and figures: seventy percent of all sites of historical interest in China lie in Shanxi province; Lu DongBing of the Tang dynasty was a local boy who gave up rank and position to practise Daoism and so become one of the Eight Immortals; Yang GuiFei was a beautiful girl who rose to become Imperial concubine to a Tang emperor; and Wang Wen was the founder of Chinese wash painting. The list of people was as numerous as the dishes in front of me, which were still arriving. Plates were not removed but were stacked at precarious angles on top of each other, the whole pile threatening to lurch to one side as Cao spun the table around so that we could try the Yellow River Carp, a whole carp fried in batter, with a cherry in its mouth and covered in a delicious red sauce, which was dripping into the Eight Treasure Black Rice, which in turn was dripping both sauces over the frogs legs and boiled peanuts.

'To the south of Yuncheng is the Salt Lake where storks are often seen,' Wu told us. 'In Ancient times the Emperor would come and sacrifice there. We will go and see it soon.'

Zhang spoke and Wu sucked on his cigarette – then translated. 'Si MayYing who wrote a guide for good kingship called *General Opinion on Ruling* was born in Yuncheng prefecture, in XiaXian County. He is a very famous historian in China, and lived during the Tang dynasty.'

The list just carried on. They were reciting each detail of local history, and I think they knew it all by heart. I smiled and nodded at each point till my cheeks ached with cramp.

But you don't have to stay in Yuncheng for long to realize that history is its biggest asset. Long ago the tides of history washed over China and left Yuncheng stranded.

When Kublai Khan moved the capital from Xian towards the eastern seaboard, then Yuncheng began to decline. With the intrusion of the Western powers into China and the trade they brought with them, the focus of the country shifted to the eastern and southern seaboards and the great Yangtse River –

giving birth to China's great modern cities of Tienjing, Shanghai and Canton. Now this little town and its grand history has been almost completely forgotten, except by the locals and the occasional tour group of overseas Chinese who come briefly to take photos of themselves in its run-down temples.

Yuncheng is in the southern toe of Shanxi province. Shanxi lies in the centre of north China, a dry dusty province built up on the thick loess soil, flat yellow earth meters deep that was blown here from Siberia during the last ice age, now eroded and crafted into steep gullies and terraced fields. The name 'Shanxi', meaning 'West of the Mountains', has a certain poetic charm, but is not entirely correct. 'In the Mountains' would be more exact as seventy per cent of the province is mountainous, and they hem Yuncheng in on all sides.

After rain, when the air is washed clean of dust, from my bedroom window I can see the peaks that lie to the south. Each ridge and scarp is so sharp that I can trace their line against the sky. Each village house is clearly visible and even the threads of smoke, faint blue in the sunlight, that trail up from their chimneys. But rain is rare so far inland, and usually the peaks dissolve into the opaque distance, and form a dim shadow across the horizon – obscured by the dust that turns everything apart from the immediate surroundings a milky off-white.

To the north too, on a really clear day, you can make out the shadows of mountains, but usually these are totally hidden from view. On maps all of these mountains have names but to people in the area, who never travel far enough away from home to need maps, they are simply known as the North and South Mountains.

Along the foot of the South Mountains there is the Salt Lake. It stretches twenty kilometres east to west and supports a local industry mining salt petre. On its northern side lies the city of Yuncheng.

Cycling through the countryside around Yuncheng, at first, I had an odd feeling that something was missing. Among fields of corn, melon and cotton, tractors and mules and mud brick houses – nowhere could I see an inch of unused land. All around, the yellow loess soil was ploughed and cultivated. Even the roadside verges were sown with wheat, or used to grow apple trees, while underneath the land was ploughed for garlic and spring onions. Where the rainwater had eroded the soil into deep gullies, these had been painstakingly terraced and every square metre was marked with neat furrows and green shoots of wheat.

The only land not planted were the irrigation channels, the narrow raised pathways that ran like tightropes between the square fields of crops. Without these the region would be subject to the cruel discipline of the weather, which over the centuries has brought famine again and again to Shanxi.

This is a landscape which has supported human life from its very beginnings, thousands of years of agricultural life, in a precarious existence between droughts and the rampages of the Yellow River as it floods every summer. Under the Emperors, survival was a battle against the elements *and* the landlord, and insecurity still dictates that every inch of precious soil be put to good use.

The three million or so people who live in Yuncheng prefecture are mainly peasants. Tight housing restrictions prevent them from moving to the town permanently, but with seasonal fluctuations in the agricultural workload, the peasants all flock to town seeking work: pulling loads on carts, building, labouring. In the winter when the water on the Salt Lake has receded, files of peasants pile up salt petre into banks and then pull carts by hand to the factories to be processed.

All the inhabitants of Yuncheng are still closely related to the countryside. Fifty years ago Yuncheng was little more than a village, a massive wall of pounded earth – protection against bandits – surrounding a cluttered interior of wooden and mud-brick buildings. Only after Liberation was the city developed and local peasants came to settle in town, drawn in from the surrounding areas to work in the new industries the Communists brought. Many of them had grown up in villages and were still bound by family responsibilities to those left behind –

and the ties of the agricultural calendar are still strong even amongst the urban dwellers.

The city wall was pulled down when the Communists liberated the area to symbolise the new peace and security that they brought, but you can still follow its course in the curve of the present street plan. But with investment in housing, education and industry over the last forty years Yuncheng has grown outwards in clumps, swamping the original village, and creating a city of low-rise blocks of flats.

The Old Town lies to the south, topping the slopes above the Salt Lake. As Yuncheng has developed the Old Town has become a poor suburb of the modern town. The roads are untarmacced, and are the same yellow-brown colour as the mud-brick single-storey houses that squeeze in on it from both sides. No concrete or blocks of flats here, only the traditional houses where all the doors and windows face into a courtyard and a large wooden gate keeps all intruders out.

Being the original town, this quarter has a completely different feel from the rest of Yuncheng. There are no neon signs or glitzy fairy lights. It has not benefitted from modern planning, but is a narrow and confusing network of streets. During the day children play in the shadows of their own houses, while the women of the family look on from their gateways, chatting whilst they knit, peel garlic or chop spring onions.

At night the families all stay inside and bolt shut the heavy wooden doors that are covered on the outside with pictures of Chinese gods. Put up at the New Year to bring good luck, they are left up to protect the family for the year, and now they are beginning to fade and peel off. These pictures are a 'country superstition' a student once told me. Quite often, instead of showing Chinese gods, they depict brave men of the Chinese armed services – soldiers, sailors and pilots, often with an astronaut thrown in for good luck. At night when the large wooden doors are shut, darkness envelops the street, except where brief chinks of light sneak out of the locked doorways.

Where the old and new town meet there is a grand old structure that I guess was once an old landlord's residence –

that class of people obliterated in mainland China by the Communists. It must have been a fine building once – high, long and rectangular like a church hall, with whole trunks of trees used as pillars and beams, and fragments of red paint remaining on the walls. Now it is used as a hardware store, and maybe this is the reason that it has escaped modernisation. Cast-iron stoves, pots and pans are piled up against exquisite latticed wooden windows, which are broken in places and papered over with tattered scraps of newspaper.

One time, whilst shopping, I saw that various timbers had been ripped out, and thinking the whole building was about to be knocked down I raced home and returned with my camera. To get around the back of the building I had to go into a work unit's compound, where I picked around the broken tiles and lengths of wood and took some photos, to the amazement of some locals who came to watch. One of the leaders of the work unit was called and he came over to investigate what the stranger foreigner was up to. When he realized I was a teacher in Yuncheng, and not a spy, he warmed to me – although he still evidently mistrusted my camera.

'It's a very beautiful building,' I said by way of explanation. 'How old is it?'

He conferred with some people in the crowd then turned back to face me. 'Five hundred years old,' he said.

I was taken back to his house where he assured himself that I was safe, whilst serving me tea and cigarettes, and asking me a barrage of questions.

He offered the cigarettes a fifth time and again I refused. It is something you learn early on in China, that men distribute cigarettes instead of shaking hands. Actually it is often a prelude to saying hello. He refused to believe that I didn't smoke – I was a man, wasn't I? I must therefore smoke.

'Don't be so formal! We're friends, no need for manners!' he told me, pressing the packet of cigarettes into my hands.

'No really – thank you – but I don't smoke,' I said, but it seemed that more proof was needed. 'No, you see, I like exercising, and smoking is no good for exercising.'

He didn't really believe me, and we ended our chat with me refusing to teach his five-year-old daughter English.

'Maybe when she's older,' I suggested politely.

A long time after that, with some foreign friends, I revisited the old hall, which hadn't been knocked down after all. It had been made into a church, and an iron cross had been set upon its top. In China Christianity is very much a minor religion, after Communism, Buddhism, Daoism, and (believe it or not) Islam. Inside the church the decorations were a strange combination of Chinese and Western. Illuminated pictures around the church showing the trials of Christ; the altar decorated with yellow cloth and strips of white gauze, and a blond blue-eyed Jesus looking compassionately down at our feet.

As we looked around we were intercepted by a young man in a modern baggy suit, who turned out to be the priest, and he invited us for a cup of tea in the vestibule. Strangers often invited us into their houses, out of generosity, mixed with curiosity about the foreigners. Inside it was just like any modern Chinese sitting room, with plastic-covered sofas and little else. A few parishioners smiled and welcomed us and filled in the history of their community.

'Christianity came to Yuncheng four hundred years ago. An Italian came spreading the Word. There has been a small group here ever since. This building used to belong to a rich landlord, who married a Christian lady. When he died, she inherited the house and made it into a church. It was shut down until recently, and we moved back here from a smaller building not far away.'

A woman came in while he was speaking, carrying a small plastic cross with a little picture of Jesus on it looking like a blond buddha, a hand raised in blessing. The priest took it, and barely pausing, blessed it, and then returned it to her. She bowed and left as he carried on.

'We are not the same as other Catholics in the world. Instead of the Pope as head of the Church, we have the Communist Party. This is the law in China.'

In China it is easy to date any building by the number of floors it has. As new technology has come in, the Chinese have learnt to build higher, but virtually all of Yuncheng's blocks of flats are four storeys or less, which makes them fairly old fashioned and out of date; a bit like Yuncheng really.

There are a few six-storey flats, rising up amongst the chimney stacks – and when we first arrived in town there was an even taller building under construction. This was the new Communist Party offices, which – face demanded it – had to be the tallest building in town. This was assured by the addition of an iron tower with a flashing light on top to add a bit of extra height to its fifteen floors.

It is also easy to tell not only the age of a building from the outside, but also what a building is used for. Residential blocks are left untiled or painted, the concrete walls drab grey, stained and dreary. Office blocks are covered in tiles that start life white, while school buildings are tiled in yellow.

The flat that we lived in was one of the drab kind, like all the others around. They were all in the same work unit, which was the college. Work units are the organisation – school, village, factory, or work place – to which each Chinese person is assigned. Our work unit was responsible for every aspect of our life: health, housing, pay, work, and general welfare.

For children their parents' work unit provides them with education, housing and healthcare. When they find work they may join a new work unit that will provide them with their own housing, childcare and pension. In a country where the rights of the group outweigh those of the individual, work units are a ready-made community, and a birth-to-grave care guarantee that with China's population growth is becoming increasingly difficult to finance.

I found living in a work unit a mixed experience – to join a large family of people was very reassuring, but stifling at the same time. There was a wonderful feeling of community, with families of three or four generations living together, and this cosy feeling was inextricably linked with a feeling of mutual support, but also with the lack of personal freedom families of any kind produce.

The work unit is also a good way of preventing massive

economic migration to the richer areas of China. It is only your work unit – and the *hukou* certificate that they provide – that entitles you to the subsidized lifestyle. Go anywhere other than your work unit and you'll have to pay the full price. Unfortunately, there are wide differences in standards between the different work units: village ones are at the bottom of the scale, and banks near the top. Schools in the Yuncheng local area are very poor – many teachers are not paid for months on end – but the banks always have enough money, as well as providing superior housing, health care and education for their workers and families. The work-unit system is good at maintaining the communities which are central to Chinese life – but with the profit-oriented criteria upon which the modern economic regimes are based it's becoming a very inefficient social structure.

Yuncheng Advanced Training College, our college, is set on the very periphery of Yuncheng, where Hedong Donglu crumbles away into the fields of wheat. Standing on my balcony I had to one side chimney stacks, the odd construction crane, and silhouettes of grey flats superimposed upon each other as they faded away to the horizon: schools, shops, houses, and office blocks – each a box of concrete. Some tall and thin, others low and squat, cubes and rectangles on a grid of roads – a city of right angles.

To the other side I could see green crops and trees which were refreshing just to look at. Amidst the haphazard cultivation, houses sprouted up at irregular intervals, sometimes congregating like mushrooms to form a small village. There was no real method in this scenery, no planning authority had worked on its design – necessity and opportunity had dictated the rural contours over the centuries. Over this scene, about three miles away, stood an old pagoda. Its upper storeys had fallen off and now the branches of a low tree stood out from its top.

It felt as if we were straddling two worlds. A modern city and centuries-old peasant agriculture – with our flat in the middle. To the left the rich bureaucrats drove cars and motor-

13

bikes, while to the right peasants ploughed the fields with a single ox or mule. Standing on my balcony I could see both worlds without even turning my head.

We were lucky that the college was so near the countryside: we could see peasants bringing their produce fresh from the fields in the early mornings for the housewives to haggle over – and for students and teachers alike it was a pleasure to turn your back on Hedong Donglu and walk out through the pile of rubbish, leaving the crowds and clamour behind. It was a common sight to see students squatting in a field of corn repeatedly drilling themselves from a textbook. Many of them felt out of place in the modern city of Yuncheng and missed the quiet lives of their villages. For others it was just a place away from their cramped dormitories and classrooms to find some peace and quiet to work in.

No doubt, in time, the city would make another push outwards in this direction – tack on another few hundred metres to the road, and the next village along would become a suburb. In the battle between old and new in China – new and modern wins hands down.

CHAPTER TWO

Lao Wai

Within minutes of lugging all our bags into our new flat there was a knocking on our open door. Our suitcases stood piled up in the hall and we hadn't even had a chance to see all the rooms ourselves when two Chinese men invited themselves in. We were two foreign teachers stranded somewhere in China, and we felt very much isolated and on our own, so we were powerless to stop them.

'Hello. You must be Justin and Mario. We are students from the Yuncheng Economic School. Teach us English, please.'

I was agog. My mind was still somewhere in Beijing trying to deal with the culture shock while my body had been sent on ahead with the luggage. Replying to their question was difficult because my brain was being stampeded by reams of new data – about the country, culture, town and people I had joined for at least the next two years. It was a struggle just to keep pace with reality so I stood uncomprehending for a few seconds. The words were clear, but I failed to register them.

'Teach us English, please.' One of the men tried again.

They must have been tipped off about the time of our arrival, and had decided to leapfrog any opposition and get in there first. If anyone would succeed with these foreigners then it would be them.

I wanted to be angry – to say 'Do you mind! I've only just arrived. I'm homesick, bewildered, excited and confused. You invite yourself into a house *I* haven't even seen yet – and then you expect me to give you an English lesson!' but I felt so dislocated that I was empty of any emotions. I just stood passive to whatever was thrown at me. Severed from our own customs and manners I was prepared to accept anything until I knew that it wasn't normal behaviour. All alone, we needed people to look after us or we'd never have fitted in, and fitting in means adapting to new customs and to their way of doing things.

In the race to get ahead in life, English was the key for them. In their eagerness to get us to teach them, I don't think we were even entirely human in their eyes. These people had never seen foreigners before in their lives, except on *Dallas* or *Dynasty*. So as foreigners in small-town China we were very much mythical figures come suddenly to life.

For us it was a rude introduction to the life we were going to lead. Here we were, only two foreigners amongst three million Chinese who all believed that by learning English they could make themselves super-rich and then go abroad and live like the people in the soaps.

This time Cao Zheng, our Waiban, was on hand to help. He came out of the bathroom where he was doing some last-minute plumbing with a hammer and leapt into action, throwing them out after a brief scuffle. They kept asking us to teach them, trying to force out that crucial 'yes' while Cao manhandled them out. The struggle turned physical and only after the door was slammed behind them did I relax.

Mario and I had joined up with VSO in a general desire to see some more of the planet before we died. Voluntary Service Overseas had always seemed to me to be a rather incongruous name – it implies a choice between here and abroad, and the word 'voluntary' conjures up images of missionary work, mud huts, and all for no wage. I have to admit that my motivation for volunteering wasn't a particularly virtuous one. I was certainly not a missionary – I did not sign up with VSO to guarantee myself a spot in Heaven – never mind anywhere else. Chinese orphans and development issues – these disturbed and upset me, but, being honest, they weren't things I'd ever lost too much sleep over.

No, I had reached that time in life when the career begins to loom larger than the exams (whichever ones they may be) and I had to choose the general course which my life would follow from then on. Sitting in my digs surrounded by old mugs of tea with rare species of fungi growing inside, I was faced with a list comprising Accounting, Teaching, Law or Management Consultancy. None were even remotely appealing as a way of filling up all my weekdays, most evenings and some weekends between now and when I reached sixty-five – and so I sat on it for a while trying to decide which I would dislike least. Then I found a VSO bookmark in a copy of *Decline and Fall* and my problem seemed, if not solved then shelved for a few years at least. I wrote to VSO to see if they needed any English teachers – and they wrote back to tell me about the development rationale behind the English teaching projects in China. The distance between China and home; the chance of doing something other than working to make someone else rich – made VSO work in China seem just the thing for me. My finals came and went – badly – I told myself that I had very cleverly burnt my bridges and filled in my VSO application form.

Mario and I shared a flat throughout our time in China. He was twenty-four and spoke English with a slight Scottish accent, having just finished two years lecturing in Spanish in Edinburgh. Not tall, but with deep green eyes and a glossy brown ponytail, he looked every inch his Chinese name – Ma LiAo – 'Proud Stallion Half a Kilometre Long.' We got on well despite the fact that we lived in such enforced physical and mental proximity, and despite the fact that he was punctual and tidy and I was not. We had come to China for roughly the same reasons – a desire to see something of the world outside our communities – although he had the added reason of having to stay outside Spain till he was thirty to avoid military conscription.

Mario and I had first met on the day of our VSO interview, before we even knew if we would be going, never mind where or with whom. The interview was held in Glasgow, and as I had to get a man to repeat himself three times before I could understand his directions to the place, I began to wonder if I would arrive safely at the interview, never mind travel to China. Inside the waiting room Mario and I had been the only non-Scots – there was a big hairy mechanic from Orkney, a librarian, a male nurse, and a few others I can't remember. Their preference for Spaniards – probably any race – over Englishmen was obvious.

Any differences between Spanish and English cultures were dwarfed by the mutual shock of Chinese culture. Compared to the Chinese with whom we lived we both had so much in common that for the first time in my life I felt a truly European citizen. But however well we got on – two Westerners alone in such a narrow society as China – we both suffered the inevitable isolation of being completely divorced from the people and worlds we each knew. There were times in Yuncheng when isolation pressed so heavily on me that I physically sickened for someone – anyone – who shared my own York-shire-centric view of the world. But it was all an incredible learning experience, and in my more lucid moments when I could remember why I'd left England, I reassured myself: I had given up home, family and country to experience another way of life.

Sharing a flat with the only other Westerner for a few hundred kilometres obviously puts some unique strains on any relationship, but Mario and I coped extremely well. We depended so much on each other at times for our sanity that I don't know how I would have coped being alone. The first way it did affect us, though, was in our decision early on not to drink alcohol except in banquets (when it was expected, and helped remove barriers between us and the hosts) or when we met up with other foreigners (when it helped us all cope with the stress of being suddenly surrounded by other Westerners). When we'd first arrived we'd had a few nights drinking the fridge out of beer. We'd talked about many things, starting with the serious, the political, the humorous – but like all drunken conversations ours spiralled down to the intimately, and – next morning – embarrassingly personal. With the enforced proximity in which we already lived, to be pouring out our deepest secrets to each other as well was just too overpowering. You can know too much about someone for comfort. Better not to drink at all.

Alcoholism is one trap that snares many ex-pats and we managed to escape that – eccentricity bordering on madness is the other, and here we weren't so good. In China we were seen as so strange that anything we did was weird, so there was a temptation to live up to that. As a completely unknown quantity you could also write your own script – act out a new part – one you could never get away with in your own peer group. Unshackled by any sobering Western influence, I led – by Western standards – a highly unusual lifestyle. The problem was that the normal and strange became completely blurred in my mind as I began to absorb Chinese attitudes and ways of thinking on top of my own, which probably contributed to the general level of surrealism that seemed to take over at times.

With no TV, radio, newspaper, bookshops – no nothing – it was important to fend off boredom and depression, and this was something we were very successful at. We actually lived in a massive subject for study: there was just so much to learn about China – language, customs, food prices, manners, art, philosophy, religion, and international postage rates – that for the first six months I don't think I ever had a spare moment. By then I had managed to persuade my parents to send me out some heavy books about China to read, which we devoured. As time went on we took up different pursuits – the universally popular ballroom dancing, basketball, photography, finally settling on *taiqi* – an art form whose perfection takes years of study.

The constant demands from people we didn't know was one of the difficulties in getting used to life in China. At any time of day or night we were the targets for attack. At any time they would telephone or come knocking and destroy our peace of mind. There is nothing more irritating than misplaced good intentions, as most of them just wanted to talk or listen to a foreigner, to ask us for help with a grammatical point, with their homework, to find out about our families – or put the phone down in a fit of giggles.

'Excuse me. I want to practise my oral English,' was a rather charmless way of starting a conversation. The poor individual would then stand there in shock. It had taken all their courage just to come up and ask that question, and now they were so overcome by the presence of a real foreigner that they quivered like a frightened animal. So in the end I ended up doing all the work in a conversation which was doomed to be dull.

For others the excitement got to be too much. My nose was too big, or my eyes were too deeply set, or maybe their blue colour unnerved them, but having made the approach, they would just giggle and turn and walk away.

In books about China I had always read of the helpfulness of the Chinese, always ready to lend assistance with an, 'Excuse me, can I help you?' or, 'Hello, sir, what country are you from?' In this case with no-one else to rescue but me, I sometimes felt that these knights-in-shining-armour followed me about waiting for a moment to pounce. I would be out exploring the local markets, using my textbook Chinese on real live people, and they would intervene – in English – breaking the spell.

When there were no aspiring English learners, or when we'd given up answering the door, we would relax on our fourth-floor balcony and overlook the lives being lived below. That lasted until we noticed all the Chinese faces in the windows of the block opposite watching us from behind curtains or through cracks in the doorways. Whenever we opened our front door the lady who lived opposite would invariably appear to sweep her doorstep or to tip her dustpan down the stairwell. She would watch our movements slyly out of the corner of her eye, or observe who was coming and going, and with whom we did things.

Walking in the street we were always the centre of attention. Girls standing in the doorways of shops would call to their friends, 'Hey, come quick, a foreigner!' and their friends would dash headlong through the doorway and fall over themselves as they pointed and waved and shouted. Mothers would pick up their children, point and say, 'Look, a foreigner!' Then the child would burst out crying. 'Don't be frightened,' the mother would coo, while I went off feeling like the Elephant Man. The peasants in town would line 'up on the street laughing or quietly curious as they watched my show: Foreigner Walks Down Street; Foreigner Stops; Foreigner Speaks Chinese; Foreigner Buys Potatoes and Cabbages; Foreigner Walks Up Street – hilarious stuff!

Whilst bargaining for food in the market against the wily salesmen, we would soon be encircled by a crowd. Curious, amused, their jostling at first felt very threatening. Our Chinese was hesitant and unsure and we were prodded, scrutinized and discussed by all around as we tried to bargain. At moments the encircling crowd would all suddenly burst out laughing at something I couldn't understand but felt was probably about me.

Once I walked into an electrical shop and I counted eleven men follow me in off the street. They pretended to look at the tape recorders as they studied every detail about me. Trying to remember it all so they could tell their children and wives and friends all about the foreigner they'd seen. I was halfway between amusement and indignation at this James Bond situation. I think their reaction would have been the same if I'd just landed from the Planet Zartob in my pink space ship with antennae sticking out of my head and I was walking up and down making strange bleeping noises. Tall, blond and blue-eyed, in China I might as well have been.

In my first week, when stardom was a new-found pleasure and still a source of amusement, I was cycling along, and as an old man drew up alongside me, his jaw dropped open in astonishment. We continued cycling together for a little while, him keeping pace with me as I tried to accelerate away. He didn't close his mouth nor blink his eyes and he looked as if he'd just come face to face with his long-dead grandfather. I smiled, said, 'Hello,' in Chinese and smiled again – but none of it registered. I tried to ignore him, laughed, and then began to feel embarrassed and a little annoyed.

I cycled faster but he followed suit and kept up alongside me, still gaping like an idiot. I went faster, and so did he. Then

21

BAM! he cycled straight into a concrete bollard. Behind, I could hear the oh!-so-satisfying sound of mangled bicycle.

The longer we stayed in Yuncheng, and began to feel at home, the more we felt angry and hurt by this seemingly ostracizing behaviour, although most of it was relatively innocent. As we settled in, our mental processes became more Chinese and we soon began to feel possessive and proud of Yuncheng, and this behaviour, understandable though it was, meant people were only seeing the differences between us. Luckily, by then I had Chinese friends whose kindness was always there to restore my faith in the nation after it had received a jolt.

A strange thing was that in the cities it was the peasants who were the most fascinated by me; out in the countryside they were unperturbed by my presence. I think it was because in the city we were seen as part of the novelty of it all: high-rise buildings, shops full of electrical goods, and foreigners. Back in the quiet countryside they had the calm self-confidence of people whose grandparents have farmed those very same fields, and maybe their great-grandparents too. People who know their grandchildren will farm there after them. My Germanic ancestors came from somewhere in central Asia – but *their* ancestors came from a site only a short bus-drive away from Yuncheng, and that gave us entirely different mind sets.

In the countryside we would walk through sleepy villages, or cycle through the fields, and the people would give us disinterested looks, then return to their labours. Even the children would carry on with their games as if we simply weren't there. So, when we were frantic with the need to escape from all the constant attention, we would set off along the causeway over the middle of Salt Lake to the quiet of the South Mountain.

The first time we went to South Mountain was on a cool, clear February day, just after our first week in Yuncheng, when Dean Wu had phoned up four students and told them to take us out for the day. They stopped us halfway along the causeway and Anthony, a very serious student, said, 'Would you like to find out about how the salt is dug up and how it is processed in the factory?'

His English was not so good, and it was obvious that he'd prepared his explanation – learning the words and reciting them to himself – from the way he spoke. But I wasn't interested in salt petre extraction or processing. I could see the green reeds on the far bank of the lake waving in the breeze, the lower slopes of the mountain striped with rows of cabbages, scattered sheep on the dry rocky slopes searching for food amidst the scrub, and then the high, unspoilt dusty brown ridges of the mountain.

'How about climbing the mountain?' I suggested.

Confusion flashed across the four faces. This had not been planned, it was not supposed to happen. What if something happened to the two foreigners? They were worried; then the excitement of doing something unexpected got the better of their concern and, as we had already set off, they had no choice but to follow us into the shadow of the mountain.

The road up the mountain was not tarmaced, but was made of hard crushed earth peppered with pebbles. It was the only link for the outlying villages to Yuncheng, so a few tractors chugged noisily over the ruts, spitting steam and water out of their open radiators. Off the causeway, the road became steeper and cycling more difficult. The road began to disappear, merging with the rough rocky land to either side, till it became impossible to cycle further. We walked into the village and the students took us to a house at random, where we walked our bikes over into the yard and left them, before setting off up the path that led up the mountain. One student went straight into the house without knocking, and then came out having changed her heels for plimsolls. I assumed that she knew the house owner. 'Have you been here before?' I asked.

'No, never,' the girl replied. 'But we will come back. I think she is a very kind lady.'

I was quite taken aback at this little episode, and smiled when I imagined the reaction in England if I walked into someone's house without knocking and asked to borrow a pair of wellies. But the Chinese – like most of the rest of the world –

do not have the same notions of private space as Westerners. They do not guard their possessions and isolation as religiously as we do, and consider our need for privacy a bit anti-social.

We climbed halfway up one of the slopes and rested on the shoulder of a ridge. Below, the view was glorious. Everything was diminutive: the village houses, the Salt Lake, the banks of salt petre that looked like waves of surf rolling across the lake frozen in time out to the chimneys of Yuncheng. One of the boys stood to face the east and performed a short *wushu* routine, a kind of *kung fu*.

'You must always face east,' he said. 'Face east and salute the rising sun.'

We returned to the South Mountain many times. To climb up through the thorny date bushes, to get out of the city and the stifling proximity of so many people, to see the greenery and hear birdsong again. Higher up the slopes, past the present village was the site where the old village used to be. After Liberation, when the threat of banditry had been removed, the villagers must have moved down from this isolated brow nearer to their fields. Now they were exchanging their mud-brick houses for two-storey brick buildings and the old village was now a ghost village. Single-storey and single-room huts set around walled courtyards, with heavy timber doors that were still padlocked, even though the walls had fallen down. Burrowed into the hillside there were also many cave houses, the poorest kind of dwelling; arched rectangular rooms went straight into the cliffs of yellow earth, cool in summer and warm in winter. Mao Tse Dung had planned the conquest of Kuomingtang China from a house such as this, now used for stabling sheep. We could have been wandering through a museum recreation of an ancient Chinese village, but recreations do not have the pathos that accompanies real life. These fallen-down huts and caves would have housed generations of families. Now they were forgotten and were gradually being buried deeper and deeper in sheep droppings. Old *kangs*, heated mud-brick beds, were breaking up, while hearths built into the walls were crumbling down.

As we walked down through the last house in the village we came across some old cottage gardens which were still maintained. In the clear chill spring day three old peasant men were taking a rest from their hoeing and digging, among the neat rows of garlic and spring onions; three old men in a garden of decayed buildings. One was sitting on a rock next to the path, another some way off under a tree and a third in another field stood resting his chin upon a hoe, completing the triangle. They were chatting about farming and the soil, but instead of coming together to talk more freely, each of them stood on their own piece of land and came no nearer. It's the Chinese equivalent of talking over the garden fence to a neighbour.

Their reaction to us, or lack of it, was refreshing in its uniqueness. Two foreigners passed between them all and they didn't even stop talking. It was as if we hadn't been there at all. We simply didn't exist in their little world.

A little way up and to the left of the old village a mountain stream had carved a deep scar between two of the peaks. Where it came out of the gully it had been divided and now fed into a large reservoir the size of a swimming pool built up against the mountainside. Our friends in Yuncheng often talked of following the stream up the mountain, hunting for freshwater crabs, which were very good fried with a little garlic. We decided one day to follow the stream into the heart of the mountains and see where it might lead us.

We set off late and found that a few young Chinese couples had also chosen the South Mountain for their hot date. On the path up from the village the men shouted and listened to the echo and threw stones around to impress the girls. We hurried on ahead, walking along the stream as it burrowed its way further into the mountain, turning and twisting around boulders as the slopes rose higher and higher on either side. From high up the path we heard the tinkle of bells and then a procession of mules filed past, slipping on the rocky path, goaded on by dark-tanned men swinging plaited lengths of rope. Each mule was carrying large white sacks of something heavy. We wondered where they might be coming from. Was there a village higher up in the mountains? What was in the sacks?

The gorge forked twice, and each time we followed the mule tracks. Coming around a corner we found the answer: an illegal gold-mining operation. Obscured by newly blasted rocks men squatted by the stream and a tired mule waited for the downward journey. The men, dressed in dusty, dark blue clothes, were digging the earthen banks of the stream. Like in old photos of the Gold Rush these dirty men with broad smiles sat smoking or panning for gold in the rock pools. At first they were as bemused to see us as we were them, which made it easy to start a chat.

'Where are you from?' they started.

'What are you doing here?' we asked.

'Gold!' one said, showing us a pan with a glittering residue of gravel lapping in a slop of water.

'What about the signs in the village? Isn't gold-mining forbidden here?'

Their answer was unashamed laughter. 'Everyone knows we are here, but with a bit of well-placed profit heads stay turned!'

We shared a drink of tea and then continued up the mountain. At last we decided to stop for lunch and climbed up one of the steep gorge slopes to see if we could see Yuncheng from there. The going was difficult, made worse by a profusion of date bushes with fierce thorns. Their branches grow with a peculiar geometry which makes them look like opened-up hexagons. We got half-way up, removed our rucksacks and the cold breeze chilled our sweaty backs as we settled down to a lunch of grapes and bananas.

A sudden BOOM! shook the ground and us. A fountain of dust and clods showered horizontally out of the mountainside just thirty yards to our left. We went over gingerly to investigate and found a series of small-mouthed tunnels which had been dug and blasted into the mountain. Two short peasants suddenly stuck their heads out of one like a pair of prairie dogs, and then dragged out a little wagon of rubble which they tipped over the edge. More goldminers.

All attempts at conversation failed. They couldn't understand us and their accents were so thick that they were incomprehensible. So, with no understanding but plenty of goodwill, we waved good-bye and hurried off as they started preparing the next bundle of explosives.

It was some time before we returned to the South Mountain again. The tourist potential of the site had not escaped the wily villagers in the meantime. Two of them sat next to the reservoir at the entrance to the gorge. One charged admission while the other sold cigarettes and bottles of water.

We climbed the mountain and from the top, looked out over the white-streaked Salt Lake where Emperors made sacrifices for the coming harvest. I was reminded of an engraving I had seen in the local museum etched on the smooth black surface of a large *stele* worked during the Yuan Dynasty, when China was under the Mongols. It showed a wall around the lake, built to protect the government salt monopoly, and lots of tiny men draining the salt petre, digging it up with shovels and putting it into wicker baskets and hand-drawn wagons. Looking down at the men working now it appeared that the methods of extraction hadn't really changed so much, although now there was a row of ugly factories dotted along the far shore to process the stuff.

We climbed down and went to the peasant lady's house where we had gone with the students that first time. As always, she invited us in – past the sleeping pig and nervous chickens in the yard – to the cool stone interior.

She chopped garlic sprouts while we sat on her ankle-high stools that had been polished smooth by generations of bony haunches and drank water from the well in her yard from porcelain bowls – chipped but probably her best – and ate peanuts, the traditional food for guests. Dirty and footsore though we were, she refreshed us enough to manage the hour's cycle home. She gave us extra peanuts as we left, filling our pockets, and then we set off back down the hill to Yuncheng.

We cycled back over the causeway at dusk, the best time, as the sun began to set. The rushes were dark against the glare of the sun, and the water a brilliant sparkle of yellow ripples.

The sun sank lower, a shining gold disc, too bright to look at directly, like a coin reflected in bright light – then faded to amber and to red. Just as in a Chinese painting, it hung heavy and scarlet in the sky above the horizon, large and bloated. It hit the layer of dust and began to disappear; gone within the minute, as if it had suddenly dropped into a pool of turgid water and had disappeared without a trace.

Sunsets in Yuncheng were always like this. A dull red sun hanging there – still there – then plop! it would sink into the murk of dust that covers Yuncheng like a blanket. We stopped our bikes and watched the display, catching every moment of it before it was gone, then cycled back in the galloping gloom.

CHAPTER THREE

Huangying! Welcome!

It was a big event for all of us, Chinese as well as foreigners: the English department banquet. Having been officially welcomed to the college, now we were to be formally welcomed to the department, and informally introduced to some of its members. Rather, introduced to all, but only talk to those with better English who were less daunted by us. It seemed that our arrival was a good excuse for banquets – and so we were passed down the hierarchy of the college: first the president and vice presidents and Party secretaries – now the English language department.

I smiled nervously, trying to look everyone in the eye, as Dean Wu introduced me to the two tables' worth of teachers and administrators.

'This is Mr Hill.' They all smiled, and he introduced them – a succession of strange names. They made my head spin, and I immediately forget them all, and concentrated on handshakes. What words couldn't say – and at this time my Chinese wasn't up to much more than 'Hello' and a few faltering sentences about shopping – maybe a handshake could.

Despite my nerves, in hindsight I see that that day meant a lot more to those of the teachers who had a real interest in English. Here we were, the only foreigners they would meet until we were replaced with a new pair of 'Big Noses'. Whatever their sphere of interest, from language to culture, we were the only source of first-hand knowledge for them. If we had questions or problems during our time in China we were assured of help and attention by the simple virtue of being foreigners. For them much depended on the impressions that they made on us, and so this was a crucial day for them.

That morning I had been drilling myself at my Chinese, waiting for twelve noon when we were due to meet up, when the phone went. It was Dean Wu. 'Hello. Justin? Come quickly! Everyone is waiting!'

I was about to tell him that Mario was still teaching, so they'd have to wait a bit longer, but the line had already gone dead.

When I arrived the 'Everyone' turned out to be Dean Wu on his own. Puffing on his cigarette, he was talking to another man who was also smoking. They carried on smoking and talking in hushed tones while I stood a polite distance away watching everything that was going on – a bicycle in each hand – wondering what on earth all the rush had been for. Students out early for lunch were strolling through the college gate, some going to the shacks that lined the pavement to eat a lunch of noodles and steamed bread, others cycling home. A few pool tables stood on the pavement and some youths in green uniforms – also smoking – were watching their friends play.

Still Dean Wu smoked and still I stood. The number three bus came along Hedong Donglu, stirring up a streamer of dust. It approached with a fanfare of horn blasts which was enough to send the lingering students and teachers scattering; all except a little boy pissing in the dirt who just avoided the careering bus by leaping to the side in mid pee. Without slowing for children or the old, the bus swung around a full 180 degrees, using the bay of the college entrance, and came to a rest facing back into town at the bus stop on the other side of the road. As the engine spluttered to a halt the rattle of loose window fittings and rusty panels also died away. Its two doors jerked open with a loud sneeze of hydraulics, and a few people pushed out. The driver climbed down from his cabin and went to sit at a nearby shack to eat his lunch. Mario arrived, and took his bicycle. We both waited. Wu finally seemed to notice us.

30

'Ah. Good. Let us go quickly!' he said, and we all pushed off and started cycling.

The restaurant was not far from the college – straight down Hedong Donglu, over the first crossroads and left at the second. Inside was a long room with four round tables and a service counter and two smaller rooms at either end, with two tables in each. All Chinese restaurants have these private banquet rooms where the more dignified hosts can entertain their guests away from the hoi polloi – *putong ren* in Chinese. An odd thing I thought then, in a communist country. But then I didn't know better: communism just alters the inequalities, it doesn't remove them.

The English department occupied both of the smaller rooms, which meant we were partying at opposite ends of the restaurant. Two tables of teachers in one room, and two of administrators and their children in the room at the other end. Wu began the introductions. First was Li ShuJi, the English department Party Secretary, with whom we shook hands. A small man, in fact very small, who we later discovered wore platform shoes, so by rights even smaller than that. He had quite bulging eyes, one with a small cataract like a pearly contact lens. I believed for quite a while that 'Li ShuJi' was his real name, but in fact it meant 'Party Secretary Li' – the party secretary of the English department.

'Vice Dean Wang.' A middle-aged woman, who I later discovered had been to Singapore for a year to study English.

'Vice Dean Hou.' Whose English greeting I found difficult to understand. Then a succession of names and smiles and handshakes that melted into a bewildering muddle. There were a number of Zhangs and Lis amongst all these, and I seated myself between two Lis at the table.

The opening ceremony of any banquet in China is the toast. Or rather three of them, although since this was a special occasion I think there were more. Dean Wu stood up and said something about a long and happy stay, then whoosh! – down went all our egg cups' worth of Shanxi Fen Jiu. This is a spirit made of sorghum, better than most Chinese paint strippers, but not much. Li ShuJi said something in Chinese that lasted long enough for the cups to be refilled, then they were raised, (and copying my first effort were clinked! in Western fashion), and the wine was tossed into the gullet. This carried on for a while; me, Mario and Cao all saying a few polite, positive and friendly words that were translated, giving us all more than enough reason to drain another cup.

After the three compulsory cups, the ladies stopped drinking, except one, a tall, burly lady who looked like a woman wrestler and who downed the cups with the rest of us. So it was with our insides on fire, we attacked the host of dishes in front of us. At least we tried to, but half a pint of fifty per cent spirits on an empty stomach doesn't do much for the chopstick control. The teacher next to me, a woman called Li DongPing, led me through the dishes.

'Peanuts, eggs and tomato, liver, a *dofu* salad – and how do you call this? In Chinese we say *songhua dan.*'

I had no idea but recognized them as Chinese One-Thousand-Year-Old Eggs.

'What's that?' I asked about another dish. It was a vegetable shaped like a large carrot. It was white and had holes running through it from top to bottom like Swiss cheese. Sliced thinly and covered in a little vinegar and sugar and, finally, chopped ginger, it had a delicious sweet-and-sour taste.

'Erm. This is the root of a flower. In Chinese we say '*liancai.*' You know?'

'Er – no. You see, my Chinese is not good at the moment.'

We sat in thoughtful silence. A silence broken by the man on my left, Li JianQiang, who contrary to the Chinese stereotype was over six foot tall, and quite well built.

'It is the root of the lotus flower,' Li JianQiang said, then gesturing towards Mr Cao, who was across the table from me, 'He is my classmate, you know. Yes,' he continued. 'We were classmates, but Cao is the "Big Man" now.' Cao's success seemed a good enough reason for a toast and we tossed one down.

'Li JianQiang has just returned from England,' said Cao, refilling our cups.

'Really?' I said. 'Where were you?' Excited in this ocean of strange reality to find myself cast adrift on the shore of something familiar, however remote.

'Nottingham,' he replied.

'Ah! Robin Hood – did you go to Sherwood Forest?' I said, getting into my stride.

'No. I didn't go.'

I was not to be put off. 'Did you go to any other places?' I said, shifting tack.

'It was very interesting. But very expensive. I did not trip at all because it was too expensive. Everything expensive. I had to find my own accommodation. Our landlord wanted a hundred pounds a week. It was very bad accommodation, so I bargained him down to sixty-five pounds. In my last term I was very lucky – I saw an advert offering free accommodation. There was an old couple who wanted a lodger to live with them. Their son was away on business most of the time and they missed having younger people around the house. So I was their son!' he laughed.

'Free?' I checked, surprised.

'Yes, entirely free. They were an Indian couple and so I think they were used to a more Chinese kind of family.'

Unfortunately I couldn't imagine lonely English parents advertising for a foreign student to come and live with them free of charge. You never know, they might steal the silver, or spit on the Axminster. Nor would any foreigner in England get such a warm welcome upon arrival as I was enjoying here – these two facts left me feeling a bit sheepish about my mean-spirited nation.

'So, how did you get to go abroad?' I asked, changing the subject.

'You know, the college, it got some World Bank funding. With the money, the college was able to send a few of the teachers abroad to study. But I think all the money has gone now.'

'Did you like England?'

'Yes, very much. You know England is very good for a man like me. If you have ability, then you can do well. I was working in an office – illegally – but I was very good at my job. I felt very good, in China I don't get that opportunity. I wanted to stay longer in England, but couldn't.'

'Why not?' I asked.

'You see, I am an only son in my family. My mother was very upset when she heard I was going to go abroad – she threatened to kill herself, she did not want her only son to leave. I do not think you can imagine, but it is the Chinese way. I couldn't stay longer than one year.'

We continued talking for a while, but my hopes about chatting about England were dashed. I had the feeling that he hadn't really seen much of the place at all. But it was more of a shame for him, I thought, since for any Chinese person a visit to the West is a once-in-a-lifetime opportunity.

It surprised me then, but with more knowledge of China later on I think I know some of the reasons for this. Just as China for some is the equivalent of forty days in the wilderness, then the West is a dream come true for a Chinese person. A potent cocktail of freedoms, decisions, money and technology – which can be too much for someone used to a more rigid lifestyle. Whereas we love solitude and Private Space, this would make the average Chinese person miserable. They have always lived in what we would call cramped conditions, always with lots of company, so a Chinese person wouldn't see solitude as a luxury, but a lonely experience without the companionship of fellow humans. Also, just as I thought in pounds and marvelled at the cheapness of China, the Chinese thought in *yuan* and marvelled at the money that they could save in the West and take home to finance a family member's education, or help look after the parents. So instead of learning English they got poorly paid illegal jobs that gave them money to take home.

I turned to the lady on the other side of me – Li DongPing. 'Do you think you will ever be able to travel to England?'

'Ah yes. It is very difficult, especially for women. Anyway, I am too old.'

She looked about thirty, and was in fact thirty-two, and, not thinking this too old, I told her so. 'And why is it especially difficult for women?' I added.

'Usually there is an age limit of thirty-five for women. Men in middle age are very energetic, but not the women. It is said that if the woman pass thirty years old, people say that – how to say – ah – they are like dried bean curd.' We laughed. 'Yeah, and it's said in talk about men, when they pass over thirty years they look like a flower – means they are very energetic.'

'But hasn't Vice Dean Wang just come back from Singapore? She must be over thirty-five, surely?'

'Yes,' she said, without elaborating.

She carried on chatting to me, which was nice because the rest of the table had reverted to using Chinese – the women gossiping amongst themselves and the men playing loud drinking games. 'You know, before this college was made, it was three colleges joined together. Our president is very old, but still very capable at everything. He didn't want to retire. He was over sixty-four, but for each year he wrote down his age one year younger. This year sixty-three, next year sixty-two and so on. Very funny, I think. If somebody wants to look younger, then we say, "Oh, you look like the President."'

More dishes arrived: fried egg and tomato, some unappetising-looking dish, which I was told was 'sea slug', but which was indistinguishable from the chopped vegetables around it, and a sweet dish of sticky black rice studded with fruits and lotus seeds.

Everyone waited for me to start each dish. 'Chi-chi-chi! Eat-eat!' they all told me, gesticulating furiously with their chopsticks. Fumbling with my chopsticks and spoon I tried to pick at each dish. Usually, I was too slow and someone would reach over, pick out the choicest part of the dish, and place it in front of me. I was having difficulty shovelling in enough food to keep them all happy.

Li DongPing continued. 'When Deng XiaoPing started the Open-door Policy – to open the door to foreign ideas and business – then the first foreign teachers came into China and they were very serious and hard-working. They give us extra work but they are not paid extra money by the colleges. My teacher, we used to call him "The Working Man", gave us many tough work. I think at times he is very strict. Sometimes we hate him. We also admire him too, especially the women.'

'Was he good-looking?' I asked.

'No, he was too serious,' she said.

'So why did the women admire him then?'

'I don't know – just because he's a man. Because we can learn a lot from him, and I think women are easier to admire somebody. But not for a boy. Boys are born with deep thoughts about what is a true man. Yeah, that's true.

'He was very serious. Stayed for another year. The woman teacher – not so! – she went back to England. She started very serious, but she became cleverer than she was at the beginning. She learnt how Chinese people behave. Chinese people don't work hard. They try to find excuses. It's true. Teachers just let students pass exams so they don't have to do retakes. She learnt to copy the Chinese way.

'I think all foreigners like travelling, is it true?' she asked, changing the subject.

'Well,' I said, 'that's because all the foreigners who don't like travelling don't come to China.'

This simple explanation seemed new to her, and she found it very amusing. 'Yeah, most teachers they come to China just for travelling. I come across many foreign teachers who have such a purpose. After their holiday they are very excited about their travel. Yeah, maybe you are right. In China there are many old things: old architecture, buildings, old things are kept in many places. It is interesting and attracts foreigners.'

'I don't really think so,' I said quickly. The glaring difference between my pagoda-bamboo-grove imaginations of China and the concrete-block reality, was very apparent. 'I think China's cities have been a great disappointment. There are hardly any old buildings at all, are there? Only those that the government has taken and said, "We will keep this for tourism." All the others have been destroyed and tall buildings have been built over them.'

She smiled. 'That's because we like flats. They are modern.

Much better than country houses. When I see pictures of European cities, there are not a lot of flats.'

'Well in Europe, you see, we don't really like flats. We like old buildings.'

Li DongPing looked confused and said, 'But I think if a city doesn't have modern buildings, high buildings or flats – then it doesn't *look* modern.'

'Yes, but we don't mind that. In England we build around the old city, whereas in China you build on top of the old town. We think that all these modern buildings are unattractive.'

'Also in China place is limited,' Li DongPing reasoned. 'More and more people. Maybe not a problem in your country. In China everyone wants to live in a city and in the east. In your England the rich live in the country and the poor in the cities. Your cities are very dirty, polluted, no?'

Perceptions of foreign countries usually lag behind reality, often getting stuck on an image that is entirely out of date, but arresting. More real than the reality. In England we're still stuck on little red books and Mao suits, or even little men with ponytails and shaven pates running opium dens. In China I began to have a feeling that they'd got stuck on the idea of the Victorian squalor of English cities. Later, I found out that Dean Wu in his course on English culture was teaching students about London smogs. I think he still lived in the steel-making Sheffield of the early sixties.

Our conversation ended as I was pulled into a drinking competition with Cao Zheng that involved sticking out one finger from your fist like in 'paper, scissors, stone'. Mrs Li explained: 'Ah yeah. You see thumb beats forefinger, forefinger beats middle finger, middle finger beats – how to say – yeah I see – ring finger, beats little finger, little finger beats thumb.'

Half-way through the game I realized Cao was cheating – waiting a fraction to see which finger I would use and then beating me. A Chinese man had warned me in Beijing that the local Chinese would be very curious to see how a foreigner would behave when drunk, and so would try to get me pissed.

The rest of the meal, with the liberal addition of Fen Jiu, went swimmingly until the final dish arrived. At a Chinese banquet, if you are not already stuffed, which is hard if everyone has been force-feeding you for the last hour and the food is so good you don't need other people to shovel it into your mouth – then the final dish is the 'filler-up'. Rice in the south of China, in Yuncheng it was noodles, soup, or *jiaozi* (dumplings). *Jiaozi* are dipped into dark vinegar before eating, a strong powerful liquid – the black treacle of vinegars. Li DongPing poured a little into my porcelain Chinese soup spoon. 'This is Shanxi vinegar. It is very famous in China.'

I started to 'fill-up' with *jiaozi*. But I needed no filling, in fact I desperately needed tipping on my head and emptying a bit. I tried to swallow my dumplings, but they would not go down, sitting, as they were, upon the layers of food I had already consumed which seemed to have overflowed my stomach. If you had cut me in half then you would have found nothing but layers of food: lotus root at the bottom, eggs, sweet-and-sour fish, black rice, vegetables, spicy dofu, deep-fried chicken, mutton soup, lotus seeds, red-cooked eggplant, with *jiaozi* sitting on the top.

I took my last *jiaozi*. 'This is all really delicious,' I said. 'But I don't think I can possibly eat another one.' A little drunk and half talking to myself.

Li DongPing and Li JianQiang leant in closer to hear me. The slippery *jiaozi* slithered out of my chopsticks, somersaulted and landed with a dull splat! into my spoonful of vinegar. The *jiaozi* stayed put, while the rich brown vinegar splashed up in all directions, landing on all the white clothing within range.

I was mortified. I apologized profusely, but they hushed me up and generously piled up my plate with extra *jiaozi* to save me (and them) the trouble of reaching for them. I ate a few more, but my stomach hurt, and I was way beyond full. I told myself that I had discovered new limits to the human physique. No body had ever consumed so much and lived. I was the first human Tardis.

We all sat back briefly, adjusting our posture to give our stomachs more room. Then, after a short pause, we were all up and out. The meal was over.

Swinging my leg over my bicycle saddle nearly gave me a

hernia and, once settled, I doubted I could reach my handlebars over my swollen stomach. I managed – just.

Duan Yu – another teacher – came alongside as Mario and I cycled back to the college. He was smiling and cheerful, while I was in real discomfort. He was one of the lucky few to have benefitted from a scholarship abroad and having been given permission to leave China, had spent a year in the USA. Unfortunately, he looked like he had as he sat on his bike in a leather jacket and mirror shades.

'Hi!' he said, looking and sounding ultra cool. 'Mario tells me that you want to learn Chinese?! You don't need to learn a language. Everyone in the world speaks English. Why waste your time?'

We believed that if we were to get the most out of China our first task was to learn the language. We were not content to confine ourselves to the English-speaking part of the population of China (teachers and students), which in Yuncheng was barely pushing double figures. Chinese friends had frequently apologized to us for not being able to speak English – the International Language – while our frustration grew at not even being able to respond to this absurd apology in Chinese.

There was some inertia on the part of the college in finding us a Chinese teacher, which a suspicious person might have taken as opposition to the idea. Maybe the college wanted us to devote all our energies to teaching – not learning? But how could we live here and not want to speak, in Chinese, to all the people we lived with and met daily? We wanted to learn as much about China as possible, and the language seemed to be the key. After a few weeks of pressure and nagging the college did finally appoint us a Chinese teacher.

Someone else I met at the English department banquet was a teacher called Li PuXiao. His life was fascinating in that in a stroke it seemed to encapsulate the history of China. He was also a Li, but as we were getting confused with all these similar names, we called him the 'Christian Guy' for obvious reasons.

Next time I met him was in the English department office, sitting quietly, with his lesson plans upon his knee, neatly written pages in a mix of Chinese characters and Roman script.

Well-cared for, they were a little dog-eared nonetheless and looked like notes he had been using since he had started teaching. He sat very composed while around him the younger teachers shouted excitedly over a game of cards. Even without the classic little Chinese goatee he had that calm wisdom that makes you feel you are in the presence of someone from a different age. I half expected him to begin each sentence with, 'Wise men say ...' But he didn't. He turned to me, gave me a little smile that twinkled with a silver-capped tooth, and said, 'I hear you are a Christian. I am a Christian.' Then he sat back and resumed his repose, exuding the contemplative inner confidence that I would expect of a saint.

In break-time, between lessons, we would often chat away, and during my stay in Yuncheng, I pieced together his life from this series of ten-minute conversations that often stopped like a soap opera on the edge of something dramatic.

'My family came from Henan Province before I was born. They came to Yuncheng to escape the famine in the 1930s. Everyone was dying. The only choice was to walk to a place where we could find food.

'I was born in 1936. My father was a peasant. He was also a Christian. Being a Christian then meant at least getting food, as the missionaries would always give food to the starving Christians. He went to work at a Protestant missionary school in Xian as a doorman. Because he worked there, I went to school there too. I was there for four years. I was thirteen when Liberation came. Xian was a very beautiful city then, much better than Yuncheng. Xian has a grid layout that dates back to the Tang Dynasty, you know. We had heard of the Communists then. They were north of Xian, and they were fighting the Japanese. We didn't know about their policies, but we respected them because they were the only people who were fighting the invaders, while the government did nothing.

'Yuncheng was very small then. Not much more than a village. Where the traffic circle is now, there used to be a high wall of earth to keep out bandits. People were very frightened of bandits – the Japanese, government troops – everything was in chaos then. After four years there I went to a seminary in

Nanjing, and then a seminary in Beijing. I was in Beijing for six years. I graduated in 1961, and went to Taiyuan to teach the Word.'

He paused. 'I helped with preaching and administration there, until the Cultural Revolution, in 1966. We were not allowed to worship then. Christianity was an imperialist evil. I wasn't severely criticized, but in the end I was sent back to Yuncheng to learn from the peasants. To rid myself of my bourgeois thoughts and to study Mao Tse Dung thought. Every day in the morning we would assemble in front of his picture and pray to Mao to help us reform ourselves.

'There were ten of us, and we were no good at farming. The peasants weren't very welcoming because there wasn't even enough food for them, and we were more empty mouths to feed. So they made us keep chickens. Our field was where the new department store is now. We kept chickens for twelve years, until 1978. Then Deng XiaoPing came to power and began to reverse the bad things that had happened. The education system was in chaos – all the teachers had been the first to be attacked and sent to the countryside. I was told that I must teach English at a middle school. Then in 1979 I started work at this college.'

During one of our talks, he asked, 'Are there many Christians in your land?'

'Yes, quite a lot.' I told him. 'Most of the people who go to church are a bit older though. I think religion is something you grow into as you get older.'

A Christian in China seemed quite an incongruous notion – almost a contradiction in terms – and so I wondered what my students thought of him.

'He is not a very good teacher,' one confided in me. 'Sometimes he just reads the Bible to us.' Something which surprised me. Weren't people in China supposed to be locked up for life for that? Obviously not.

But apart from the quality of his teaching, the students always seemed to run out of things to say about the Christian Guy, as if they weren't sure what to make of him. I don't think this reticence was because he was a Christian – Christianity

41

in China is catching on, especially amongst women in the countryside. 'Because they are more superstitious,' I was told by way of explanation – maybe they were uncomfortable about saying anything bad about the most senior member of staff; maybe because he had had such a dubious past – all that time spent with Western Imperialists; or because he seemed to keep himself to himself. Whatever the reason, they always changed the subject and started to talk about his son. 'His son is very famous, he is very skilled in QiGong. QiGong is the skill of using your body's Qi (force). He can do many things with it – break rocks, burn paper, and even heal you. It's true.'

The Christian Guy didn't live in the college, and unfortunately we didn't see him much. I don't think we were ever likely to be in Yuncheng long enough to get to know him properly. He was one of those people who knew we were busy, and of course far too busy to see someone like him, and so kept himself to himself. Towards the end of my stay, though, he did call me over and asked me to get him a tape of hymns from the 'Adventists of the Seventh Day', with lyrics and music. I wrote home for this, but heard nothing more. Either my family thought I had Found Jesus in China and disapproved, or there weren't any such tapes available in York High Street. It was hard to explain to him how in the West – where everything and anything can be bought – I couldn't get him the tape he wanted. Still, I felt bad for failing to get him the one thing he ever asked from me.

CHAPTER FOUR

Deep Throat

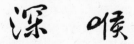

Another teacher whose English was good enough and who was inclined to visit us was a rather unusual figure also called Li, whom we named 'Deep Throat.' This was on account of his deep croaking voice caused by a persistent throat infection which ought to have stopped him smoking but which didn't.

Like all Chinese people his head seemed too large for his slight body, but this effect was made all the more obvious by another unusual feature of his. He had a great scraggly beard that reached round from sideburn to sideburn and covered pretty much everything in between in its chaotic growth.

He had a particular fascination with what he called 'the sordid side of life' and he promised us many times that he would take us to experience the seedy side of China. 'I think people in your country will find it interesting. Write it down, tell them.'

When he found that we didn't much like being called 'LaoWai,' he lectured us. 'It is a polite name. "Lao" means old – it is a term of respect, and "Wai" means "foreigner." I always called my teacher "LaoWai".'

I explained to him that 'WOG – 'Westernised Oriental Gentleman' was once also considered to be polite. But meanings change. I don't think that he liked being told by a foreigner how he should use his own language in his own country, which was fair enough, but then I didn't much like being shouted at by all the locals.

We each stuck to our guns, and from that moment on he

only referred to us as 'LaoWai.' We never took up his offer to take us out to see the social filth of Yuncheng, so he took it upon himself to come to our house and introduce it to us.

He started his first embassy off by presenting us each with a book that he had written. 'I have dedicated my new book to you. I thank you for the help that you have given. When it is printed I will give you a copy each.'

We hadn't helped him and the old book he gave us – *The One Thousand Two Hundred and Fifty-Five Uses of 'Of'* – was hardly destined for the bestseller list. The only reason he'd put the dedication in was to help it sell – claiming that foreigners had helped him write it.

'I publish many books. Too many teachers here waste their lives, I – I study and write. I will introduce you to China. If you want to learn about China, then I think that the minimum you must stay is at least three years. We can go into the countryside. I will show you the poor people. You know you must not believe what you read about China in your newspapers. The "Economic Miracle" has not happened in the countryside. It has not helped the peasants much. You know, things haven't really changed so much since 1949. You should write some articles to tell your people – you could interview old people, write about the One Child Policy, the Economic Miracle.'

'What about politics?' I asked, and like a recurrent theme, our conversation came to Tiananmen Square. 1989, 'The Event' of 4 June, came up quite frequently in conversation with students, but their explanations of what happened all sounded the same, almost rehearsed, mirroring the official view.

Deep Throat was matter of fact. 'Many of the teachers were criticized after Tiananmen, so they dislike Deng Xiao Ping. In 1989 college students and teachers went out and shouted "Down with Deng Xiao Ping." One of our students was arrested. This year he has returned. He is a student now in the Chinese department. Teachers also dislike Li Pung. Li Pung is the most hated man in China – he ordered in the tanks, you know. You see, many people are unhappy because of *guanxi* – connections – and corruption, which give some people jobs with power, and they use that power to make money. The police are also very unpopular. They are criminals themselves! If your brother is in prison, to get him out you must send your sister to the police station to sleep with the policeman.'

He found this very funny. Getting onto the topic of the police seemed to twig something in his mind, and he continued in his deep, croaking voice, 'You know, before you arrived we were visited by the Chief of Police. He came to talk to the teachers and students. He told us how we should behave with a foreigner. But he has never met a foreigner! All he did was repeat old wives' tales that he'd heard. Very amusing, we thought! We have all had foreign teachers, you see. He told us what we should or shouldn't say. He told us that we must not betray the Motherland and tell you any secrets. I think there are no secrets in Yuncheng. We asked him what secrets we mustn't tell you. But he didn't know either.'

It was all very interesting, but a phone call from a friend of his meant that he had to leave before he could reveal anything really sordid.

Next time he came round he opened up a bit more and asked us if we had any pornographic magazines.

'In Taiyuan my English teacher, he gave me many magazines – *Playboy*, *Esquire* – many beautiful girls. Peter – the American teacher – he was my friend. When he left he gave me all his store of magazines. I have kept them in my house, you know. There I have many magazines. Very interesting.'

This led him onto the subject of Chinese girls. 'You should marry a Chinese girl,' he said. 'Chinese girls make good wives. They're good cooks, and serve you well. I think you would like them.'

I got up and went out to get cups of tea for all of us, and after Deep Throat had left I found out that he had chosen that moment to offer to take Mario to a local brothel. 'I think for fifty *yuan* I could find a girl for you,' he had said. Obviously he considered me too young for a brothel, and the matter of the proposed trip was dropped upon my return. But Deep Throat continued to enlighten us on the subject in general.

'Brothels!' he said. 'Oh yes. There are many brothels in Yuncheng. Many hairdressers are also houses full of young girls,' he said. 'Look – especially in the evening – hairdressers with the doors open and many girls sitting there and chatting. That is a brothel.'

Soon a friend of his, Shen Zong, joined us, and as the Chinese are very thick-skinned guests it seemed that we were there for the evening. However bored you look or however many hints you make, without coming out and saying, 'Sorry, you must leave now!' a guest will seldom get the message.

Deep Throat and his friend were a real pair, their interests almost identical. 'We will teach you many cultural things,' Deep Throat said. 'My friend Shen Zong is a great scholar. He is a genius! He knows many things, English, QiGong, Yoga, Daoism, Buddhism, Confucius. He is now writing a book, *Journey to the West*, it will be in many volumes.' Shen Zong stood and smiled as his friend gave him this glowing introduction. However, it soon became apparent that he and Deep Throat shared a fascination with sex.

'My friend,' Deep Throat said, 'he had many girlfriends when he was young. His parents were very unhappy with him and made him marry his current wife. They chose her for him, it was all organized by the parents. She and Shen Zong are not happy, though.'

'I love my wife,' Shen Zong said hollowly. 'But she does not love me.'

'My friend – he does not love his wife. I know these things.' Deep Throat countered in his deep voice.

'I love her, and I love my son,' Shen Zong said with a smile that made no attempt to convince us. In fact, his utter indifference to the topic of his wife or son, showing neither love or hatred, made me feel uneasy.

'Why doesn't she love you?' Mario asked.

Shen Zong shrugged. But Deep Throat put in – with evident delight at getting back to his favourite subject – 'His wife is not very – adventurous. My friend, he likes to watch yellow videos. Sex is very important to him. I give him my magazines and he shows them to his wife when they are in bed, to excite her, make her do things. But she won't learn. They are not happy together. They only stay together for the child. If they tried to separate, then their families and friends would all try to force them to stay together.'

Shen Zong sat smiling through this analysis of his marriage and made no attempt to deny any of it. If they were expecting us to share with them equally lurid tales, they left disappointed.

'Hi! Come in, come in. No, don't worry. It's very dirty in here – don't worry, come in!'

Dean Wu came around to see us the other night and we had to pull him through the doorway as he tried to take off his shoes outside. Although not large, he was quite strong, and he used all of this strength to resist us.

'Ah,' he said, turning to go through into our sitting room, pointing at the carpet and looking at his shoes questioningly. In China a carpet is such a luxury that only foreigners would tread on it with shoes.

'Never mind, Dean Wu,' Mario said and pushed him through the door, and then forced him down into a seat.

'Cup of tea, Dean Wu?' I offered. Most Chinese never bother to offer but just plonk a cup down in front of you. But offering cups of tea is a nice British way of starting a conversation, a habit I still hadn't given up.

'No, thank you,' he said, so I went out and brought him a cup of tea. I put it down in front of him.

He pushed it away. 'No, thank you.'

I pushed it back to him. He forced it back and during the little tussle it spilled over the table. I pushed it back and there it stayed. The basic formalities over, business could start.

'So what can we do for you, Dean Wu?'

Each culture has its own peculiarities, but China has more than most. One custom I found difficult at first was that a door opened is the equivalent of an invitation inside – once opened the Chinese guest walks in, invited or not. This presents the problem of unwanted guests having to be persuaded outside again without causing offence. The Western habit of talking to someone who is standing on your doorstep and not letting them in is so rude to the Chinese mind as to be unthinkable. This can lead to a number of misunderstandings. Standing in the doorway with *very* unwanted visitors outside I was often literally knocked off my feet as they barged through me.

The use of physical force was one of the hardest things to handle in China. Etiquette with chopsticks was nothing compared to learning to cope with the polite use of physical force, which, like it, or not and I didn't, is considered normal. If someone is hesitating over a decision, then lay hands on him, decide for him, and literally force him into it. Any struggles on his part are only out of politeness, so if he resists, then push even harder.

Now this sounds fun, and once mastered it sometimes was, but for a Westerner who is uncomfortable with strangers even touching them (as most Westerners are) there is nothing as alarming as the use of physical force.

The first time I came across this was early on when Mario and I had invited some students around for a get-to-know-each-other cup of tea. Our pupils – all mature students in in-service teacher training – arrived and we asked them to help themselves to the bowls of nuts and biscuits we had put out. We had already learnt by then that the Chinese never help themselves to anything – that's impolite on their part. Instead it is the host's job to encourage, cajole, blackmail, and if all else fails, force-feed a guest, who, for politeness' sake, must refuse everything.

Seeing that they weren't going to eat or drink anything without some persuasion, I picked up a bowl of peanuts, and stood up, ready to exhaust myself in an effort to get the students to tuck in.

'Mr Hill, please sit down,' Kang Jie, one of the students, said. I didn't, and so he reached over, put his hands on my shoulders, and with a gentle but surprisingly forceful shove, pushed me back onto my seat. I was too shocked to react as he unpeeled my fingers from the bowl and returned it to the coffee table.

My look of bewilderment went unnoticed, except by Mario,

who decided that where I had failed he would succeed. He picked up the bowl, stood up to offer it around, and before his knees had time to fully straighten, Kang Jie came over, placed his hands on Mario's shoulders and pushed him back into his seat.

For a virtual stranger, in your own house, to whollup! you back into your seat was beyond belief. I told myself this was a new country, with new manners. They work for the Chinese as well as Western manners do for us.

But even when I expected to be thrown around it never failed to irritate me. Buying tickets to a park. I went to pay and had my hand rudely shoved out of the way by a female student half my size who then proceeded to pay for me; getting into a car a more-than-firm shove from behind almost launched me out of the opposite window; I had countless fights over who should carry bags, which I always ended up losing and not really knowing how. In my bemused state I would remind myself that next time I would remember to use more than what *I* considered to be polite force, much more.

It took us quite a while to settle with a Chinese teacher. Most Chinese people have no experience of teaching foreign learners, a skill most of us in the cosmopolitan West take for granted. Our first teacher just wanted to teach us children's songs – and we soon found out why. She took us out for a dreadful evening at a high-class karaoke bar where I was pressurised into singing the Chinese equivalent of 'Three Blind Mice'. I felt like a grotesque child prodigy, a performing monkey there to entertain her husband and friends. It was the most humiliating moment I ever had in China, but at least I got it over with early. The song went on and on until eventually I was presented with a bouquet of plastic flowers as I stepped off the stage. I remember thinking that a crap bunch of plastic flowers was small consolation for what I'd just been through, but the crowning insult was yet to come – after five minutes they were summarily taken away from me to be given to the singer who'd just finished. That little old thing called 'Face' again.

When that teacher disappeared to supervise students on

teaching practice we were relieved to be rid of her – but without a Chinese teacher. We had a stand-in teacher for a few weeks who went to Henan Province to get married – then we were handed onto Wang QunXia.

I had been playing ping-pong in the old people's club at the time. The old people's club wasn't even necessarily for old people, but was just a bare room with one ping-pong table, ordinary tables and chairs and a chess set. The old played chess there while everyone else went to play ping-pong. I was called out and introduced to QunXia. She was quite tall, ungainly, with lopsided glasses held together with Sellotape, and fluoride-stained teeth. She looked like a class train spotter, but she remained our Chinese teacher for the rest of our time in China.

QunXia was twenty-four when she started teaching us and lived in the college where her father was a lecturer in Chinese. As the child of a teacher she had good *guanxi* – connections – with the college and after graduating in Chinese got a job working as an assistant in one of the offices. She had studied English at school for seven years, but it was very minimal. Taking her new appointment very seriously, for us she learnt one word, 'Wrong!' and, being very strict with us, she used it regularly. She tested us weekly, and punished us with her mispronounced '*Rrrong!*' if she thought we were not working hard enough.

'*Rrrong!*'

A voice on the telephone. 'Hello. Justin? Justin? Wait there. I am coming over. Wait there.'

Two hours later Cao, our WaiBan, knocked on the door, and walked in. Picking up a conversation which we hadn't had, he said, 'The shower. How is it?'

'Not very good, I'm afraid. It worked for ten minutes. But then it stopped.'

'A chair. Chair?'

I gave him a chair and he went to work on the shower with his hammer. It was a fill-up-heat-up-trickle-drip shower, made in China. Cao was hammering on it and the sound of metal on metal echoed through the flat.

As if roused from slumber by the noise, Dean Wu appeared at the door.

'Hello, Dean Wu.'

'Is someone here?' he said, ready to disappear unnoticed if we had guests.

'No, no. Just Mr Cao – repairing our shower.'

'O,' he said, the Chinese equivalent of 'I see', then went into the bathroom. Their voices mingled in incomprehensible staccato Chinese as they talked about the problem.

Wu returned. 'I think the shower is broken. You know, I told them. I said they must, I said they *must* have a shower. Surely! I know that foreigners must have a shower.' He hit his fist against his palm to emphasise his words, then gave Cao a severe ticking off for failing to serve our needs properly, a display designed to impress and reassure us that they were taking the problem seriously, which actually left us acutely embarrassed.

Cao was sweating a little, splattered with dirty water from the pipes, clicking his tongue. 'Sorry. Not good. Not good.' He held up a piece of pipe. 'This is blocked. I will return this evening.' Then he went out.

They both returned that evening. Cao went to work on the shower, while we sat with Dean Wu.

'Did you have a nice time when you were in England, Dean Wu?'

'Oh, yes, surely,' he said in a way which made us wonder if he'd not quite understood.

'Where did you go?'

'Ah. When I was in England I went to see Professor Empson. Do you know Professor Empson?' he asked. I didn't, so he spelt out the name for me.

'Empson worked in China, you know. He was a lecturer in Beijing. He invited all the Chinese students in Britain to his house for a meal. He was very kind. That was when I lived in Sheffield with Mrs Williamson. One day we drove to the Isle of Man. It was very green. Very beautiful. We had a – picnic. I remember it all very clearly. It is my favourite day in England. Surely!'

It was strange to see this little man joking and reminiscing about his time in England in 1965 and 6, up to the start of the Cultural Revolution, when he was recalled to a China which was in the throes of a madness that would last ten years. He told us once that he had not suffered too badly during that time, even though he had previously lived and studied abroad, because he was still quite young. Maybe it was only by playing the fool that he had managed to get as far as he had.

Cao came out of the bathroom, as dirty as before, and we all went to check on the shower, which was dripping again at its usual rate. Dripping precariously near to the electric plug.

'Mr Cao, I think this is very dangerous. I think this should be moved away from the water,' I said.

Cao was unperturbed and tapped the electricity socket thoughtfully with his screwdriver. His wet screwdriver, held in a wet hand. Dean Wu stepped closer to investigate the problem properly, while Mario and I took a step backwards. We expected sparks to fly at any moment, but there were none. Cao turned off the shower and I stepped in to unplug it, then we all went for a cup of tea.

'Cup of tea?'

'No, thank you,' they said.

'Go on. Have one.'

'No, thank you.'

'Have one. Really – we're having one.'

They stopped arguing, which I took to be an affirmative, so I put the kettle on the stove and lit the gas.

'I think you should see the countryside,' Dean Wu announced. He had a habit of promising all kinds of things that never came to be – but this sounded good, and so we edged to the front of our seats and nodded enthusiastically to encourage him, and hoped he didn't just think that we were being polite.

'You know, in the countryside celebrations are very noisy. *Bla! Bla! Bla!*' (He imitated a pipe player leading a wedding procession.) 'And many many firecrackers. Surely!' He continued plucking ideas out of the air, egged on to even grander promises by our enthusiasm. Turning to Mr Cao he said, 'We must send them to see a country wedding. Country weddings are very colourful. Many people – noise. *Bla! Bla! Bla!* We will also arrange a funeral. Very interesting, and you can go and take photographs. Surely!'

The way he said 'arrange a funeral' was disturbingly Mafia-like and it didn't sound as appealing as the wedding. Two foreigners photographing the grieving widow and sobbing children – I'm not sure we would be keen on that idea.

'Would you like to visit a real village family? We will visit my wife's parents. They live near the pagoda you can see from your balcony,' said Cao.

'Yes please!' we said together.

It was decided. Wu and Cao went off in Chinese, talking quickly and loudly, till Mr Cao suddenly announced in English, 'I am the master of my own house!'

'I think you are a hen-pecked husband!' retorted Dean Wu laughing. Turning to us he said, 'When I was a student I read *Rip Van Winkle*. That story taught me two words "nostalgia" and "hen-pecked husband"! Mr Cao is a hen-pecked husband!'

We had had a few chats with Mr Cao, mainly brought about by things going wrong in the flat. Our shower had remained a constant source of work for the poor man, as in our first six months we had only managed to have three showers. He would repair it and each time he would return from the bathroom stained and splashed and declare he had solved the problem. Then it would work for five minutes before stopping again mysteriously. Each time he came he would sit and talk a little.

Once he told us about his mother. She had gone to his father's house when she was eight, and married his father when she was thirteen. His father had been Communist Party head of a village near Yuncheng which was now a suburb. The village was actually on the way into town from the college, still distinguishable from the centre because everyone there lived in brick compound houses, not flats, and still had farmland outside the city.

Another time he told us how happy he was to be married. He had met his wife when he was twenty-nine and she was twenty-one. He saw her, liked her, and got a friend to introduce her to him. They 'talked a lot' for about six months before they got married. When we joked about divorce he declared that divorce would be 'very dangerous' for him and his wife. 'People would put a lot of pressure on me,' he said, darkly.

One day I met him in the street, around pay day. Cao was cycling to lunch with his little son, who was too shy to say, 'Hello, Uncle,' to me despite several promptings, but turned away and started crying.

It's an effect I have on Chinese children when I smile, first used with ruthless ferocity on the Beijing Underground. Embittered by the horrified looks my pleasant smiles provoked I systematically and deliberately reduced a whole carriage full of staring toddlers to tears by smiling at them all. Blond, wide-eyed and big-nosed I looked like a demon; in much the same way that our devils are swarthy with slit eyes.

'Are you free on Sunday?' Cao asked. 'Come to my in-laws. They live near the pagoda, you know.'

We agreed, and although it was pay day, he cycled off without giving me my wages.

On Saturday morning just before lunch there was a knock at the door and Mr Cao walked in with another man, carrying a large red plastic bath between them. They pushed past me, put it in the bathroom, and left. As Cao passed back out of the door, he gripped my arm.

'Tomorrow,' he said. 'Wait here and I will come for you.' Then he disappeared.

Cao's wife's village is just to the northeast of Yuncheng, near a town called AnYi. Until the end of the Qing Dynasty in 1911, it was AnYi and not Yuncheng that was capital of the area, and the broken-topped pagoda was a relic from those days.

Over the barren, dusty winter fields lay a layer of frost, as the temperature had gone into freefall the Wednesday earlier. I thought we were going by bus, so when Mr Cao came to collect us and said, 'No gloves!' I didn't bother to take them.

We didn't bus it, but cycled, and I spent the entire journey regretting having left my gloves behind. My fingers were introducing me to new extremes of cold-induced pain as we rode along the busy road. Old men and peasants cycled leisurely at just about walking pace, while lorries loaded with sacks of coal and scrap metal swept past with wind-blown peasants perched on top. They blared their horns as they roared past in a swirl of dust. A few scooters dodged between us all, and a few we overtook.

To either side of the road were ponds for farming fish. Amidst all the noise a man rowed out over one in a boat, gently rippling the surface as he cast a net into the water. We glimpsed the pagoda over the buildings, its top crumbling away. Entering the village with the pagoda still visible above us, we followed Mr Cao as he cycled down a side road awash with liquid mud, lined with stalls of fruit, vegetables and whole sides of pork. Soon he turned off again onto a drier track where the puddles and the deep tyre tracks had dried solid.

'These houses are over one hundred years old,' he said, pointing to the leaning mud-brick cottages either side.

We passed one left-hand turn – no, the next one – yes! – and there was the pagoda in view at the end of an alley. From top to bottom of the structure, which was three times the height of the surrounding houses, ran a wide fissure. The pagoda stood in a circle of broken bricks and rubbish, bounded on all sides by mud-brick houses. At its front was the original stone gateway, its lintels still intact, but missing the surrounding wall that would give the locked gates a purpose.

We cycled up to the gate, parked our bikes and walked around the pagoda.

'Falling stones,' Cao said in warning.

On the western side of the pagoda was an engraved stone tablet, the width and height of a mediaeval church door. Maybe the engravings were Buddhist scriptures, or the name of the man who built it, but yellow spray paint now covered the otherwise pristine characters. On the opposite side to the tablet was a doorway that stank of piss. Looking up, I could see there were many windows or doorways further up the tower, but inside and out there seemed to be no way of actually climbing it.

Mario and Cao started talking to a group of boys who had followed us here. Cao signalled to me and we set off down an alley, following one of the boys through a gate into a courtyard. Cao popped his head through the front door of one of the houses then came out and said, 'There are no old men here. We go.' So we left and went into the next house.

Inside, the main living room was spacious but bare, the large wooden dressing table holding the room's only ornaments: a large rusty mirror, candles flanking the statue of a goddess, and a large black-and-white death photo of an old Chinese man – probably the grandfather of the rotund middle-aged man who appeared and ushered us to sit down. We sat at a low table surrounded by ankle-high stools and questioned him through Cao. All the while his large Hitachi TV – very out of place in a wattle-and-mud hut – blasted out, almost making the old building rattle in its foundations.

He told us the pagoda's name, which was so complicated I immediately forgot it. 'You know,' Cao said, 'the Japanese used the tower as a machine-gun post when they came in 1938. It was built in the Tang dynasty, but he doesn't know what it was for. In 1920 the pagoda was split wide open by an earthquake. Another earthquake in 1924 closed it up again.'

As we left there was a profusion of goodwill and backslapping, but very little understanding. The man walked us to our bikes, and stood waving till we cycled around the corner on our way to see Mr Cao's in-laws.

Their house was fairly similar to the one we had come from: just two rooms, the main room serving as kitchen, dining room and most other things, while the much smaller end room was a bedroom. We were sat down, and fed with sweets, peanuts, and local pastries stuffed with date paste and encrusted with coloured sugar.

As we munched with bulging cheeks, Cao chatted to his in-laws. He and his father-in-law smoking as his mother-in-law – a lady who was to die six months later of cancer – made the *jiaozi* stuffing of minced pork and fragrant chives and then kneaded the dough.

As she started to roll out the dough, Cao jumped up and

said, 'Come. We will go. We will go and see my Grandparents' house. It is very old.'

It was a short walk down a twisting alleyway to the Grandparents' house. From the outside it didn't look very different from the other village houses – made of mud bricks, with carved wooden beams supporting a grey-tiled roof, and all the surfaces covered with a generous layer of age. But the Grandparents' house was clotted with cobwebs that clung around the eaves, and the windows were not made of glass but still latticed and papered over with old newspapers.

'It is one hundred and fifty years old. Inside is old furniture,' said Cao, letting himself in.

There it was. Sturdy furniture, black with age, except where it had been polished smooth by long-dead hands and bony bottoms, and the rich grain of the wood shone out. The furniture was more elegant than anything we had seen before. Tall and slender, all the joints reinforced with small brackets of black iron.

There was no ceiling in the house, just an empty space up to the dark, slanting roof. Across the rafters there were spread lots of bamboo poles twenty metres long that ran almost the whole length of the house. There was no sign of the Grandparents.

I was wondering what on earth all the poles were for, when Cao said, 'Come,' and took us behind a curtained doorway into the small sleeping area. Across one half of the room lay the old fashioned *kang* – a brick bed heated from beneath by a small stove. The *kang*'s interior was divided from the rest of the room by a latticed wood-and-paper screen, which had a square opening in it. In the gap sat the small grandmother, cross-legged, wearing black padded trousers and jacket, and large round spectacles, one lens of which had a crack running from top to bottom. She made no sign as we came in, and Cao told us to sit. The grandfather sat on a stool next to the bed, warming himself by a free-standing stove. He had long stubble on his chin and wore a Mao suit and blue cap. They both looked older than the house itself.

We could have been visiting Qing Dynasty China – except

for the small colour TV and the reproduction Edwardian paintings of little girls and puppies that were pinned onto the mud-plastered wall. We said hello and sat smiling at each other, then the grandfather went out and came back with some family photos.

The first was a picture of his father's family long before he had been born. A line of figures, some standing, some seated, all looking out from their dark-embroidered robes with pale moon faces. He pointed to his father, still a young man, in the second row on the right-hand side. The large family group looked rigidly ahead without smiling, ladies with painted silk fans open to the camera, while the face of a baby in the arms of a fierce matriarch in the centre of the picture was a blur of movement.

Another photo featured the grandfather himself in the early 1940s, when he had been commandeered into working for the Japanese railway: a group of eight white-uniformed Chinese men with him on the end, and in front, three Japanese Army officers in khaki uniforms and caps, each with short whips in hand and one with a samurai sword.

'The Japanese arrived in 1938 and left in 1946. Eight years later,' Cao said by way of explanation.

You don't have to spend too long in China to realise that the usual sentiment towards the Japanese is not particularly friendly. The atrocities they committed during the Second World War in China were as horrific as Hitler's in Europe – and the Chinese will not forget. But as Cao had said so little I wondered what his attitude was to people like the grandfather who in some way had helped the invaders, and why he was being so reticent about condemning the Japanese. Perhaps he didn't want to be disrespectful to this old gentleman, or he didn't want us to feel alienated by any anti-foreigner sentiment.

We were given more sweets as Cao chatted away to the grandparents in Chinese. If we stopped eating for an instant the old man picked through the pile and unwrapped the best ones for us.

I was full already, but now it was time to go and have our *jiaozi*.

Only we three ate, Cao, Mario and I, while the rest of the family cooked and replaced our cooling bowls of *jiaozi* with fresh hot ones. Bowl after bowl. I was stuffed to the eyeballs, and on refusing, was implored by the mother not to be polite but to honour her by eating another bowl. Throughout all of this she apologized for her poverty, the common food, and the rustic conditions, telling me that China was still a developing country.

At last the flow of *jiaozi* stopped, and bowls of the water the *jiaozi* had been boiled in were brought to wash it all down.

'Drink,' Cao said. 'It is good. Healthy. Good for your stomach.' Cao ate another few bowls and I couldn't understand how he could put so much more food than me into his so-much-smaller body.

Goodbyes were short, and I was quickly out trying to swing my leg over my saddle – it was painful leaning forward to reach my handlebars. We had been here for two months now, and this was the first time we had been into a Chinese home and eaten with Chinese people. As we cycled out of the compound gateway and back to Yuncheng, I felt that at last I had crossed the threshold, and was just beginning to get to know China.

CHAPTER FIVE

ChunTian: Spring

Spring in Yuncheng is heralded by the onset of desert storms that come charging down from the north-west, bringing what looks and feels like half the Gobi Desert with them.

Their arrival is quite sudden, and tonight this one disturbed me as I started to fall asleep. The windows in their crude frames rattled loudly, and outside I could hear the tinkle as smashing panes of glass were ripped out of their loose frames by the strength of the roaring wind. The windows in my room – large things with multiple panes of glass loosely nailed into their crumbling wooden frames – had been a source of constant irritation, especially in the winter when the already inadequate heating was made irrelevant by icy draughts that caused the curtains to billow when the wind gusted. I tried everything, and now, despite the reams of tape that were stuck over every conceivable crack and crevice, I could still smell and taste the fine loess dust that is blasted past window, frame, and Sellotape by the force of the wind.

Next morning I had to go to the post office, fifteen minutes' cycle into town. The sky was a rich blue but despite the sunshine the air had a definite winter bite to it. My bicycle's tyres were, as always, too flat for cycling. But in China bicycle repair men are never too far away.

In fact there was one at this, the sleepy end of Hedong Donglu: a husband-and-wife team. He repaired bikes and motorbikes and she could achieve wonders with a derelict pair of shoes. So now I stopped there, and as always I got special treatment because I was foreign.

He checked the valve, taking it out and examining the rubber casing. Of course it was broken. He put on a new one, pumped up the tyres, and then I got to pay him my 'special price.' This could be anything – cheaper, the same, or more expensive than everyone else, and I'd been here so long now that I didn't really care – but he always reassured me that it was special. Hushed tones, an intimate look and comradely smile told me I'd been given the best treatment.

Stories abound in the Chinese newspapers about people who have made fortunes doing obscure jobs like this: a Beijing man who made 1000 *yuan* a month collecting beer-bottle tops, someone who funded his university education by collecting aluminium cans. Everybody knows someone who has become rich, everyone wants to become rich. But then there's always someone richer, someone making more money. A college of education wasn't the best place for a foreigner to observe the effects of the Chinese Socialist Market Economy – a nice-sounding name for unfettered capitalism – but most of my colleagues seemed unable to understand the changes that are happening in China, or if they could, were unable to take advantage of them. Maybe some of them had the entre-preneurial drive educated out of them, relying too much on their education and not business skills.

It's a problem that's widely acknowledged in China. A colleague told me, 'You see, the children see that the people who are rich – they are not well educated. They see that the educated people like teachers and lecturers are poor, and they think, "Why should I work hard?" '

The students often gossiped about the bicycle repair couple.

'He is very rich. Of course. Yes. Maybe 800 *yuan* a month. Three times as much as a teacher. That is a good job.'

But somehow I could not equate this dirty, sunburnt couple whose clothes were so grimy and oil-stained that their original colour was almost, but not quite, unrecognisable, with one of the new-rich of China. 'If they were rich then surely they'd wear better clothes?' I suggested.

'No. They are too mean. And if they wore good clothes then people would know how rich they are and pay less,' I was told.

61

I ignored this as *Hong Yan Bing* – 'Red-Eye Disease' – jealousy. But then I wondered. In the last few months I had seen the man riding a motorbike – a clapped-out old thing that must have been used as a prop in a World War Two film – but a motorbike nonetheless. Maybe it was true. He must have been doing alright.

Cycling into town I created the usual reaction. Foreigner in town! I could feel the sense of excitement I left in my wake. Most did nothing much, but enough stopped, shouted, stared dumbly, or ran to get their friends to look. Calls of 'Hallooo', 'Lao Wai', and other phrases that I deliberately tried not to learn came rushing after me. Before coming to China I had expected this, and for the first while it didn't bother me so much. It would abate, they would get used to seeing me, I thought. But they didn't, or if they did, there were always newcomers to town who had to start afresh. The longer I'd been here the more my circus-freak status ground on my nerves.

I'd been warned about this by other old China hands. 'When everything's all new and freaky to you, then you don't mind them thinking the same about you. But when you feel at home, naturalized, part of the community, that's when it upsets you,' one said. 'Then being treated like a non-human drives you mad.'

Unfortunately this had come true for me. I cursed and swore, a string of four-letter words under my breath, leaving the attention behind but cycling ever faster into more attention. It was silly really, but I could spend days, or even weeks, without venturing into the town at all just because I didn't feel up to the reaction I'd provoke. The relative security of the college or home was preferable to the outside world. Living your life constantly on show – when everything you do or say is monitored and talked about and every acquaintance is vetted – is extremely exhausting. Constantly having the fact that I was a foreigner drummed into me left me feeling embittered towards China.

'In England I was normal,' I told myself. 'I *will* be normal again.'

Today in town I had a definite mission, to post a letter home. Too often my trips into town were like this – lightning strikes – in and out before my patience was exhausted and frustration turned to anger. Most Chinese bureaucrats, if treated nicely, were fine, with the notable exception of my local post office staff, who had been trained in hell. As I cycled into town I was preparing myself for whatever they'd throw at me.

A gang of middle-aged women in their uniforms and peaked hats. In fact it was the same uniform as that of the army and the police – except theirs was blue not green. I could have been paranoid – I wasn't when I came, but it had plenty of chances to develop – but I was sure they deliberately annoyed me. Ignorant of the existence of a small-parcel rate, in fact ignorant of so many things – I had no choice but to put up with them. Previous excuses for not sending my mail had been that my envelopes were the wrong size, and that I could only use envelopes bought from this post office not the one near the college, and even that I had written my address in the wrong-coloured ink; I was supposed to write in black.

The Yuncheng postal staff were a maddening example of the Chinese work ethic in action, if that's the right word. In China, counter staff are not there to serve customers but just to get paid. Now, willing this transaction to go smoothly I handed my letter over to the lady. She leered at it, snarled at me, flung it back, and started to count through a thick book of receipts. She thumbed through the pad of paper, added up the totals, and then cross checked. I knew she would not suffer any interruptions. She was out of service until the problem – me – went away. A throng pushed up all around me, all shoving their letters through at her. She ignored us all as she started counting again. Sweat trickled down from my armpit as I nudged people who were pressing round me, forcefully enough to make them back away a little. This was enough to drive me to violence, but I knew that I had no choice but to accept it if I wanted my mail to pass to and fro without more hassle.

She looked up, I smiled, said 'England!' and she considered for a moment – then took my letter, told me the price, and made a joke to the next lady that I wouldn't want to understand even if I could. The operation appeared complete.

I told myself that it could have been worse as I left, relieved to have got it all over with.

Outside there were drifts of dust all over town, a memento of last night's winds. It was a good enough reason for a city spring clean, when 'Volunteers' spruced up their work-unit compounds, brushing the dust into the streets. Teams of women swept the roads, and used the dirt to fill in the numerous potholes. The concrete bollards that were connected by metal poles and bisected each lane, protecting cyclists from motorised traffic, (or was it the other way round?) were painted by a rag-taggle band of peasants.

Despite their obvious effort and the fun everyone was having sweeping brush-loads of dirt everywhere, it was a grand waste of time. Dust in Yuncheng is like water in Venice. You can sweep it up, tip it over your neighbour's wall, or beat it into the potholes, but come the next breath of air it'll be all over the place again. The talcum consistency of the loess dust makes it too fine to stay anywhere for long, and now all the frenetic broom work and sweeping had created clouds of dust that were inevitably settling on the freshly painted white bollards, returning them to their dirty shade minutes after they had been cleaned up.

Yesterday we were invited to play football by some students. By 4.30 PM the news had got around the college. Mario and I walked down to the sports ground and saw a crowd, three people deep, encircling the football pitch, the front row squatting on their haunches like expectant crows. They saw us coming, and all clapped as we walked on to the pitch.

'Oh hell!' I thought. 'I can't even play football.'

My public humiliation was made worse because Mario could play. Very well. By his fifth goal – all dazzling solo efforts – I cursed my luck. Luckily for me the students, although they were individually quite skilful, had no concept of team play. Their passes were lazy, overconfident and predictable and if they did get clear with the ball then they tried to be too fancy and ended up falling over themselves. In many ways Chinese football seemed to be a live demonstration of the Chaos Theory – the ball was bounced around like in a pin-ball machine and all the players rushed after it *en masse* without any apparent game plan. Even for someone as bad as me, they were relatively easy to pressurise into mistakes.

The final whistle went, and the teacher in charge came over. His English was thick-accented and delivered one syllable at a time.

'Hel-lo. My name is Lu JunYi. Welcome you to Chi-na.' His chest was heaving with the exertion and the effort of talking to us.

'Thank you. I'm Justin. This is Mario,' I said. He frowned and I could see I'd lost him already. 'Justin! Mario!' I said pointing to each of us in turn.

There was a long pause, before he said, 'Thank you. Goodbye,' and went off, very pleased with himself.

We set off and an interested crowd followed us halfway home, before turning aside to have dinner, and give other people room to look.

Last night we had our major breakthrough in the Chinese language – quite a momentous event for us after two months of being here. There was so much that we wanted to do – buy our own food and cook for ourselves, talk to the people we met in the streets, say something more than 'Hello' to our neighbours, just begin to interact normally in this society – but couldn't because we couldn't speak Chinese.

The conditions for last night's breakthrough were in some ways ideal – we had had a couple of beers and the two men who were chatting to us were very relaxed despite the fact we were Westerners – and to top it all they seemed to know our Chinese textbook off by heart. They asked all the right questions – even in the right order. It was perfect, an instrumental lesson in how much you could say with very little.

We were sitting in Hedong Square on a warm dark evening whilst the chaotic noises and activity of the nightlife swirled rather confusingly around us. Even after eight weeks, life here was still so new that every day was something of a learning experience – which made every minute of life immensely exciting and exhausting at the same time. We sat down at one of the small tables and chairs of bamboo and ordered two beers. They were brought and then we were left alone to drink. The salesman – a grizzled old peasant with a stained open shirt and a quiet temperament – surprised us by not calling all his pals over to come and look at us, nor did he sit and stare. He gave us our beer and two plastic cups still awash with water (a common practice designed, I could only guess, to prove that they have been cleaned) and then wandered off to serve some other customers.

After an hour or so he did come over – and we had our first good chat in our new language. We said who we were and why we were in Yuncheng, and he told us about himself. He had four pool tables which he rented out whilst serving people beer and tea. He earned about 300 *yuan* a month, which was more than the college lecturers. We told him how much we earned a month – which he said wasn't enough and that the college should pay us more, how many brothers and sisters we had and that we weren't married. He wanted to know how much we could earn in England and when we told him he wanted to know why we came to China for so little money? We told him China was a very interesting country and that we had come here to learn about it.

As the darkness deepened a group of Shaolin monks came over to listen. Shaolin Temple is the most famous *kung fu* teaching monastery in China, but this group were little more than itinerant performers travelling from town to town smashing bricks and logs with different parts of their bodies. They didn't seem particularly holy, sitting in their yellow robes and shaven pates, giggling, and I began to feel that religious vocations might not be taken so seriously in China. But a group of shrouded monks seemed an apt audience for this special evening, which, now, only one day after, had already begun to take on an almost religious significance for us, offering us a glimmer of hope that someday we would be able to talk

66

fluent Chinese and begin to integrate more naturally into Yuncheng society.

The one thing that gives Yuncheng a respite from the dust is rain. But by the time the droplets have reached ground level they are already dirty, having washed through the air which is hazy with dust. The first drops vanish into the parched soil, disappearing as if they had never existed. When the topsoil is damp, it takes on the consistency of a mud-pack and sticks tenaciously to everything. Given more rain, which is very unusual as the climate here is practically a desert, the gutters become awash with a deep brown liquid like the lakes and rivers in Charlie's chocolate factory. This is the same consistency as the neighbouring Yellow River, which always looks like a torrent of bubbling, turgid chocolate.

When the rain fell as heavily as this then our breathing was free from dust, and the South Mountain was clear to view, but it brought along new problems of its own: by the roadside a wall collapsed because its foundations had been washed away; a large section of field slipped down across the upper end of Hedong Donglu; in the college sports ground there were large craters where underground streams washed through and the ground above imploded; a similar effect could be seen on the Tarmac roads as their foundations washed away, and the day's traffic rumbled over the surface which gradually sank deeper and deeper, finally cracking open and falling into the hollows beneath.

The Chinese do not like rain and never venture out if it is raining. This they can afford to do as it only rains once a month at best. Twice a month in the late summer rainy season. For me rain was a welcome release in many ways. I pulled down my umbrella over my head as I walked the empty streets, feeling completely sheltered from unwanted attention. I didn't know if this was the whole reason, or the fact that it was good to be outside, smelling the rich scents of earth, streets, and flowers that the dampness suddenly unlocked – but I always headed outside in the rain. Thinking of home.

I was so firmly grounded in the day-to-day realities of China, that England felt unreal to me now. Letters, telling me of episodes in other people's lives seemed to come from a dream world. I couldn't even imagine myself in England any more – just like I couldn't imagine myself in China before I arrived. China dominated my life so much that I couldn't even imagine myself leaving it – now I was settled, the trauma of uprooting myself again daunted me.

Yuncheng Bank of China have a problem, and I am the only man who can solve it. The problem is here in front of me. Two Bank of England notes printed on thick cloth, claiming to be worth £500,000 each. Dean Wu, whose daughter works at the bank, has brought them in for me to check.

'Are these joke money?' I ask him. I've been away so long that at first I'm not so sure if we have notes for this much or not, and if we do, what £500,000 banknotes look like.

'No, they are real. Are they real?' he asks, smoking thoughtfully, waiting for my answer.

Maybe they are real. They might be real. England is now so unfamiliar to me, I find myself sounding very uncertain. But a quick check proves they cannot be real. Gibberish on the back, and a picture of the Queen with a gaudy gold painted necklace and crown, dated 1933 – when we had a king.

With this evidence I pronounce them, in front of everyone, to be false. They are whisked away as Wu's daughter rushes back to the bank.

'So where did you get them from?' I ask Dean Wu, who is retelling the story to some students in Chinese.

'Oh, you see, a Hong Kong man has tried to cash these at the bank here in Yuncheng. Only you could tell us if they were real or not. Now you have confirmed their – authenticity!'

I later found out that they had gone to the flat first to ask Mario, and he had given the same answer as me, and proved it by showing them a real twenty-pound note. Still, it never hurts to double check.

At our first college sports day Mario and I were the focus of a lot of attention and giggles, and all the races we ran were keenly watched. As foreigners this was to be expected. What was remarkable was that one other person got more attention than us.

This person's name was Ma XiaoDan, an art student. When he was nine years old he had lost both arms, and his commendable effort at coming third in the hundred metres despite having no arms caused unashamed hilarity in the crowd. I did not understand the laughter, to me it seemed disgusting, but no-one seemed upset by it, and teachers and students laughed as openly as all the others.

'An armless man running looks funny – so we laugh,' a student said with simple logic. Ma XiaoDan's running was unusual, and laughter was the response.

That he too was treated as a freak created a bond of mutual sympathy between us, and soon we were exchanging how are yous, long before I knew anything more about him. Then one of my students, Zhu Gui, phoned to tell me that one of the art department students had an invitation for us and could they come around after lunch?

We had been invited to a couple of the art students' exhibitions before and had been encouraged to write something short and wise in their visitors' books to give a foreigner's view of their work. It was a pleasure to oblige. Would it be another graduation show? Special visits usually had some hidden agenda, and telephoning for permission to come round was definitely suspicious. Mario decided that it would be students from the performance part of the department wanting some Western music tapes. I thought that some painters would want to use us as models. Mario and I were still trying to guess what it might be when there was a knock at the door.

We were both wrong. It was Zhu Gui, with Ma XiaoDan – and he didn't want anything from us at all – in fact quite the opposite. As we ushered him to a seat there were the usual pleasantries, enthusiastic nodding and smiling that were needed to fill the place of conversation.

'Ma XiaoDan is from my home town,' Zhu Gui began. 'When he lost his arms, he began to paint using his feet. Next week there will be an exhibition of his work in the Yuncheng

Museum. XiaoDan would like to invite you to the opening ceremony.'

We were delighted and agreed, and then congratulated him on his running ability.

'He was at the National Handicapped Games, running two hundred metres,' said Zhu Gui. 'He is also vice president of our district's organization for handicapped people.'

The following week we arrived early for the exhibition. There were a few extrovert art department students I recognized from the basketball court, and members of Ma XiaoDan's family. We had our photo taken outside the museum with his friends and father and then went to see the pictures.

Inside the courtyard a group of deaf children gathered around their teacher who was talking to them in sign language. They burst into a frenzied chatter of hand signals when they saw us. It was quite odd to be the centre of such silent observation, equally odd because I was as curious about their behaviour as they were about mine.

There was one group of paintings in his exhibition that really drew my attention: *Chun-Xia-Qun-Dong – Spring, Summer, Autumn, Winter* – a traditional theme in Chinese ink painting which shows a rural scene through the four seasons. Typically Chinese, they depict the mythical world of the peasant living in harmony with the bamboo groves, mist-wreathed peaks and limpid pools. They are simple, timeless and utterly enchanting. But it really was the feeling of being welcomed as a freak in the company of other freaks that overcame me and made me feel quite weepy.

I had just been out to buy some fruit for a friend, Shi YongMei, who had invited us over to her house for lunch. There was a dust storm blowing against me as I cycled almost blind, my eyes streaming gritty tears.

At eleven o'clock we met up with Dean Wu who had also been invited, and went down the road to Shi YongMei's work unit.

We were invited into the living room – the best room that also doubled as their daughter's bedroom – and we were given fruit, sweets and peanuts. We refused all these goodies, and joined Dean Wu in an impromptu tour of the flat. This un-guest-like behaviour – refusing food and not sitting down – caused a flurry of panic amongst the womenfolk, who thankfully did not try to wrestle us into our seats, but looked at us full of awe, unsure what to do.

There was another bedroom, with a double bed in it, a bathroom and kitchen. The main hallway was converted into a mini classroom with a blackboard, desks and chairs. Shi YongMei's father, now retired, had been the head of the music department in the college, and to supplement his pension now taught music to children.

The women – Shi YongMei, her mother, and a friend who'd come over to help on this big day, were all in the kitchen. We offered to go and help, which brought on an even greater onset of panic, as the idea implied that we were not being cared for properly as guests and were having to do things for ourselves. We were seated again, Shi YongMei peeling apples and bananas which she then presented to us faster than we could eat them. Soon Dean Wu, Shi YongMei's father and her husband joined us, leaving the ladies in the kitchen working on the food.

The husband worked at the electrical plant as an engineer.

'Are you busy?' I asked.

'No,' he said, with a little laugh. 'I am never busy, but I still have to go to work. You see, there are twelve of us on each shift, but maybe three of us could do the work, so we just sit around and smoke. Cigarettes! I never smoked a single cigarette until I started work, but I had to do something to fill the time. I couldn't drink tea all day – I'd spend the whole day pissing! – so I began smoking.'

'So did you get this flat when you started work here?'

'Oh no, when we got married we had to live with my parents for four years. Then we got this flat from my work unit,' he told us, unscrewing a bottle of *baijiu* – Chinese firewater. 'We must finish all this bottle today,' he said, and started laughing at the two very worried-looking foreigners.

One of the pleasures of living in China was that it never ceased to surprise, so when I began to think that now, surely, I must have a fairly rounded idea of life here, then it unlocked another secret for me, which upset everything I thought before and was tantalizing enough to keep me going until next time.

We'd been using a swimming pool in town for a while, and in return for free swims we were required in a very ad-hoc manner to visit the swimming pool keeper's son's film shack. The swimming pool was off the main street, down a mud track, and the son's shack was through one of the doorways that opened off this road. In a little room with blacked-out windows that was so hot inside that even the mosquitoes were trying to get out, we could watch all the films we liked for two *yuan*. The room was no bigger than my bedroom, and often seated thirty people. But the screen was no plain video and television job. This was a surround-sound-wide-flat-screen laser-disc-player affair.

I watched with incredulity as the son took a small suitcase from under his bed and, after clicking open all the various locks and clasps, showed us his collection of laser discs. There were, of course, all the sex and violence films that Hollywood devotes itself to.

'Could we see one now?' we asked, almost giddy with the thought of seeing a western film.

The son shook his head. 'After eight.' Then, pointing to the man and woman on the cover and graphically demonstrating sexual intercourse with his fingers, said, 'There are too many small children.'

The entrance to the cinema was covered by a thick black quilt to soundproof the room. From inside I could hear the explosions, grunts, shots and cries of a run-of-the-mill Hong Kong kung fu film. Too young for sex, but not for violence.

'Never for violence!' The owner laughed.

That evening we watched the film, a fairly recent Hollywood blockbuster. It started with sex, had lots of violence in between, then ended with sex.

Watching this kind of picture I felt that I had grown quite apart from my native culture during the months in China. Now I was an outsider from it, I found I did not share the same beliefs as my friends and family at home, and I was not a member of the world that they lived in. What I was seeing – sex, violence, a hunger for money – seemed to me to be very wrong. But it hadn't seemed so in England. There it all seemed normal. That I had such different views of the kind of films I had previously enjoyed worried me. Was I becoming Chinese? Or was I getting a new perspective into the West? One stifles individuality and personal freedoms, the other encourages these at the expense of society as a whole. I didn't have any answers but I knew both were wrong.

In keeping with our declining visits to the little room, however, our access to the swimming pool was dwindling too. 'No coal. No heating. The water's dirty. No water,' were the excuses given until we gave up trying.

An American friend, new to China, once told me that she couldn't get into the country. Couldn't get behind the Happyland façade they presented to outsiders. The Mary Poppins land where Our Chinese People are kind, polite and beautiful.

This was certainly a problem for me, living in China, especially when so much time was spent with students. Although they were over eighteen years old their lives were ruled by Confucian principles: they believed that in return for their service and humility their masters would perform their role correctly. This ancient principle still underlies the Communist Party's ideology. Once I showed my students *A Room with a View* – confident that the scene where the men play naked in a forest pool was not too risqué for them. But the silence of moral outrage that descended as the men began to undress made me feel acutely embarrassed – and to my astonishment it was me who turned scarlet with humiliation. Two or three mature students actually walked out of the room. Personally, I think there is no more natural and amusing scene, regardless of the buttocks and occasional glimpses of male genitalia, but they were obviously unhappy. I thought, no wonder I sometimes find their topics of conversation rather limited.

At times I felt that there was no real depth to the Chinese society I knew. No substance. Everyone seemed to have the same opinion on the Past, Present and Future – views that were either naive or untrue. There was no talk of any scandal and no dissent about the government or society. The education system did not equip people with inquisitive minds, so they were taught to obey instructions without asking why. Sex seemed non-existent – leaving a big question mark over the population boom – and it looked like these characteristics would not change during my time there. I would hate China to become like Britain, but I just felt that there was no grit in life here. There seemed to be such a lack of vitality, conviction or purpose in the people, other than that of wanting to become rich. Chinese people have a history of being submissive to their rulers, and the lesson of Tiananmen Square was that the people are not allowed to criticize the Party's rule. Idealism, democratic change, increased political accountability were all taboo subjects. The only channel left for their energies was making money.

The daily evidence supported this belief – greater familiarity and friendship with the people did not lead me to a hidden world of sex, drugs and rock 'n' roll. Where were their ambitions and desires? With a few exceptions friendship with Chinese people was just more of the same, a multitude of voices all saying the same thing.

That was until we found Song Jiang. Or rather discovered what it was he had to give. He encouraged us to persevere – and as time went on we found more people who were prepared to allow us into their private lives.

Song Jiang was a teacher in our English department who had only recently returned from Canada, where he had been studying for two-and-a-half years.

The first time we went to his house, we were quite drunk. He had given us an open invitation, and after a few beers we decided to take him up on his offer. He sobered us up with cup after cup of sweet black coffee while we sat around his table and chatted. His first question was, 'How old do you think I am?'

Used to adding a few years on to the age of Chinese people, we answered in unison, 'twenty-five.'

'Actually, I am thirty-seven,' he replied. 'After I left school it was the Cultural Revolution. I was a train driver for seven years. There was nothing to do, so I taught myself to play the piano. Then I began to teach myself English. In 1978 some of the colleges reopened. Each work unit could send a worker – and so I got a place to study at Xian. I've been teaching now for nine years. Here, have a look at this!' he said, passing over a book of English short stories printed in 1948. 'I am translating this at the moment. The President likes me and he told me that I must do a few translations, then the college can make me an associate professor.'

At that moment the electricity went so we sat in candlelight, the darkness all around us and the deep silence making it feel like we were talking deep into the night. This atmosphere, the candles and our conversation, made our meeting feel very conspiratorial.

'You know, I was in Canada. I was there during the 1989 Incident. I watched everything that happened. It was very worrying. None of my letters were allowed through. I got a few letters from my wife so I knew she was alright. She phoned me once, and we talked for one minute then she was cut off. The Canadian government was offering all Chinese people asylum, but my wife was pleading for me to come home. What could I do? I had to return to look after my wife.

'You know, I have had many arguments with the college. Because the colleges defied the government in 1989 they were targeted for re-education, and there are still compulsory re-education meetings. I refuse to go. The meetings are a waste of time. All that happens is that the Party secretary sits and reads from the newspapers – whatever they have reported – the latest speeches from Zhang Ze Ming or Li Pung. We have four hours of meetings a week, and because I don't go then my pay is docked. I don't care – they can have the money – I won't go to their meetings.'

The electricity returned and I could see that Mario was in as much shock as myself. We had been there a while already and no one apart from Deep Throat had given, even in the strictest confidence, anything except the official Party line. Here

Tiananmen had been brought up without prompting from us, and that was only for warm-ups.

In my mind I could hear the clangs! as the secret door that hid Chinese society came swinging open. So there really was so much more than had been let on. Now I knew it all seemed very obvious, but before, when no-one admitted or even referred to it how could I know? It was as if a huge conspiracy had been unveiled by one insider – Song Jiang.

Hedong Square has a lively market in the summer nights. As the midday heat increases then the daytime markets close and turn into evening markets instead. Between the two rows of shacks in the square where men furiously manipulate the frying noodles, everyone surges about under a starlit sky, and a yellowed moon just past full ripeness hangs low in the eastern sky. Girls are out walking in their pretty frocks, dabbing sweat from their upper lips with minutely folded handkerchiefs. People selling pieces of five-spice rabbit from their panniers walk up and down forlornly calling out, advertising their wares.

We had our own 'noodle man', or rather a noodle couple. We always went to them, for the simple reason that when we first arrived he was the only one who didn't try to charge us double. His noodles weren't even that good, but when everyone was out to cheat you for being a dumb foreigner the smallest kindness was gladly repaid, and now he profited nicely from our continued custom.

A fellow teacher, unfamiliar with the possibilities of the nighttime food market, told me that she had once gone to the square and that she had asked someone which was the best noodle place to go to. The passer-by pointed out our noodle man and said that he was the best because the foreigners went there.

We looked for him in his usual spot in the market, but tonight he was not here. We asked a few of the other shack owners where he was.

A wily old man next door, who was wearing a cap like Rip Van Winkle's, was pleased to tell us: 'He doesn't have a licence. No licence no cook. Come here – my noodles are the most delicious,' he said. 'Come here! My noodles are the best in town!'

In among the Chinese – couples out to eat, mothers feeding their children, students beginning to evolve into adults, young men out to drink and talk – among all the bustle, noise, lights and darkness we somehow fitted in. In such a mixed bunch, all with their own business to see to, the level of attention was refreshingly mild, and usually we could sit and eat in peace.

Once we actually sat engulfed in a crowd of people who were watching an argument, oblivious to the two *LaoWais* sitting right underneath their noses.

The argument was between a short, stout middle-aged woman, who looked like someone who would rarely boil over, and a shack owner who sold kebabs of meat and vegetables from his glass cabinet on wheels. They cursed and swore, shouted and insulted each other for a few minutes with the volume of abuse rising. A large crowd of docile observers gathered in the shadowy night. An audience of ghosts while the two in the middle screamed insults that sounded like machine-gun fire, spotlighted in the eerie light of a swinging lightbulb. The woman went off, returned, left again and returned once more. Nobody in the audience moved to intervene, just watched dumbly.

It is strange how arguments are resolved in different societies. In the West a person is likely to 'lose face' by not fighting, and so we resort to violence much earlier than the Chinese, who lose face by not winning. So in China arguments involve long periods of shouting which only rarely spill over into violence. If they do, it is sudden and explosive. This argument had reached the explosive stage. Ten minutes of cursing, and the woman flipped her lid and started smashing each glass panel on the man's cabinet. Then the man lost all rational control. He dashed off, wild with fury, grabbed a wooden stool and charged back with it raised above his head. He brought it down to smash the brains out of the woman on the very spot.

At this instant, as the man was in half swing and the woman a fraction of a second from joining her ancestors, the previously inert crowd rushed suddenly in. Ten raised hands stopped the blow from falling, then twenty arms pushed him back, and a tide of people swept the two combatants apart.

I'd seen something similar once. That time the weapon had been not a stool but a cleaver. I was convinced that I was about to witness murder when the public intervened. Now that I'd seen it a second time I began to get a sense of its grand theatre, like a melodramatic opera. People could swing cleavers and stools with all their venom at others, confident in the knowledge that they'd always be stopped. Then everyone could leave the scene with face intact.

'I tried to kill her,' the man could say. 'If everyone hadn't got in the way then I would have showed her.' While the woman would tell her friends, 'I stood up to him, and he couldn't take it. Tried to hit me – but everyone agreed with me and fought him off.'

A very Chinese solution.

Yuncheng has trebled in size in the last sixteen years, and so the old centre of town – with its department stores and schools – is relegated now to a suburb.

Peasants flock to the city, especially during the agricultural low season, but most do not stay long. There is no heavy industry in Yuncheng, and so they head further afield to China's major cities: Beijing, Tianjing, Shanghai, Guandong. A few who do remain join the ranks of salesmen at the roadside. These people are a random bunch: peasants from far off and from local villages, unemployed city folk and occasionally one of last year's students turns up too, sheepish and unwilling to talk. Whatever else education gives them, it also provides them with unrealistic expectations and invariably their hopes are fruitless. So it is of particular embarrassment for them to meet me.

Some of the salespeople bring their own produce in early in the morning, cycling in along mud tracks with their reed panniers full of carefully padded eggs, fruit, or vegetables. But most buy it from wholesalers in the alleys in town. One street is packed with mountains of melons, cabbages, potatoes, and spring onions selling by the sackload to middlemen. These sell from anything available, usually the backs of rickshaws or on pieces of sackcloth spread over the road. As the day progresses they edge further and further into the road till by midday they form a line down the middle.

There was one man I met, in his early twenties, wearing army trousers and an old suit jacket, who had a smattering of English. He spoke badly – slowly forming each word before forcing it out – but with patience we could have simple conversations. I think he learned and practised things to tell me in case we should meet.

And so I pieced together fragments of his life. English had been his favourite subject at school, and he had been the best in his village. He had failed his school exams, but instead of staying in his village, he had left to seek work.

One day he produced a notebook from his pocket, a diary full of Chinese characters and on the opposite pages their English translation.

A friend in Beijing who had taught me a little Chinese had compared the different writing systems. 'Chinese characters are drawings, a cartoon story. Western writing is phonetic, each page so many sounds – like a symphony.' Here on the page I could appreciate this. The stylized Chinese characters and the Western writing, which did resemble music notation.

As with most Chinese, this salesman was, as Dean Wu liked to say, 'Deaf and dumb. He can barely hear or speak English, although he can read and write.'

I didn't have time to go through the whole notebook, and so went through the first passages; his life story: after failing his college exams, he had gone to Beijing and Tianjing to paint doorways. He decided that this was not a good life, and went to a local tourist mountain, HuaShan, where he worked – at what I'm not sure – but he was not well paid, so he returned to Yuncheng. He was planning a trip to Guandong soon with his brother. There they hoped to become rich. Standing over his sackcloth with tomatoes and aubergines I gave him an impromptu English lesson surrounded by other curious vegetable sellers.

*

'Hi, Song Jiang,' I said as he appeared in the department office. I hadn't seen him for a while. One night I phoned his flat and his wife, a policewoman, told me that he was doing business in Xian.

'Hi, Justin! I haven't seen you for a long time.'

'No. How are things?'

'Not so good. There is a rumour that Deng XiaoPing has died, so the Taiyuan stock market has crashed. We have lost a lot of money. Also we have two Japanese cars that we cannot sell.'

'How did you get those?'

'You see, the Navy smuggles them in from Japan and sells them on the dockside. We bought two, but it is quite difficult to sell them without the necessary papers.'

'The Navy is smuggling cars?' I asked in surprise.

'Of course,' smiled Song Jiang.

To ensure the survival of the economic reforms in China the leadership have wooed the PLA – People's Liberation Army – drawing them into the new markets. The PLA is now the biggest financial body in China, with its fingers, hands and arms deeply embedded in the money pot. Not just servicing arms industries but more lucrative financial concerns. A recent crackdown on drugs, prostitution and illegal gambling in Canton resulted in a number of nightclubs and karaoke bars being shut down – most of them owned by the PLA. I guess they're still liberating the people, but in rather different ways.

It's a pattern throughout China. In order to guarantee the success of the economic reforms, the support of the governing class is needed: Communist Party members, high-level bureaucrats, and army leaders. No better way to ensure the reforms' survival than to let them get rich first.

Time permitting, we often joined the old men who played tennis at the courts near Hedong Square. Duan Yu, the mirror-shaded teacher of English, had taken us down first and introduced us to the 'club'. His wife, a petite solicitor, was a keen player, but otherwise the tennis scene in Yuncheng had a distinctly geriatric feel to it. All the players, except for a few grandchildren and newcomers like Duan Yu, were over sixty. During the Cultural Revolution, tennis was one of those foreign games, the playing of which would leave people open to 'criticism', a dubious euphemism for intimidation, beatings and arbitrary imprisonment.

The tennis club members were a comfortable group to be with. They had an air of jovial camaraderie and took the presence of foreigners in their midst with a calmness that was the direct opposite of everyone else in China. In fact in general I found the older generation were the least excited by our presence, partly due to the confidence that old age brings, but also because they had had more experience of foreigners, in the days before Liberation or the Cultural Revolution.

As people watched the games there was a tranquil silence except for the sound of the ball being knocked back and forth. That was until someone missed a shot, hit a dud, or in any other way slipped up, when everyone would collapse into fits of laughter.

As a Westerner I found this embarrassing at first, but it was good-natured humour, without the face-conscious tension of the younger Chinese. Laughter is very catchy, and I soon found I was joining in with all the rest. Indeed, I began to worry that I had become China-ised, and that back in England I would cause mortal offence by hooting with laughter at other people's mistakes.

One player stuck out from the others. I don't know his real name because he was always described as 'Taiwan *ren*' – 'Taiwanese man' – I think he had taken the appellation as a title.

His designer white tracksuit, expensive composite racquet, slicked-back hair, self-important attitude and large build stacked up on top of his stomach were in complete contrast to the native Chinese. They wore cheap plimsolls, played in whatever clothes they had, and were Lowry stick-men compared to this well-fed goliath.

Although his name was Taiwan *ren*, his blood was actually more local than most of the other players, who had been sent here during the Cultural Revolution from the richer provinces like Shandong and Hubei, to help build up the hinterland. Yuncheng was his '*LaoJia*' – his hometown – a word that has more significance for Chinese than for Westerners. *LaoJia* implies the very earth your ancestors have tilled and been buried in for generations. So it was natural that this old Taiwan *ren* should come here to die, now welcomed by a government eager for foreign capital. The Taiwan *ren* was seventy-five now, so he would have been about thirty when he fled to Taiwan. As a landlord or capitalist he had no doubt been chased out of China by the efforts of some of the old men here.

Another member of the 'club' was Lao Gao, a lecturer from our college, who'd been sent here from Shandong during the Cultural Revolution. When the madness had finally ended he had been caught up through marriage into this new community so he never made it back home to his family.

The day before the workers' May Day holiday he came up to us and invited us to play the next morning. 'Tennis tournament?! Tomorrow morning – OK – fine, we'll play.'

It was kind of him to think of us, but we still grumbled about the endemic lack of warning in China. It was too late to put in some practice, and, even worse, we had to be up at 6:30 AM on a Sunday morning.

It was not a very big affair, just six pairs of players who all played each other in a round robin. It was strange to be competing with the town's geriatrics – like joining your grandad and his friends for a game – what made it worse was that we lost our first match 6–2.

The wizened appearance of the opposition was very deceptive. Although admittedly a little slow on their feet, their brains and skills were still sharp enough. Confusing spins and surgical precision more than made up for their lack of speed. They did tire quickly though, and by our second match our opposition were beginning to flag. We sat on benches along the side of the court, watching, while Taiwan *ren* sent his daughter off to buy drinks and ice creams for everyone. The sun got hotter and hotter, and we sheltered under tracksuit tops trying to reduce the glare. At eleven we stopped and rested until five when the temperature was a little more gentle, but still hotter than a hot English summer's day.

I felt as if I was watching a Sunday-afternoon cricket match – no pressure and no worries. The old men seemed calmly to accept our presence, an event that is terribly rare in China. We were so strange-looking to them and our cultures so different that acceptance was something I thought I'd never feel in China. This desert of emotion left me gasping for someone to treat me normally – and made moments like this so precious. Outside the perimeter fence a handful of peasants looked in – reminding me of hungry convicts looking through to a different world. But inside everyone was treating us as if we were normal, neither fawning, grasping, curious, or obsessed by us. For a few hours I actually felt like a normal person.

Mario was called over to referee the next match, and one of the old men came over to sit with me. We chatted a little, then sat without speaking, just keeping each other company. He looked fifty but was in fact seventy. A retired teacher. He had joined the Communist Party because he wanted to help drive the Japanese out of his country.

As the afternoon turned into evening a dust storm whipped up, and the competition ended as everyone hurried home, the Chinese on bicycles, and the Taiwan *ren* on his moped. It had been such a pleasant day – away from all the attention and pressures that I thought to myself, 'How can I ever leave China?'

We crossed Hedong Donglu as the sun set in a ball of red at the eastern end of the street while the moon rose in the west, tinted a pale rose by the reflected sunlight.

CHAPTER SIX

Guanxi

Our duties at the college were generally to improve the communicative language skills of the student teachers, who would go on to be English teachers in their home towns or villages. Mr Wu, Mr Cao, and all the other English department teachers had been taught by Western teachers during their studies, and so had at least been exposed to the peculiarities of foreigners. For my students it was very different. The first time any of them had seen a foreigner was when I walked into class at the beginning of term. They were like schoolboys learning Latin suddenly having Julius Caesar walk into the class for a chat.

As I walked down the corridor I could hear an excited babble of voices that went suddenly silent as I walked in and put my books down on the desk.

'Good morning!' I said loud and clear, and broke the spell.

En masse they shot up. 'Good morning!' they chorused loudly back, then sat down, some still staring at me intently, others smiling with pleasure at their first successful interaction with a foreigner in a language they'd been learning for seven years.

Unfortunately, for a long time we didn't progress much further than that.

China is such a unique and compelling country that I had an insatiable hunger to learn everything I could about it. I was interested in everything Chinese – philosophy, calligraphy, paintings, history, but this stuff was beyond their range – as it would have been with their British equivalents, young adults fresh from school. Nearly all the students were peasant children, or lived in the small market towns around Yuncheng.

Even though millions of Chinese live in some of the largest cities on earth – Shanghai: twelve million, ChongQing: fourteen million – China is still in many ways an agricultural society, with about seventy per cent of the 1.2 billion population living and working in what is still a labour-intensive agricultural economy. The peasants have tough lives, in which such things as freedom, choice, and personal self-fulfilment are alien concepts.

So it was that our students' holidays were spent working in the fields, and during the term there were two breaks in which the students went home to gather in the harvest, those from the south of Shanxi leaving first as the harvest swept northwards.

While it lasted it dominated the country. The news centred on the country's crops and farmers, giving daily reports on the quantity brought in so far. In each village the wheat harvest lasted nearly a week, everyone up at five AM and working in teams to cut the wheat with sickles. Sometimes the government would send machines to help, but they were unreliable and there were too few to go around. So the cutting, threshing and sacking was all done by hand.

As well as wheat, many families also grew cotton, which was backbreaking to collect, or apples, and in the autumn a harvest of maize. Whenever needed the students would sneak off home, and return to college covered in cuts and scratches and calluses – testament to farming methods extinct in England for at least two generations – while I would try to teach them English.

Unfortunately many of the students didn't want to study English at all, but they had no say in what, or where they studied after school. Each year the regional education authority looks at the school examination results and assigns each student to a college and a subject.

Sometimes this made the task of motivating the students quite hopeless. Trying to invigorate one student with a sense of purpose, and not having much success, I said, 'So, don't you want to study English?'

'No,' she answered. 'I don't like English – I want to study maths.' Her answer left me quite disconsolate – surely my lessons weren't that bad? I mean maths!

But then there were students at the opposite extreme – those who were super-keen: 'Now I get more interested in different ideas between Western peoples and Chinese,' a student called Zhu Gui once told me. 'English takes me into another world, a very beautiful one. It widens my view. I love the language! More than that – it may be the most useful language in the world.'

Despite the flowery adjectives what he was saying was and is true. For him – a peasant's son from rural China – English, the World Service, the books we gave him to read, what we said and the beliefs we expressed must have been a treasure trove of alternative thinking. In this kind of small town, English was his hot-line to a different world, revealing another realm of possibilities to him.

These keen students were very rewarding but they often became a bit over-zealous. Wanting to spend all their free time – every minute of it – improving their English, they were desperate to take advantage of the two foreigners who had appeared in Yuncheng to teach, and in the process proceeded to devour every minute of our time. It was a difficult problem to deal with. There weren't enough foreign teachers to spread between them all, and so many of them left with their dreams unrealized. We could have chosen any one of them, and in the two years that they spent in the college we could have made them almost perfect. It was an unpleasant and strange feeling to hold this power over someone else's future and one that I tried to ignore.

I wanted to talk about China's present situation – Deng's Socialist Market Economy, Mao and his Cultural Revolution, Child infanticide and the One-child policy, Tibet, Tiananmen Square – as these seemed the big issues facing modern China. But for a long time I was wary about broaching such subjects, until I had their trust and until I was sure that it wouldn't cause offence.

But, again, my students were the wrong people to ask, as very few of them had learnt to see life clearly for themselves yet, and what I got back was a mixture of hearsay, Party propaganda, truth and rumour. They hadn't been exposed to the range of experiences that would allow them to test the validity of the ideas and notions taught to them as children, so in groups they usually settled for the Party line – which went something like, 'Yes, there are many problems still which we must address, but this is necessary if China is to become a modern nation.' And making China a 'modern country' seemed to justify most things.

They were astonished to find a foreigner in their midst – as astonished as I was to find myself living in small-town China – and so these questions were a way of maintaining communication while they all got over the shock.

To them I was something of an unknown quantity in a country where the Party tells people what to say and believe – and everyone says the right thing, whether they believe it or not. They have an innate knowledge of what subjects to speak about or avoid, or of how to say things according to polite etiquette, but they knew that I was a complete novice and like a loaded gun I might go off unexpectedly and cause irretrievable loss of face. So they developed a style of questioning which was their way of reassuring themselves that I was safe – like you would prod a sleeping bear.

How many countries had I been to?

Did I love the Chinese people?

Had I been to the Great Wall?

Could I use chopsticks?

Their questions were very safe. Routine answers were expected and given.

The endless rounds of questions, repeated over and over and often asked by the same people was a Chinese way of honouring me. By making someone answer question after question about themselves you make them feel important. But I knew I was getting somewhere when I was talking about Everest one day and I was stopped in mid-track by a student saying, 'No.

Edmund Hillary was not the first person to climb Everest. It was a Chinese man.'

This was the first time we had progressed from platitudes to real interaction. This breakthrough was followed up by one of those questions that paradoxically gave me more of an insight into their lives than my answer revealed about mine. It was in the last term of their two-year course. After six weeks' teaching practice which would be the only preparation for their lifelong career as teachers, one student raised her hand and asked me, 'Mr Hill, does the government in your country assign you to a job?'

How do you start to describe freedom to people who cannot imagine it? They were fascinated when I explained as well as I could the system whereby people in Britain get jobs.

No, the government does not tell you where you can work. Nor do you automatically join the same factory or company as your parents. Instead you go to a job centre, or information centre, look at the different opportunities, or requirements for work, fill in an application form from which the company or whatever decides whether they want you or not. If they like you, they might ask you to an interview, and depending on how you do in the interview, then you will or won't get the job.

They listened rapt and wide-eyed as if I was describing jewels and treasures from Aladdin's Cave. 'It is very different in our China,' I was told. 'To get a good job in China you must have *guanxi* – good relations.'

I had heard of *guanxi* before I came to China, but then it had seemed like a more advanced version of the Old School Tie in England. It wasn't until I had been here for a while that I realized how fully it pervades the whole of Chinese society. Basically, it means that if you help someone, they owe you a favour, and favours have to be returned if you are to stay friendly. From seeming an almost cosy cultural peculiarity, with my growing awareness and knowledge of China, *guanxi* hung around like a bad smell, colouring my view of everything. I grew to feel that *guanxi* was the root of all evil in China – resulting in rank corruption and making the powerful rich, and subduing and disenabling the rest. Worst of all, it made me cynical about people's generosity: I looked behind their actions and wondered what were they really after?

The problem with *guanxi* is that it blurs the distinction between what in Britain would be seen as acceptable and unacceptable corruption. My moral map became blurred, my codes of behaviour a little frayed at the edges. Much sooner than I had imagined, I began using *guanxi* – and once you've started it's not so easy to be damning. The first time I remember consciously using it was when we wanted to show our students *Top of the Pops* as part of some work we'd been doing on British culture. First of all we went through the official channels – the English department, who contacted the video department, who told us that there were 'technical difficulties' – basically we were to forget the idea.

A few months later, as our embryonic Chinese was developing, we discovered that there were 'bad relations' between the English and video departments – no *guanxi*. A few days after this discovery we met the man responsible for the video room, Yen LaoShi. We stopped, chatted, and he seemed very pleasant. We made a point of saying hello whenever we met him, always asking him if he was busy today, which was another question we knew in Chinese. A little later we went directly to his office and – getting a student to translate – asked if we could use the video room because bla bla bla, and course, he would be very welcome to come along if he wanted to watch as well.

No problem.

A few weeks later we went to ask if we could have one of the college's spare video recorders in our flat for previewing videos for lessons – no problem, of course!

This backdoor dealing was exactly the sort of thing we'd been warned against doing at VSO training weekends in the UK. We were exploiting our power as white-skinned Westerners to get things our local colleagues couldn't necessarily get, and so reinforcing attitudes that Westerners are somehow superior to, and more capable than, the Chinese.

No doubt that principle was right – but theory and real life are different things entirely. In China *guanxi* is the lubricant that oils all social interaction – you don't have to dedicate your life to it, but you simply cannot avoid it. Not to co-operate with *guanxi* would be plain bad manners, and peculiar in the extreme.

Most of my students were from peasant families, so they would tell me mournfully, 'I will become a teacher. My parents are peasants. They have no *guanxi*.' For them Yuncheng was the local New York, the bright lights, big city, where they came for two years to study before being sent back by the local government to teach in their own towns. It gave them a glimpse of the new China, of the opportunities that existed for other people who did have *guanxi*, before they were sent to a school in their backward neighbourhood, where they would remain till they retired at sixty.

'So what is a good job in China?' I asked. The answer was a sad reflection on the modern state of affairs. My students all aspired to work a) in a bank, or b) in the post office, or c) in the railways. These were the jobs where work was easy, with prestige and money. One of them told me why:

'The banks have a good wage. In a bank we would start on maybe 600 *yuan*. But a teacher earns maybe 150 *yuan* per month, and where we live the local government cannot afford to pay the teachers. Banks are rich and can provide houses to newly married couples and there are many other advantages. They are also very secure, jobs for life.'

They said the same for the post office and railway system, these had 'many other advantages,' though what these were the students didn't really seem to know.

I found it hard to tell whether this was just a case of *Hong Yen Bing* – good old-fashioned envy of others, or really based on truth.

Another thing that I found quite shocking was that the students who managed to get jobs, or who had *guanxi*, refused to talk about it. 'If we have *guanxi*, then we do not tell anyone. We cannot even tell our deskmates,' one student said, and many others nodded. For me, they had seemed like any other class of students, with a fair mix of friends and a few enemies, but a general sense of camaraderie. Now, when everyone was looking for a job, I could sense the mistrust. Ironically, in a country which prides itself in making everyone equal, it doesn't do to incite jealousy in others.

I asked one girl if she would become a teacher. 'No,' she said.

'What will you be, then?'

'I don't know. My father is trying to find me a job. He is going around his friends at the moment, giving them presents. But he has little *guanxi*, he is a lecturer. I think I will become a teacher,' she moaned.

That a twenty-two-year-old girl should have no say in her future career, which would be decided by which of her father's friends would accept gifts in return for a job, couldn't be right, I thought. But it was something that she accepted as quite normal. When I asked her what she considered a good job she replied, 'One where I have to do nothing.'

English Corner, the conversation part of our classes, was the safe meeting ground for students to talk to us about anything they wanted. The idea was that everyone, whatever their level, would find someone to have a chat with in English. Reality was a planet away from this ideal. Mario and I would sit down and immediately be surrounded by a circle of students who would interrogate us for the allotted two hours.

The first English Corner was held outside on a cold spring afternoon with the sun bright in the windswept sky, but giving no warmth at all. Mario and I took half of the hundred-strong crowd each and told everyone about our families, ability with chopsticks, and how much we liked China, over and over for two hours, till the cold froze our ears, noses and toes and we had to go inside. It could only get better.

There was always the threat of a Great Wall question, our code for the most popular question we were asked, and one student, a mature student called Zhang BaoAn, would always ask me, and then Mario, the same question. Every week she would arrive at the back of the crowd, edge forward and then announce in a loud clear voice. 'Mr Hill, do you cook for yourself?'

And every time I would tell her, and she would nod, 'Thank you,' and then go and ask Mario the same question. I began to wonder if she was going to offer to come and look after us – to cook and suchlike – but she never did.

'Do you miss your home?'

'Not yet.'

'Can you use chopsticks?'

'Yes.'

'You are very brave.'

'No. I don't think so.'

'England is very beautiful. Am I right?'

'Some parts are beautiful.'

'Have you been to the Great Wall?'

'Yes.'

'Can we be good friends?'

'Yes, I hope so.'

'Do you like Chinese food?'

'Yes. It's delicious.'

'Can you cook for yourself?'

'Yes. Most people in the West can cook.'

'You are very clever.'

'Umm.'

'Can you speak Chinese?'

'A little.'

'Can you say something for us?'

(In Chinese.) 'Hello. How are you?' Loud laughter and giggles.

'Your Chinese is very good.'

'You are very clever.'

'Can you advise us how to learn English better.'

Questions with variables were especially popular among the students with weaker English.

'What did you do at university on Sunday?' would lead to a spate of similar questions. Students too shy to think of their own questions, or not sure how to approach the strange foreigner sitting in front of them, saw that this particular one worked, or at least I responded, so they made it their own.

Then they would proudly ask, 'What did you do at university on Tuesdays?'

One student had a repertoire of only one question: every time I met him I knew he would ask me, 'Mr Hill, do you think the Great Wall is very beautiful?'

To add a little interest to our conversations I tried to vary my answers a bit. They ranged from 'OK,' to 'Absolutely amazing!' and each time he smiled, getting lost after the first word, but saying, 'Thank you,' and leaving happy after another successful communication.

Thankfully our better students were always there and we did move onto more interesting topics as we learnt more about each other. Their questions were often very revealing about their own lives.

'What do you call your brother?'

'By his name,' I said, 'And you?'

'In my family we don't call each other by name, but by our titles. Big Brother, Big Sister, Little Sister. My Father calls my Mother "Wife" and she calls him "Husband".'

'Did you have to do morning exercises at your university?' The idea made me laugh.

'Were you criticized at university if your dormitory was dirty?'

'We didn't live in dorms,' I said.

'The college have just made strict rules about our dorms. Either sex is not allowed into the other's dorm buildings. We are not allowed pictures on our walls, and are not allowed curtains over our beds.'

'Do you love your Motherland?'

'Why do the British like fighting so much?' one student asked, and this question rather surprised me. Hadn't the Empire been a benevolent operation, to raise the other peoples of the world to the standards of our Western civilization – the White Man's Burden? Obviously from the other end of the gun it looked quite different.

'I think the British always attack other people,' another said.

'The British are very clever,' a third student said. 'The British only fight on other people's soils.'

93

It is often difficult hearing other people's opinions of your country, especially when they are bad. Britain has a fairly undistinguished record in China, as in much of the rest of the world. At my school, the naval bombardments on undefended Chinese cities got only a minor mention under the euphemistic title 'gunboat diplomacy.' But the Chinese spent a disproportionate amount of time studying the Western imperialist policy in China. One of the explanations for this is wounded pride. One hundred years ago the Chinese perceived themselves as the most enlightened, civilized and advanced nation – in fact the *only* civilization in a world of hostile barbarians. Repeated defeats at the hands of Westerners and Japanese have grated deep on the Chinese psyche.

'Every child knows the "Eight Attack-China Countries",' a friend once told me. 'From this high (he indicated toddler level) we are taught about the eight imperialist powers who attacked China.'

The only consolation for Britain is that our intrusion into China was nothing compared to that of the Japanese in 1937. 'Chinese and Japanese political leaders are close,' a student said. 'But not the people. Yuncheng was occupied by the Japanese until 1945. I think the Japanese are very terrible. I think if the Japanese are given a seat on the UN Security Council, it will be very dangerous for us.'

All my students had inherited their parents' and grandparents' hatred of what they considered the demonic Japanese. They saw the current investment of Japanese firms in China not as new business, but as reparations due for the wartime misery and destruction they inflicted on China – a long-awaited apology.

The insights continued when a girl told us how when she was smaller she used to play near the railway tracks in Yuncheng. There she sometimes found the remains of unwanted baby girls who had been tossed from passing trains. Victims of the One-Child Policy.

As well as criticizing other developing countries for overpopulation, the Western governments and media like haranguing China over the One-Child Policy. But it's a worrying fact that something like sixty per cent of China's population is under twenty years old – and will be coming to child-bearing age in a matter of years. With 700 million people having two or three children, China's 1.2 billion population could double in a few decades. The problem, however, is that in China siring children is not only a pleasure, but also the duty of every mating couple. Not to propagate your family line is disrespectful to your ancestors – and amongst the Chinese, respecting your ancestors is still important.

In China only male children can carry on the family line – daughters leave the family when they marry and any children they have belong to their husband's clan. As well as continuing the family name, sons are more able to help with the heavy farm work and when their parents are too old to work the fields they will care for them. So when the One-Child Policy was first introduced, infanticide and the abandonment of disabled and female babies became a nationwide problem – although it is impossible to say how widespread it was. So the government was forced to make the rules more lenient, letting some couples have two children.

That was about as much as our students told us. More than that was hard to find out – the Chinese do not share the West's growing preoccupation with exposing and discussing national, social or personal problems, especially not to foreigners. It would result in a loss of national face.

At another English Corner a boy told us how most villages still had matchmakers to arrange weddings.

'A 2,500 *yuan* dowry is cheap for a wife,' he said. '5,000 *yuan* is usual, sometimes even 10,000 *yuan*. In some villages they are very backward. Girls are married very young. Some girls in my class in school left to marry.'

'Did you know any of these girls?'

'Yes,' he said. 'But I don't remember their names. They left school very young and we never saw them again. I can remember their faces, they were married as early as eight years old. Then they stopped coming to school. From that age on, little girls sometimes dropped out to get married.'

The legal age of marriage in China is twenty-one for a girl and twenty-four for a boy. But many students talked of classmates in their villages who already had children. The age for marriage is decided in Beijing, which is a long way both distance-wise and mentally from the peasants of China, where law enforcement is left to officials who don't really understand the reasoning behind them, or who are simply corrupt.

'I want to go to America, because it is the strongest of countries,' a student announced one day. I told him that although many Chinese people thought that Britain and America were the same, they were quite different, that Britain was much more conservative than America.

'China is also conservative,' I was told. 'Yes. Boys and girls are not allowed to fall in love, or touch. They are kept separate and play away from each other.'

'Isn't that unnatural? Bad?' I suggested tentatively, although at my all-boys school I hadn't thought so at all.

The girl, who was from a village in the mountains, wrote on a piece of paper the words 'sexual freedom' and furtively showed it to me only, then crumpled it up in her hand.

'I think it is good we are conservative here,' she said.

Hong Kong also featured largely in the minds of the students, who seemed to feel that there would be a war with Britain over the colony. Unlike in the UK, the problems over Hong Kong are keenly felt in China. All the Chinese yearn for unity and stability and so when they talked of Hong Kong and Macau and Taiwan they talked like people who had lost a family member. All these places were, by rights, Chinese. They were theirs, always would be theirs and should be returned to the Motherland.

Once, three students brought some pieces that they wanted to read to me.

'Why have you written it all down?'

'We can't speak to you, we get too nervous,' one said.

I encouraged them a little – which was what they had been

waiting for – and then they held up their pieces and began reading one by one.

'China is a developing country. She has splendid achievements now and a bright future, as well as a long and beautiful history. Now, more and more people have begun to realize the importance of China all over the world. China is a large country and is playing an important role in the world. Our five thousand years of history have showed the world her greatness. We have the Four Inventions: Paper, Printing, Gunpowder, and the Compass. It was the Chinese who invented them first. They made a notable impact on the world. Because of China's wonders and her kindness, generosity and gentleness, she began to be invaded. Maybe you have been to the Great Wall? Can you imagine that it is with their hands that the Chinese built it to keep the intruders from the interior? During the Qing Dynasty our treasures and wonderful buildings were destroyed by foreign Imperialists. We were shot by our own gunpowder. From then on China was reduced to poverty, but she didn't yield, she began to defend herself, fighting for her rights and position. Before, China was a closed country. Now she has opened the door wide to the world. Responding to the Party's call, we are working hard to build a socialist country with Chinese characteristics. Under their leadership, and after ten years' hard work, we have achieved lots in many fields. Especially our economy. In the old days people didn't have enough to eat, not enough fuel to drive the cold off. Now more and more electrical goods are arising. You can see more cars in the streets. I think with our hard-working people, China will become richer and richer, stronger and stronger.'

The next began, 'China has a long history. She is one of the sources of world civilization. The Yellow River is the cradle of the Chinese people. All of our Chinese people have yellow skins just like our *HuangHe*, our Mother Yellow River. I've only seen the river from the train. It was so splendid and beautiful as the wild water was carrying a lot of yellow soil as it rolled quickly and ran fast to the remote East Sea. After Liberation and especially the Open-Door Policy, China has almost turned round her poor and backwards appearance. The people's living standard has risen greatly. In the street the people's clothes are colourful and varied. The furniture and decorations inside people's houses are modern. Some people even have their own cars. The future of China is something that concerns every Chinese person. All of us hope that China becomes rich and strong. But the way is hard and needs a long time. On the way education is very important. "Education is the basic plan for the next hundred years" is the slogan of our government and we have a duty to carry it out.'

I listened to the last. 'Yuncheng is my home. It is a small city. When I was young, it was not a rich place, but since the reform and opening up of China, the small town has had a great deal of changes. Now, if you want to go to the street you can go by taxi, or by round-city bus. If you want to get in touch with others, even people far away, you can use the public phone. Yuncheng is a big base for wheat, and its foreign trade is very flourishing. The people here are very simple and honest, they treat people very kindly. If you are in trouble they will do their best to help you. They respect their elders and love the young; they unite and help each other. Yuncheng is just a small city, but it may reflect the whole country. Under the lead of our government the Chinese people unite as one and make big strides forwards towards the higher aims.'

English Corners often failed to take off and become even mildly interesting, so I listened to these pieces with a touch of boredom. Open-door Policy, yellow skins, Liberation, government slogans; Our simple-honest-hardworking-respectful-helpful-kind-polite-and-immensely-repetitive Chinese People!

I wanted to tell them that I felt China had stagnated. These were just things that they had been taught, reasons to be proud of being Chinese. Maybe in a few hundred years the situation would be reversed and grubby little English boys would be proudly telling their Chinese or Japanese guests about the great inventions of Britain – steam locomotion, the telephone and penicillin.

But beyond first reactions I sometimes found some of the things they said about their lives very revealing and touching. 'In the old days people didn't have enough to eat – not enough fuel to drive the cold off ... after ten years' hard work we have achieved lots in many fields ... turned round her poor and backward appearance ... more and more electrical goods are arising ... more cars in the streets ... furniture and decorations inside people's homes are modern ... in the street people's clothes are more varied and colourful.' But there were undertones that disturbed me too: 'Chinese people will unite as one and make big strides towards higher aims ... China will become rich and strong ... China will become richer and richer, stronger and stronger.' Compared to the Middle East or Far East we in the West have been uncivilised wretches since history began – except for the last three hundred years or so, and I can understand how that fact must rankle with the Chinese. But maybe these scales are beginning to tip back now, and it won't be too long before they settle at their former equilibrium, with the East on top.

Most students had *Duixiangs* – a term describing their betrothed, whom some of them chose for themselves, and these were often the only members of the opposite sex they could safely be seen with without arousing the attention of gossip mongers. One female student, Zhang YuFeng, who often came to see us to talk or borrow books, was always accompanied by her *duixiang*, who would wait at the bottom of the stairs until she returned.

'Why does he do this?' we asked once.

'Because he loves me,' she answered.

'Is it not because he doesn't trust you?'

Her answer was an embarrassed laugh.

Usually girls came to visit us in threes. Part of the reason for this was the close surveillance of our flat. It wasn't an organized watch, just the sharp eyes of the neighbours on our staircase; seven suspicious housewives with nothing better to do who met up at the bottom of the stairs to gossip when the sun was out. But the other students were very quick to attack girls who came to visit us, accusing them of trying to seduce us, and of trying to get a passport out of China. If two girls came we might be having a foursome, so groups of three or more were safer.

Chao Xia was a very keen student, who used any excuse to come to practise her English – and we used up our list of get-outs on her many times over. It was impossible to keep her away. Eventually she became like a piece of familiar furniture and we began to feel almost kindly towards her and miss her if she hadn't come calling for a day or two.

One morning I'd seen her waiting at the bus stop at 10 AM. At 2:30 she was still standing, with her hands in her pockets, scuffing pebbles with her foot. She was standing a little way apart from the pool players on this cold blustery spring day.

It turned out that she was waiting for a prospective *duixiang*. 'This boy saw a photo of me, and then my classmate, Yao QingXue, told him something about me, and he wanted to meet me. She was our *maipuo* – matchmaker. I went up to Linfen two weeks ago. He is quite tall, one metre seventy-nine centimetres, and works at an engineering factory, I don't really know at what. But I don't know if I like him. I must decide before graduation in three months' time.'

I was very surprised that one of my students was arranging her marriage already, and asked her round to the flat to tell me about it.

'So you don't like any Yuncheng boys?' I teased.

'Oh, I do, but Linfen is better than Yuncheng,' she said.

It turned out that that afternoon he never arrived. He did arrive the weekend after, though, and she came around to my flat to tell me what had happened. Her manner had changed – shifted from that of a single girl to that of a woman who has a man she is responsible for.

'I told my father and he was very angry. He asked "Do you love him?" He criticized me. He is very strict. He thinks the *maipuo* is not reliable. I told him that we'd only met once. He doesn't really know much about the family. He's afraid that they will cheat me. My mother will go to Linfen and see the family, to check out their situation. I think they are richer than my family. They have good *guanxi*. They have said that they can move my *hukou* (registration certificate) to Linfen and find me a good job there. I must decide if I like him, though. They're also worried that I might cheat them. I think they are

very kind and that is good for me, because if I marry, I will
live with his family.'

'So are you going to get married?' I asked, surprised that a
girl who had never really had a proper boyfriend before was
already so deep in the process of getting married.

'Oh no. I will work in Linfen and do some things with the
family. Then we will decide about marriage.'

It was a big step though, and her chances of another
good marriage would be reduced if she pulled out of this
arrangement. It's said in China that a girl's love is like the
food, it should be of the freshest kind. A girl is not worth so
much if she's been involved before, and with your future job
prospects depending on your in-law's *guanxi*, then it's risky.

'So will you go and live with them?' I asked.

'Yes, but my father thinks that we must be very careful.
Sometimes the girl is cheated. Some girls are sold by the family
and sent away somewhere. In Shanghai it is cheaper to buy a
wife from the country than to marry a local girl. After this it
is very difficult for them to return to their families. If they
return, then they will be a disgrace to them.

'Some people are very *kaifang* (open minded). Two young
people love each other. They kiss or something, and no
wedding – live together. I am not very *kaifang*. Some people do
shihun – trial marriages – but it is not good, I think. Many
men use this as a chance to live with a girl and then leave
them. They are always evil people. You know, society has
changed. My neighbour says, "Why not have another Mao?
To politicize society, to stop bad society." In Chairman Mao's
time society was good and peoples' minds were good – but
now they have become bad.'

She continued, 'Like marriage. Marriages are now a bad
custom. You must have a meal – very expensive. Once this
was just for friends, now relatives and people at work will
complain if they are not invited for a banquet. This custom is
only good for restaurants. This month my father has gone to
three weddings – my cousin's brother, an uncle's sister, and a
colleague's. We have a very large extended family. My father
must give money as a present. Usually twenty *yuan* or forty

yuan if it is a relative. A close relative should be 100 *yuan* or 150 *yuan*. Many times a month makes this very expensive. My father only earns 200 *yuan* a month ...'

'When you get married, you must borrow much money, and spend the next ten years paying it off. Twenty years ago you would give a watch or sewing machine. Now we have the '*Si Da Jian*' – 'Four Big Things' – washing machine, fridge, gas stove and air conditioning. Sometimes even the '*Ba Da Jian*' – 'Eight Big Things,' extractor fan, scooter – it is terrible.'

'So what about the boy? How did your meeting go?' I said.

'Yes, good. But he is very shy. He is very tall, and because I am short, my father is afraid that his relatives will criticize me. If one is short and one is tall then maybe they will say it will not be a lucky marriage. He does not express himself very well. He has written three letters to me. He is not well-educated, as he only had one or two years in senior school. In China, your handwriting is very important, but his handwriting is not very good.'

'So what will happen next then?' I asked.

'My father must agree, I know. But when he met the boy's father then they got on. They had had similar experiences during the Cultural Revolution, and so they were good friends. My father told me what I should write in a letter and say that if they satisfied my conditions then we could carry on seeing each other. Firstly, the boy should get a better job. Secondly, the relatives may not criticize me; maybe they are very superstitious, say bad things about us because he is tall and I am short. Thirdly, my parents are afraid he will leave me, so we must promise to be together for at least ten to twenty years.

'I wrote all this and said that if he can promise these things, then I agree to go into a deeper relationship with him. When he received the letter, the boy was very worried. He wrote again – he said, "If you want to go to Linfen I don't know if you'd like me, we can see." I think it is bad to say that to a girl. If I say "yes" then he will think that I will use him to get a good job, but won't marry him. You know most of his questions are "with purpose". There is a famous romantic writer in China called Qiang Xiao. If you read her, then you won't find any realistic lovers – they are all fantasy people. In her books there is usually a love triangle. He will love her, and she will make him jealous by talking to a friend. So he must give her flowers. I am not like that. You know, I have deep feelings.'

Listening to her and from my knowledge of her, I guessed she was as emotionally untested as most Westerners are in their early teens. 'Because I have no experience of relationships,' she told me, 'then my father tells me what I should do.'

Cao Xia told me of the other two romances that she had had so far in her twenty-one years of life.

'When I was at school, then I had deep feelings for a boy. He was very kind to me and we both liked English. We would both do our homework together. Because he was kind to me, I thought he had feelings for me. But it was just because he was kind. I later found out that he had a different girlfriend.

'The second was a boy at college. He liked me. We would talk, and I knew he liked me. But he was from a village, so had no future. You know that I am not a greedy girl, I don't care for money, but I know that a good future is very important. Too many girls they give their love to a boy, and then later their families will separate them.'

Both non-starters really.

'Did you kiss either of them?'

'No. I have not had that experience yet,' she said, going red and giggling.

Something the students could not understand was how I could leave my family for so long. Although many of the peasant children had left home to become weekly boarders in their local school at the age of thirteen, the city children, for the most part, had never spent a night away from their families.

It had been a big step for me to drop everything and come to China, but in many ways I was closer to my family than I had been in England. With a letter each week from my parents, it was more than I had or had even wanted when at university. Often late, these long-awaited letters filtered through the vagaries of the international postage system – they finally delivered four sides of information, news, good wishes and advice. I read each letter over and over, till I almost knew them by heart – and with my mind's eye I would follow their lives as they continued along their familiar lines and would wonder why my life had jumped so suddenly to a new world, which my letters to them could never adequately describe.

One girl, after looking through my photos of home, actually burst into tears. The pathos of a photo of me saying goodbye to my mother was just too much for her, and she sniffed through her tears, 'You have such a lovely home. You must miss them so much.'

The younger students, between seventeen and twenty-three, seemed to be physically adults, but were still children at heart. The same applies to anyone growing up, I'm sure, but in China maturity happens so much later than elsewhere. The boys would put on a kind of bravado involving smoking and comparing how many bottles of beer each could drink. They would wear their suits with pride, learn to chainsmoke without being sick, but behind all this there seemed to be no real maturity.

Wang YueSheng, for example, was quite a character. Slim, good-looking and quite charming in a puppyish way, he treated us like his elder brothers.

'Have you ever been in love?' he'd ask. Then he would tell me some fanciful tale of a lost love in his life. Another time he confided to me the story of a great adventure he had had whilst at middle-school: 'I went out at night and drank a bottle of beer. My head spun and so I lay down to sleep at a bus stop. Before the sun rose, I woke up and shivered so much that I thought that I would die. My head was still spinning but I managed to climb the gate of my school and go to my dorm. None of my dorm mates knew that I had been out. You are the first person I have told.'

Amongst the girls there was a determined and modern-minded minority who privately professed that they would neither marry nor have children, but the weight of their family's opinion was against them, and under these pressures or the vagaries of falling in love, I doubted that many would reach thirty both unmarried and childless.

But they nonetheless enjoyed playing the role of silent housekeeper that society had prepared them for. When they came around to visit us they liked to pour us tea, look attentive when we spoke, and to refuse to sit down or eat more than a mouthful – and then pour us some more tea. 'A woman's place is in the home,' they would tell us, while many said that of all things in life they wished to give birth to a baby boy, as that was the pinnacle of motherly achievement and would keep their future in-laws happy.

One girl, a short, sturdy, serious peasant girl, who was a true Party patriot and looked as though she'd have 'Bred For Victory' under Chairman Mao's drive to increase China's manpower and feed his factories (now distinctly frowned upon), told me in a serious voice, which left me reprimanded for even suggesting the frivolous idea to her: 'Twenty-two is too young for a boyfriend. I must study hard instead.'

During my time in China, the students were forced to work to pay for their education. Before it had been almost free, in return for life-long service as a teacher. If you didn't become a teacher in the end, then you would have to repay the entire cost. However, the college had now decided to apply the dictats of the Socialist Market Economy into its workings. The money given to the students, forty-six *yuan* per month, would be cut to forty *yuan* and the extra money would be used as a cash reward for the better students. The next year, the forty *yuan* would be cut to twenty, and each extra twenty-six *yuan* pooled as prize-money for the best students.

One student, whose ambition was to 'be like Mr Hill' and travel, went around selling socks and gloves to children in local schools. He had earned himself nearly 100 *yuan*, but instead of using it for travelling, this money now had to go on his food and accommodation.

At the same time, the compulsory unpaid labour which was demanded of all students was increased. However, delivering coal or moving houses brick by brick to a new location for a teacher gave the students vital *guanxi* with them, which might come in handy at examination time.

The department's Communist Party secretary, Li ShuJi, was a short man, even for the Chinese, so short that he had difficulty riding his bicycle, set up a kind of tutor agency for the local area. He got *guanxi* from others by finding good students to tutor their children, and students, many of whom were unpaid, got *guanxi* with him for accepting. They could hardly refuse. The students often complained to us, but had no real choice but to accept their lot.

We also had a few mature students – serving teachers who had been sent back to college against their will, leaving wives, husbands, and children at home. They were difficult to teach as they were here in order to qualify for a pay-rise, and were not really interested in improving their English skills. They were housed and treated like the younger students – morning exercises, compulsory attendance at lessons, compulsory evening study – more like Western schoolchildren than mature students at university. In the evenings we would play Chinese chess and chat with them. They told us about their lives at home, their plots of land, which most of them were renting out to other people in the villages, while one had started a shop. Many had not been paid by their local authorities for months. Those who grew crops grew mainly wheat or cotton. During the harvest, they would take time off classes to help in the village, sowing or reaping or winnowing.

Most had two children, and a few had three. A bald man with a high forehead introduced me to his village.

'We have 2,800 people. One school with thirty-five teachers and four hundred students. There are ten cars, three factories – one making machine parts, one canning fruit and one making things for the government. Welcome you to my village!'

'Are any of you in the Communist Party?' I asked one night.

'No. Full membership is very difficult. Last year only two students out of 120 got into the Party.

But their English was very poor, and it was not until later on with students we had taught from the beginning of their time at the college, that we began to form deeper friendships.

The best insight we had into their lives was when we were

invited to the house of a student, Zhang XinAi, for the weekend. Dean Wu had suggested we visit the countryside, and said he would tell the students that we wanted to do so. But he made many offers, none of which ever came to anything. Thankfully, he had still not managed to arrange a funeral, but at banquets after a few drinks he would regularly say, 'Ah. You must come to my house. You can see a traditional family meal! My wife will cook *jiaozi* and many, many delicious foods! Homemade food is always the best!'

But these meals never materialized. It was a bizarre ritual and as time went by the fantasy became more elaborate. We discussed menus, *jiaozi* fillings, and even set dates – though it was a complete fantasy. The alcohol-induced camaraderie brought us together to play with the idea; but, sober, it always amused, and confused me. It was just for effect, to impress me.

So it was quite a shock a few weeks later when Zhang XinAi and Zheng YouCai, two final-year students, came around and invited us to visit XiaXian county. We stood and peered at the map on the wall, an unintelligible mix of lines, dots and Chinese characters.

'My home is near there,' she said, pointing to a dot not too far away. 'This is XiaXian town.'

The appointed Saturday arrived, a hot and sunny day at the end of May.

We met up at the front of the college, three students and two foreigners, and cycled out of Yuncheng. Soon the dirt and noise of construction and cars, the throngs of cyclists and pedestrians who made anything but a crawl through the streets impossible, were left behind and we were out on the country road. There was still a constant flow of traffic – the big DongFeng lorries, occasional cars with their privileged passengers, and the village traffic of chugging tractors with their spitting open radiators. All careering along the road, splitting our eardrums with their screeching horns.

The students at first were quite nervous, and a little shy of cycling alongside us. Then Zhang XinAi came up. 'This is a great honour for our village. You are the first foreigners to visit since 1945,' she said.

'Who were the last foreigners?' I asked.

'Japanese soldiers,' she answered, without elaborating. Japanese soldiers in 1939-45 were hardly just passing visitors – they massacred their way through China – but it would have been considered unlucky to talk about it just before our visit.

The village was about twenty kilometres from Yuncheng. On the way we passed through a small town which was nothing more than a line of modern concrete garages housing a selection of shops and businesses. People stopped dead in their tracks as we cycled past. A dirty man, who was so oily that his clothes were only just recognizable, stopped welding and sat back on a large tyre and stared as we cycled past only yards from him. His mouth fell open and I half expected him to rub his eyes as if they were utterly deceiving him – no doubt expecting us all to disappear when he opened them again.

In Yuncheng the people were now thankfully almost used to having a foreigner appear around the corner, or cycle past them. But here in this sleepy wayside town they no more expected a blond giant to cycle past them than they expected their dead father to sit down at the dinner table and ask them to pass the salt. In the reactions of the people as we passed, the name we were often given, 'foreign ghost' seemed quite apt.

When we left the village, to either side of the road lay fields of melon, corn, apples and maize.

'Our classmate, Zhang XinAi's family have many apple trees,' one said, 'and they are very rich.'

'You must come to YongJi, my hometown,' Zheng YouCai said. 'In my town there is a very tall pagoda on a hill. My aunt works there and we can go there and spend the night under the trees. It is best in the spring, when all the flowers are out.' We cycled on a little way in silence, thinking of the flowers and sleeping out. 'There is a story about the pagoda from the Tang dynasty. It is called the "Romance of the Western Chamber." '

This was a different pagoda to the one we had visited with Cao. The Yuncheng area is dotted with temples and pagodas, reminders of the time when it was the centre of the Chinese empire. We had heard the story: a boy on his way to the Imperial civil service exam in Xian stops off at a temple on the way. Girl staying there with mother. Boy hears girl singing over a wall. Both fall in love, girl and boy contrive to meet with the help of the girl's servant. Girl's mother finds out. Bans them from meeting. Boy helps to fight off some bandits, and in the end mother agrees to the marriage if he passes the exams. The young hero goes off to take his exams upon which his and the girl's love depends ... and that's where it finishes. That story was considered so degenerate and subversive at the time that it was banned until 1911, and the end of the Qing dynasty.

'We are nearly there,' Zhang XinAi said. 'My village is just down this path.'

We turned off the Tarmac, and onto a rutted dirt track going between two fields of rape. Her village, a sprawl of mud-brick houses, lay about one kilometre away. If the welder's reaction had been one of incomprehension at the sight of us, then to the two teenaged boys with patched and faded trousers who we passed on the track, we were something nearing the supernatural. They saw Zhang XinAi, said 'Hello', then noticed the two of us cycling behind. They stopped their bikes and watched in wonder. They were still staring as we reached the nearest houses, then they began to shout over and over, 'Halloo! Halloo! Halloo!'

We didn't meet anyone else on the way except a young man carrying a plough over his shoulders. He nodded to us as a group and failed to notice Mario or me at all. Despite our clothes and new bikes, I don't think that he considered the possibility of foreigners ever cycling through his own village.

We reached the gate of Zhang XinAi's house and walked in. The road led into a small dirt courtyard, shaded by a cherry tree and bordered on three sides by a single-storey mud-brick house roofed with grey tiles. On the fourth side a gateway opened onto a short barbican construction, with another gate, and near this was a well. To the left of the gateway another section had been added to the compound, with another well, and the family's squat toilet, the contents of which slid into an open-air cesspit, which was used to fertilize their fields. The sunken pigsty held two short-snouted and bristly black pigs, four feet long and so fat that their bellies trailed on the floor and their flesh overhung their beady eyes. At the far-end was a two-storey barn with hay in it and farm implements stacked against the walls. In the middle of this was an antique grinding machine that looked as if it belonged in a sepia photo but which the family still used to grind their corn into flour. Around this and between the buildings ran a high brick wall, enclosing the compound.

Zhang XinAi's old mother, a square woman with large breasts swinging under her traditional shoulder-fastening Chinese top, and who was also slightly deaf, came out to welcome us, and her old father pushed us aside and walked our bikes inside.

A low square table, that didn't even reach my knee, and stools not much higher than my ankle, were produced, and we were sat down in the shade and fed peanuts and chipped mugs of green tea with the tea leaves floating on top.

A bucket was lowered and pulled back up the well. 'You must be very tired, please have a wash,' said Zhang XinAi, scooping up some sparkling clear water in a bowl for us.

We wiped away the sweat and dust from our faces, then we returned to shelling our peanuts and sipping our tea as our hosts disappeared to cook for us.

It had been peculiar at first being entertained by Chinese hosts. I had expected to chat and get to know the people who had so generously invited us to their home. Instead we had had a succession of neighbours (people from adjacent blocks of flats), neighbours (people from our stairwell), and neighbours (the family who lived directly underneath us) but we didn't meet the women of the family until after the meal. They continued cooking and ate plain rice while we were fed on all kinds of vegetables and meats and fish and *jiaozi* and then more of the same. The people who lived below us, the Li family, had a daughter who was an English lecturer in our college but as the father was too embarrassed by the fact that he couldn't speak English and so welcome us properly, he also remained in the kitchen and left the duty of host to his son-in-law and daughter.

The news that two foreigners were in the village spread like wildfire. A crowd of children came cautiously into the gateway and watched us, turning to run excitedly away if we so much as looked at them or made a move in their direction.

With the arrival of some adults, the children became a bit braver and stood in a semi-circle around us, some wide-eyed, others laughing and joking, while the adults asked us the usual round of questions. The Yuncheng population got excited enough when they saw us, but here we felt like explorers who had just 'discovered' the village, the people were so thrilled and confused and honoured by our arrival – the first foreigners they had ever seen. They were delighted that we could understand their local accent, and then answer them in standard Chinese. 'Your Chinese is better than ours!' they laughed, and unusually, I was soon enjoying being such a celebrity.

We ate a very filling lunch while everyone apologized for the poverty of the food and surroundings. 'Because our village is off the main road we are poor. There is another village like ours, but they are on the main road and so they can sell their crops much easier than we can,' said mother.

After a rest we were taken on a tour of the village.

'This is my cousin's field,' said Zhang XinAi, and it struck me that half the village was family. 'Would you like to have a look?'

We followed her into a hothouse which had been built using mud bricks and plastic sheets, and pushed through the jungle of cucumber plants to meet her cousin.

'Cucumbers are getting a good price this year, so my cousin is very rich,' Zhang XinAi told us.

We were then taken to the village shrine, where the elders of the village met us. They took us on a tour of the two-storey building which on the second floor, housed a very gaudy god: a mannequin dressed in a fur hat and shiny red-and-yellow clothes, sitting on a gold-painted throne. Incense was lit, and after the village elders had bowed their heads three times, we were offered the chance to do the same. 'Bow your head three times and make a wish,' Zhang XinAi told us. I did, feeling very strange to be kneeling for the first time in front of a 'heathen' idol.

'There used to be many shrines in our village, but they were destroyed during the Cultural Revolution. This was only built recently with money from the village. It is not used often, though every year in the spring we have a big festival here, with music and firecrackers and a fair – it is very popular. You must come. It is on the nineteenth day of the second month. That is the time when the god's spirit visits us. We have a long procession to welcome him into the village, and again to send him on his way. During those three days women who want babies will come and pray to him.'

That evening was a quiet affair away from the crowds and the attentions of the villagers. Father handed us bowls of well water to wash ourselves with, and then went over to the old cherry tree and started shaking it. Fat dark cherries rained down, and we picked up the profusion of fruits from the ground, washed them, and sat back to eat.

As evening fell, Zhang XinAi's father went in to fetch his lightbulb – the only one in the house, and as we moved to the table for dinner and then back to sit under the tree, he removed the lightbulb and screwed it into the nearest socket.

'Usually we go to sleep with the dark. My parents are very hard-working, they get up at four AM to work in the fields,' Zhang XinAi explained.

'This is where you will sleep,' she told us later, showing us our bedroom. 'This is where my elder brother and his wife slept on their marriage night. It is special because of that.'

I looked around the room before going to bed. The walls were made of a rough mud brick, but there were bright red blankets and pillows on the bed. Over the dressing table was a large red Double Happiness character. In a little side room were large storage jars of vinegar and rice and flour, wooden lids askew. There was a strange feel to this matrimonial room. The bed looked hard and uncomfortable, and the still warm night made sleep elusive.

CHAPTER SEVEN

DaiYu

Up the eight flights of concrete steps to our plain door – the only one not adorned with curling strips of red paper painted with gold characters, which were left over from Spring Festival – and inside. The click as our door shut behind us brought a reassuring peace.

We had just returned from a 'surprise' meal out, which was more like a kidnapping than an invitation. Chen Da, a computer lecturer with an obsession to get abroad, had started joining my classes, and had mentioned that his house was near the football pitch where we sweated away our afternoons. After he spoke there was a pause as he giggled nervously and studied my reaction. I seized this opportunity to head off an evening with someone I didn't really like much. In China, as well as being a painful night out, this would have the added dis-advantage of his having *guanxi* with me, ie the right to reciprocate a visit.

'Well, if I play football,' I said, 'I might pop over for a cup of tea sometime,' with heavy emphasis on the '*if*', '*might*' and '*sometime*', and the whole lot said in the most downbeat tone possible.

The problem with what we think are carefully worded hedges and negative tones is that cultural differences mean that an obvious 'no' is maybe not so obvious in another language and the poor bloke might not really understand what you are saying.

That evening, returning from the sports field, Chen Da came

running up after us. Breathless, and a little excited, he smiled with relief at having found us, although his tone was reproachful. 'Have you forgotten? Dinner is ready for you. My wife is waiting for us.'

After this inauspicious start the evening went downhill. The whole night Chen Da giggled and laughed as if he were a little deranged, while his calm and gentle wife cooked in the kitchen and smiled tolerantly at her husband.

When Chinese conversation falters it turns to money matters as quickly as the English turn to the weather. Money has a more prominent place in Chinese culture, and a more important role in defining status, so to talk about it isn't considered bad manners at all. We soon found out about the earnings of half of his extended family: he earned 300 *yuan* a month for six hours' teaching a week, and his wife a greater – but unspecified – sum. They had been classmates at primary school, their parents had been friends, and they had decided when they were still young that the two would marry.

'You know it is my uncle's funeral this weekend,' he laughed. 'Yes! Yes!'

'Why is that funny?' I asked. 'I hope you wouldn't laugh at your father's funeral?'

He giggled and said, 'No, of course not. My parents adopted me – Ha! They were distant relatives of my family. My family had too many children, and so I, as the youngest was sent to be adopted.'

The dishes arrived one by one, seven in all. Boiled nuts, lotus root, strong salty pickles, lumps of turnip and bony meat in a clear broth.

'This is very kind of you – to go to so much effort.' Mario said.

Chen Da exploded into maniacal laughter. Eventually he managed to say, 'This is normal, we eat like this every night – hee, hee, hee.'

I felt he was lying in an effort to impress us. Appearance is very important to the Chinese: designer goods seem to have been specially created for the Easterner's notions of 'face.' Ostentation which seems tasteless to me is common: pure wool labels are not discreetly displayed on the inside of garments but are emblazoned onto the chest like a Lacoste crocodile, while the maker's labels are sewn on the outside cuff of all suits.

The complexities of 'face' to a Westerner are infinite – whole books could be written on the subject – but what mattered to me was that he was lying about such an absurd little thing that any further attempts at searching conversation seemed futile.

This selfconsciousness also applies to China's being a developing nation; even complete strangers would regularly apologize to us for the country's 'backwardness'. Just imagine the suffering I, as a Westerner must be enduring. However, apologies were always tinged with a national pride: someday soon China would not be backward, but, as promised by the Communist Party whose proclamations were swallowed like those of Moses on the Rock, would join the ranks of modern nations. 'Stand in the East like a strong lion,' as a student put it. I felt Chen Da was trying to put himself on a level with his imagined view of England, using the amount of meat served at dinner to show he was a man of quality.

This chip on his shoulder was irritating, but his demonic laughter was far more grating.

'All Spanish girls are very beautiful,' Chen Da said to Mario.

'Some Spanish girls are pretty. Some are ugly,' Mario said flatly. 'Most are neither. It is just the same as China.'

'Some Spanish girls are pretty – ha! Ha! Ha! Some are ugly – yes, yes – some are ugly. Ha! Ha! Ha!'

All evening he kept returning to the subject of learning English. He had been learning for ten years, and he would be ready in two more for the exam which he had to pass before he could go onto a waiting list to go abroad. Each avenue led to the same thing – our offer to teach him English – something we didn't do. So each conversation fell emptily away into silence. After the meal he peeled two apples for us both, refilled our cups of tea, but we still didn't offer. I could see him despairing, giggling as he wondered to himself how obvious he had to make it before we would understand. Dying to ask us directly, but too nervous in case we said no – the tension only made him giggle more.

I looked at his wife, knitting quietly in the corner by the kitchen door. A long-suffering wife with a husband wasting money on his crazed obsession with getting abroad. She was the moderating influence on him, a full-time job, I think.

We left without offering lessons, and Chen Da fell over himself as he showed us out, consoling himself that if he hadn't got lessons then at least he'd got nearer his goal. He laughed nervously as he welcomed us to his house at any time – we were always welcome he shouted, wringing his hands as we turned to wave to him one last time. Then he clapped his hands, waved, and returned indoors.

Walking back to the flat, a group of rowdy young men playing pool at the college gate went completely silent when they saw us. Two of them leapt up and walked over to get a closer look. The night before we had gone for a bottle of beer and dish of peanuts at one of the local restaurants. Within a minute of sitting down the doorway was spilling over with awed Chinese faces and bodies, jostling for a better look. Even the window was splattered with faces pressed up against it, peering in.

To get away from all this was an immense relief. Behind our front door we were buffered against China, which only intruded on our minds as the muffled sounds from the flat below, shouts or a knock on the door.

This seclusion lasted until I turned on the TV – which showed two bears doing synchronized dancing accompanied by an hysterical commentary. Sometimes, *Life on Earth* would be dubbed with a voice like a football commentator's. This probably made it more accessible to the average peasant, and I could just imagine what they were saying. 'Yep, that dumb horse is going to get it now – wow, that's a big lion! He's got it! Yes, he's got it! Did you see that! Hell, was that fun!' But, true to form, they hadn't even dubbed it properly. You could still hear David Attenborough's voice between the bursts of speech. Living abroad, I felt I sometimes had to put cultural sensitivity on hold, just to let off some steam. It's wrong, but it helps.

'Bloody China! Typical of a nation that puts sugar in its toothpaste,' I would sometimes curse, 'Simply can't get anything right! Useless sods.'

Mario tolerated my outbursts – and never mentioned them again. They passed like drunken indiscretions – and having released the valve I felt guilty but much calmer.

Much later on, when I had been in Yuncheng nearly two years, I was pushed through a jostling Chinese crowd and so many pressures were building up that I lost my patience. 'Out of the way you bloody chinks!' I hissed – then pulled myself up short. I objected to Lao Wai, and knew how irritating and hurtful it was to be called racial names – and here I was calling them chinks! As being abroad had certainly opened my eyes to how foreigners are treated in England – and it's not particularly well – I decided I couldn't have it both ways, and began to re-examine my English attitudes.

I went to the kitchen for a cup of tea. Our gas bottle had run out and the college had no spares. I had told Cao that morning and he had promised us that a delivery would arrive from Xian next week. Meanwhile, we had been given an electric ring to cook on, a thing that looked like a stretched spring, set in a cracked earthen case. That the wires were unprotected I quickly discovered by electrocuting myself, and that the flat's electrics were inadequate to cope with it I found out next as the wires that led up the wall burst into flames. Hot plastic dripped down in burning droplets and a poisonous black smoke billowed up to the ceiling. I closed the door, pulled out the plug – which was pouring melted plastic out of the screw holes and was almost too hot to touch – then phoned Mr Cao.

'You wait. I will come.'

He did, the next morning, bringing the college handyman to insulate the wire in extra-thick coating. As the man worked we three went to have a chat.

'Are you busy?'

Cao clicked his tongue. 'Oh yes, very busy you know.'

Then he leapt up and left.

I put on the kettle for a relaxing cup of jasmine tea, and after five minutes our newly repaired kettle fused the electrics in the entire flat. The lights went out and the tape player slurred to a halt and a smell of burning plastic drifted down from our fuse box. There was no water or electricity and, when I telephoned Mr Cao, the lady in the office said that he'd just left to visit his parents-in-law in AnYi.

'Oh, there's a girl called Lin DaiYu coming around tonight at seven,' Mario told me as we walked back from the football pitch that afternoon. There was an audible clang as my heart dropped.

After an evening with Chen Da, I was completely off mixing with the Chinese in a social setting. And the previous week I'd had to hide in my bedroom from three uninvited guests who came calling at 10.30 PM and made Chen Da look like the ultimate social animal.

'No, she's not like that,' Mario continued, noticing my alarm. 'A bit different.'

'Well,' I said. 'I'm having nothing to do with it. You invited her – you entertain her!'

She came. Just as we sat down to eat our dinner of sand-wiches – knock, knock knock! – a polite tap at the door, different from the hammering of most Chinese people. Mario had persuaded her into a seat and they were already talking before I arrived with the obligatory cup of tea. Contrary to expectations she needed no repeated encouragement to drink her tea, but, flustered and a little bewildered, she took it and slurped loudly, sieving the floating green leaves through her teeth.

She wore thick black nylon ski pants, and a pink coat with pink false fur around the collar. Mario and I sat on the sofa, DaiYu in front of us looking very small on her chair. She was maybe in her early twenties, but still looked diminutive, like a child wearing her mother's clothes.

'So why do you want to learn English?' Mario asked.

'I want to go abroad and have many children,' she said

sadly. 'In China we are only allowed one child. It is the government policy. But I love children. I have a little nephew. He is – oh! – so funny,' she said with affection, clapping her hands together. 'I would like to have six children – all boys! I think I can be more natural with children.

'If you help me with my English I can teach you how to make *jiaozi*,' she laughed, and unlike most other Chinese girls didn't put her hand to cover her teeth as she did.

'But how good are your *jiaozi*?' I asked.

'My *jiaozi* are very good. My mother tells me my cooking is very good.'

'Well then, why not come over this weekend?'

'I am going home this weekend. My mother phoned me this evening and said that she misses me very much. I am going home to see her.'

She chatted to us in Chinese, talking slowly and keeping things simple enough for us to understand a little. The fact that she had come alone to our flat convinced us that she was in her twenties. It was a shock to hear her tell us how old she was. I switched back to English to check that I hadn't misunderstood.

'Seventeen?!'

The joke was reversed when she estimated us to be in our early forties, twenty years older than we were.

'When you come to my house I will banquet you!' she said – and the turn of phrase had a particular charm. 'You will like my home – it is near the Yellow River.'

'Is the river really yellow?' I asked.

'Oh yes, of course!' she laughed, 'I think you are funny!'

At 9.15 PM, a very late time for a lone Chinese girl to be visiting single men, DaiYu got up. 'Now I think ... I must leave.'

She looked nervous, or unsure, as if she wanted to say something more but couldn't. We also wanted to say more – but couldn't say it simply enough in English so we smiled and said earnestly, 'You must come back and teach us to make *jiaozi*. Please do!'

It was arranged that she would come on Monday.

From then on we entrusted ourselves to DaiYu as she attempted to introduce us to her Yuncheng and Chinese life. She had an ever-ready store of friends, or 'very nice ladies' whom she would take us to see, and translated for us whenever our Chinese faltered, as it mostly did. After I expressed an interest in Chinese tea, DaiYu returned and told us how she had found us a new friend. A very kind woman who had a tea shop. We should go and visit her. We went, and came away with two kinds of tea. Longjing and Jinghong Health Tea.

'This is very good,' DaiYu said. 'It will help you lose weight.'

My size was of great interest to the Chinese. Plump in a way most Westerners are, I felt like a monstrosity when compared to them. Older people often gave me the thumbs-up and said 'Shenti hao' – 'You've a good body.' The younger people took it upon themselves to help me with my obesity problem.

'I find it useful to cook. If I cook, then I don't eat as much,' one girl told me at English Corner, our conversation class.

Others were not so polite. One evening after a particularly enormous banquet, I lay on my bed with my belt undone, and with my stomach bulging, trying to give it as much room as possible. The phone rang. It was Li DongPing. 'Hi. Err – are you busy?'

'No.' I said, hoping she wasn't going to invite me round for dinner.

'Why not come around for an informal talk?'

It had been a good day, so hefting my stomach up and waddling like a pregnant woman, I walked over to her block and up the three flights of stairs.

'Hi, come in! Sit down!'

I did, glad to take the weight (which since lunch felt like it had doubled) off my feet.

'You look very breathless, why is that?' Li DongPing said, 'is it because you are so fat?'

Playing ping-pong on a spring evening that was warmer than most English summer days, a lady approached me. I was hot and sweaty and, concerned about my health, she spoke the immortal line: 'Mr Hill. Summer is not the friend of the Fat Man.'

Each time my girth was abused I silently swore. Now DaiYu was at it. I examined the box, which described the tea as, 'fragrant, strong, good taste – no harm to human body, easy to make tea, good medical therapy, a new product in Chinese traditional food therapy research.' The health properties were listed on the back – 'Fat-lowering, weight-losing, halitosis-allaying, clears away heat to stop itching, relaxes the bowels, it is especially useful to cure obesity, halitosis, itching, constipation.'

It was exactly like the blurb on a packet of potato crisps I had been given once. 'Healthy food', it had said. 'Ideal for young and old, especially for people who want to lose weight.'

Whenever we touched upon the subject of Chinese health care it always provided an interesting insight into Chinese life. Mario, as a vegetarian, was constantly nagged by the officials of the college for not eating meat.

'You must eat meat – it will make you stronger. You're too thin – here have some chicken, it's OK isn't it? It's not meat ...?' and to prove their point, they said I was big because I ate meat. If Mario did lose weight in Yuncheng whilst he was in the care of the college, it would mean a loss of face on their part. To have a foreigner wasting away would make people think that the college wasn't looking after him properly. But the truth was we were eating better than we had ever done – a diet of stir-fried, boiled and steamed fresh vegetables and noodles. Not a processed foodstuff in sight.

Whatever the truth about eating meat, it was a curious fact that I was never ill during term time, but Mario had a few scattered illnesses that served to worry the college even more, and encouraged them to try and reform his peculiar diet.

Even a sporting injury was ample evidence of his need to eat meat – as Cao told him after he'd twisted an ankle playing basketball. The ankle was badly swollen and the doctor was called – as much to show how seriously the college took Mario's welfare as from concern for the gravity of his condition. The doctor had a real hands-on approach: the offending joint was given a ten-minute massage, then three long acupuncture needles were inserted in various points on his leg.

'Do they hurt?' I asked Mario.

'Yes – a little,' he said. A fourth needle was inserted into his left buttock. 'Oh!' he said, 'I can't feel anything now.'

Another time Mario had a hoarse rasping cough that stubbornly refused to go away. He had been put on an intravenous drip for an hour or two a day, with Mrs Li LingZhen turning up to do her knitting and keep him company – but neither the drip nor the female care helped.

Song Jiang met us one day when Mario was still barking like a bronchial seal. He stopped to chat and told us that he had a friend in the hospital who was very skilled in massage and herbal medicine.

'The college doctor – she is not highly thought of,' he said. 'My friend, he is very skilled in Chinese medicine. In Chinese medicine we treat the whole body. Western medicine just treats the ill limb or body part – only treats it in isolation. Illness is a result of an imbalance – it is no good treating the illness if the imbalance remains – you will just become ill again.'

It sounded interesting, so Mario agreed to be taken off every afternoon for a vigorous chest massage, and to be given a dark herbal medicine to drink every morning. The sachet of leaves, twigs and roots needed to be boiled for three hours, so Song Jiang's wife got up at 5 AM to do this, then delivered the cup before Mario started teaching. I had a sip, and found it unpleasant enough to cure anything – except, it seemed, the cough. It went inexorably on – neither life-threatening nor being cured – irritating enough for me and I wasn't even suffering from it.

DaiYu came around after a weekend at home with something she'd got from her mother's dispensary – a bottle of ginseng tablets. 'They are very good,' she said. 'They will cure your cough.'

Thankfully for us all the cough did eventually go, but whether it was because of the herbs, massage, ginseng or from natural causes I couldn't tell you.

The Chinese preoccupation is not so much with their health as with treating themselves with medicine. Private clinics must be one of the most common kinds of business in any street in

China. There is no embarrassment about being ill or taking medicine – often the fact is flaunted. A very popular medicine for a minor skin problem is an ointment that has a lurid purple colour. Whatever the actual complaint was I could never see – it was usually so small – but the treatment left a massively obvious purple stain for a few days which the treated person never seemed to be embarrassed by, but left unwashed for maximum effect.

The variety of health treatments, some valid and others entirely bogus, seems to be much wider in China than in the West. Herbs, acupuncture, massage – I've even seen an old woman give her son a *QiGong* massage. QiGong is quite an esoteric skill, taking a lifetime to master. The *Qi* massage consists of manipulating the other person's *Qi*, smoothing out inequalities and imbalances without touching his or her body. The masseur's hands move, pushing and kneading the air, but never touching. My students believed it worked, having seen QiGong tricks performed on TV, but I have my doubts.

DaiYu had also started to teach us to make *jiaozi*. We had decided to make beef dumplings, and in buying the mince she had got to know a restaurant owner who was also 'a very kind woman'. We started going regularly to this Hui restaurant, the Hui – Muslim Chinese – being the largest of the country's minorities. It was an interesting place, with a very different feel to Han restaurants. Here people looked more like us; or rather, we didn't look so weird. Although most of China's Muslims are Hui, there are over ten Muslim peoples in total – Khazaks, Uigers, Tajiks – many of Indo-European and Turkish stock, but all falling into China's vast land mass. This restaurant, with all these races, was as cosmopolitan as Yuncheng got.

The owner was a tall Hui woman who looked more Turkish than Chinese, who had lived in Xingjiang all her life but had recently come here with her father-in-law because he was from Yuncheng and he wanted to die here. Noodles were her speciality, and she served us up large bowls of them with delicious sauces poured over them.

One night after a meal of noodles DaiYu, Mario and I sat by candlelight through a power cut and talked. DaiYu told us many things about herself – how she wanted to be free, how she danced alone in her room, how she hated the Chinese obsession with money, how she had once loved a boy but how he had been killed in a motorcycle accident. What she was telling us was so unlike anything I'd heard in China before that I felt it was too strange to be true. But then truth in China especially is a very subjective notion. I couldn't tell if she was imagining these things to reinvent herself or whether she was the first and only person to talk to us honestly. Maybe these events in her life were true, just that now, with us, she was interpreting them in a new light.

Whether she had been before or not, DaiYu seemed to be becoming more and more of a misfit in her own society, and as such was naturally drawn to us as outsiders in the local community. Maybe it would be the same for us when we returned home changed. As we talked that evening the room had a very un-national feel. We were not in China, and DaiYu was not a local. We were outside our nationalities, and it was a thrilling feeling – but one we would only feel with DaiYu.

DaiYu read our palms. 'Mario will have a longish life but a short career. You will also marry twice!' she said. It was not good news to Mario, who didn't relish the idea of getting married even once.

'Justin will have a long, happy life and marriage – but a very short career,' she said, after examining my palm. She seemed to get all the important bits in the right order and her prediction suited me fine.

DaiYu was, I think, quite lonely. When she had passed her exams for the college her mother had chosen what subject she should study, and had decided that DaiYu would study electronics, as this was a modern subject. Chinese youth, in fact most of the population, seem quite happy to entrust their futures to their respective superiors: children to parents, parents to their parents, and everyone to the Communist Party. DaiYu didn't enjoy her subject, and didn't fit in with her classmates. She didn't really know what she wanted, but she knew it wasn't this. Just before starting at college she had gone on a holiday to TianJing where she had met a hotel manager who'd said that if she improved her English then she could go and work there. And so new possibilities must have opened up in her mind beyond her small market town, a sleepy satellite of Yuncheng.

In Tianjing she'd seen the sea for the first time. 'I sat so long in the sun gazing out to sea that my mother pretended not to recognize me because she said I was so dark!' she laughed, and I found it strange to imagine a country so vast that you can live there and never see the sea till you're seventeen years old. What a mysterious sensation to have at that age – the size of it, the shifting waves, the salt smell and the sound of surf on sand.

With us she discovered all kinds of new ideas and approaches to life which, unlike our students, she was prepared to try out. Her more open mind was in part due to her family. Her mother was a pharmacist in her local town, and her father a doctor. Both had been sent here from their native provinces to help the locals. She was the youngest child, and had been a little spoilt by her family.

One day in the market we had seen some embroidered slippers and DaiYu told us that her grandmother had worn similar shoes.

'My grandmother had very little feet. They were very ugly. When she was seven years old she was forced to walk upon her bound feet, though the pain made her cry. I only ever saw them without the bandages a few times,' she told us. 'She was embarrassed to show them to us as they were from Old China before Liberation and Old China things were not good. All the toes were bent under the foot to the middle, except the big toe. She could walk on them alright and it wasn't too painful.'

The phone rang. It was DaiYu, inviting us to a disco that night. 'A disco? Why not,' I said.

We met DaiYu and her friend at the front gate of the college. Her friend's name was Hui Ming. She was an art student who hoped to go to Beijing to study English. She wore black leggings tucked into white booties, and a black jacket, and she didn't talk but instead gave us a rather lopsided smile.

We set off in the rolling gloom straight down Hedong Donglu.

'Is it far?' we asked.

'No, not far,' DaiYu said, without elaborating. After ten minutes of slow cycling she pointed ahead. 'There it is!'

Over the crossroads stood another of the multi-purpose concrete boxes, but this one had a canopy of fairy lights over the doorway – tiny lights all sparkling in the twilight.

'This is very new. Maybe it is the first disco in town,' DaiYu said as we locked up our bicycles.

It hadn't taken me too long to get used to the Chinese 'maybe'. 'Maybe we will go for lunch now.' 'Maybe I will come around this evening.' 'Maybe' meaning 'fairly definitely'. A useful word in a country as face-conscious as China, always giving an escape route in case the speaker is proved to be wrong.

It seemed that the entire local youth had flocked there. They were queuing excitedly, pushing through the doors up the stairs, past a beleaguered ticket saleswoman who seemed to have been chosen more for her fragile Chinese beauty than for her ability to take money, find the right change and then return the change and ticket to the customer. We were pushed up a plain concrete staircase, gritty underfoot with sand mixed with cigarette butts, spit and worse. The music got louder and louder, till we spilled out into a large room. This was the disco.

The dance floor, which took up the middle of the room, was empty, while down both sides of the room seventy-odd people were scattered at single rows of tables.

They seemed a very different group from the excited crowd at the door. The girls sat ram-rod straight, very composed, with bored expressions, staring into nowhere. The boys were equally rigid in their dark suits – not knowing what to do at a disco, and paralysed with the fear of getting it wrong. I toyed with the idea that all the interesting people had been siphoned off to a different room where they were now having a wild party. But I dismissed that idea. No, this was it.

We joined a pair of young men at a table, members of

the up-and-coming generation. True children of the 'Modern China'. Their suits had designer labels sewn onto their sleeves, to demonstrate clearly how expensive the suit was without having to worry about anything like cut or style. They held up their red plastic mugs which had COFFEE on them in white block capitals, as if in a cheap commercial, showing off their sophistication as they drank a Western drink, and tried to smoke their cigarettes like James Dean. They were so involved in their 'image' that I doubted they had half a personality between them.

That fear turned out to be right. They were from Xian, capital of the next-door province, which had a population of a few million, and as they talked to us they turned their noses up at DaiYu and Hui Ming and everyone else in the room who they considered their rustic countrymen, not even worthy of their disdain.

'Yuncheng is too small. Too rural. Too dirty. You should go to Xian,' one told us. 'There are many foreigners there. Many tall buildings.'

I would have liked to be able to tell them that rural, dirty, backward Yuncheng was everything I'd come to China for, but as yet my Chinese wasn't up to that. Luckily this retarded little disco was too much for their rich sensibilities and they left soon after.

The pop music had also been too much and so, when the first waltz of the evening came on, accompanied by flashing lights and a spinning mirror ball, the empty dance floor was suddenly swamped.

We noticed that Hui Ming was spending a lot of time dancing with a tall Chinese man aged about fifty whose waist had thickened and stiffened like an old tree.

'I think that old man likes your friend,' I said, joking. DaiYu's response shocked me.

'Yes. It is one thing I don't like about her. She wants to sleep with many men before marriage.'

Hui Ming carried on dancing with her older man while a group of men came over to the table next to ours. The music switched to karaoke, and – if it were possible – the volume was turned up a notch. The karaoke was painful: it made the Eurovision Song Contest look like a fine arts competition. Mournful love songs accompanied by videos showing pretty couples getting rapturous at the sight of each other in the surf, in a meadow, on a bridge. Then falling out of love with tearful, pouting looks, followed by delirium as they fell together again.

Someone tapped me on the shoulder, one of a group of rowdy men sitting behind us. They were all in green uniforms, which doesn't necessarily mean anything in China, where a major sideline of the police or army is to flog military clothing at the streetside.

I turned round to talk to whoever it was who'd tapped me – and came nose to nose with a grinning Chinese youth. Yellowed teeth bit a cigarette that was close enough to warm my chin. The smoke and beer fumes helped to nullify the stench of his hot breath. He shouted at me in garbled Chinese. His alcohol-fuzzed brain found it difficult to comprehend that I couldn't understand him. But with the karaoke singer in full voice and all the other noise I couldn't even hear him and turned away again.

A moment later the whole table had joined us, and my cigarette-smoking friend kindly put his arm around my shoulders and smiled his toothy smile, exhaling all over me, which felt like being washed in filthy dishwater.

'Where are you from?'

'How many people in your family?'

'Are you married?'

'How old are you?'

'How much money do you earn each month?'

'Have you got used to life in China?'

We were bombarded with the eager questions that are the preliminary for any kind of social contact in China, then it was our turn to ask questions.

They were all pissed, and so when they told me that they were undercover policemen on a drugs raid I didn't really take them too seriously.

'But someone has tipped off the drug dealers,' one of them continued. 'You know drugs?' He took a piece of chewing gum wrapper and imitated snorting from it. 'If we find any dealers then bang! we will shoot them.' The speaker and another 'policeman' were in plain clothes, but they clapped a third, in uniform, on the back.

'Bang! Bang! Bang!' they laughed.

The uniformed policeman looked very young, and a little shy, as he looked at his large hands and spoke. 'I am nineteen,' he said quietly.

'What do you do?' I asked, which made the plain-clothed policemen even more excited. 'Bang! Bang!' they laughed and clapped him on the back again.

He was a quiet figure amongst the circle of inebriated and excited men. He drew a breath. 'I am an executioner,' he said with embarrassment, smiling vaguely at his hands in apology. 'I go around the local districts and shoot bad people. I have killed two people.'

There was a pause while he rubbed away a stain from his thick hands, then he spoke again. 'I do not like my job.'

The other policeman, who was still hugging me, and whose breath had not improved during the conversation, asked, 'How many bottles of beer can you drink?'

'Oh, a few, I think,' I said. More beer was ordered, glasses filled, and then '*Gan Bei!*' and we drained our cups in one go. '*Gan Bei! Gan Bei!*' we carried on till I'd lost count and no longer cared.

'Come! We will go and eat.' They picked us up and pulled us along with them. Outside it was dreary and cold, a sliver of moon shining in a star-encrusted sky, over the silhouettes of chimneys and blocks of flats.

It was a short cycle to the town square – Hedong Square. Hedong Square, now off to one side of town, lies at the projected centre of a future Yuncheng: a modern high-rise city with broad avenues teeming with cars and traffic. Now, every morning the square sways with ballroom dancers and the graceful movements of *taiqi*. During the day it sleeps, coming alive at night when vendors cycle their restaurants-on-wheels into town and then set up shack. Tents are erected, and lightbulbs are strung from overhead wires, while the idle, the drunk and late-night workers and their friends gather to talk earnestly, unable to sleep.

The air was rich with the smell of spiced mutton kebabs spitting fat over the glowing braziers, frying noodles, and the sounds of the scrape of stirred woks, the shouts of the vendors and the loud banter of drinking games as bottles of Chinese spirits were quickly emptied.

Our friends led us past bursts of flame from burning woks, straight to one of the shacks. A gust of wind breathed life into the square, the tents flapped, while the lightbulbs danced like fireflies on their wires, casting lurid shadows on the tent and the dust curled up like salamanders. We crunched grit with our fried noodles topped with egg, tomatoes and green peppers and kebabs of mutton spiced with cumin and red chilli.

'Eat, eat,' they said, offering more when I was already full.

At 9.15 AM last Sunday morning someone knocked loudly on our front door. We ignored them, and we listened to their disappointed steps retreat down the stairs. Five minutes later they returned with what sounded like reinforcements, and they knocked on the door again, louder this time. By ten I had had breakfast and was settling down to read the *Guardian Weekly*, which gave us all the news, albeit two weeks late. My newspapers were very special, a pleasure that was also my only connection to the world outside. I liked to sit and read undisturbed for a morning at least – but today wasn't going to be my day. The knockers returned and left, but then the phone rang and I was foolish enough to answer it: students.

'Hello, Mr Hill. Are you busy? We will come around immediately.'

Three girls arrived soon after, stepping lightly over their shoes which they'd left on the doorstep and letting themselves into our lounge where they sat down. Hom Ya, Jing Chen and Qu Xia, whose name meant Autumn Cloud. Mario played Chinese chess with Hom Ya, and lost. Jing Chen and Qu Xia asked me the same questions they'd heard others ask me at English Corner.

'What Chinese people have you heard of?'

'Mao, Deng and Confucius,' I said. 'Oh, and the Last Emperor, Pu Yi.'

'I love Chairman Mao the best of all these,' Jing Chen told me. 'Because he expelled the foreign invaders.'

'Do you think that China needs defending now?'

'Yes. Our China is a peaceful nation, but we must defend ourselves.'

'Who do you think would invade China?'

'Japan or America. They are violent peoples. Mao was very great. He defeated the Japanese.'

'But what about the Cultural Revolution, or the Great Leap Forward?' I asked.

'Of course Chairman Mao made many mistakes. I think he was seventy per cent good and thirty per cent bad,' Qu Xia said, then changed the subject. 'We have brought some tickets for you to come to the cinema. Would you like to come?'

Announced in that fashion, I didn't think we had much choice but to accept, so I put down my newspaper and followed them to the cinema.

Chinese cinemas are very different from your average twelve-screen complex. Bare concrete walls, and the babble of noise always at ear-splitting pitch as everyone talks to friends – generally at the other side of the cinema. The audience quietened a little when the film started, but all around in the semi-darkness we could hear the sounds of hawking, smoking, talking, laughing and spitting.

Spitting is endemic in China, where grotching up lumps of phlegm is considered to be quite a healthy habit. A Chinese person will hawk loudly for a number of seconds, swill the result around his or her mouth, repeat the process, and then let the offending phlegm dribble down from the lower lip onto the floor. After the noisy build-up, you are led to expect that the contents will be spat violently out. But having to watch the lump of phlegm drooling off the lower lip makes it as unpleasant to watch as it is to listen to.

During my first virgin days walking down a Beijing street I was mulling over the likelihood of a romance or even a dalliance during my two years in China. A stunning Chinese lady appeared around the corner: high heels, swishing trousers, a petite figure and a face straight from a Ming-dynasty mural. The prospect of romance loomed suddenly large. Then, three steps away from me, this beauty hawked and spat out a gobbet right next to my feet. My heart sank as she passed me by with a faint 'whish' of her clothes.

Back in the cinema we were being treated to a dubbed 1950s Hollywood comedy, the glitz and orchestrated plot giving a truly bizarre impression of the West to these small-town Chinese who were watching in awe.

I was unlucky enough to have a chain-smoker with acute bronchitis sitting behind me, one who had obviously break-fasted on raw garlic that morning. He puffed on each cigarette till he choked and wheezed then broke out into a fit of coughing so severe I thought he might die. After half an hour of having his hot garlic breath spluttering down my bare neck I wished he would. I turned up my collar as far as it would go and leant forward as far as possible. I was nervously aware of every noise around me, and when someone on my left in the darkness began hawking and spitting I drew my feet in as close as possible to avoid any lumps of lung that might fly my way.

This trip to the cinema was turning into a cruel test for my Western sensibilities. Then, at last, the words THE END came up on the screen and the Chinese audience, to a man, jumped up and began stampeding for the exits. The two narrow doors inevitably became jammed with people angry at being crushed in the mob, so I took an unfair use of my size advantage and broke free into the welcome bright, clean air.

DaiYu, like the college authorities, and the drugs policemen we'd met at the disco, all offered to take us to GuanDi temple, the birth place of GuanYu, the Chinese War god. However, DaiYu was the only one who took the offer any further. After so many hollow words it was actually a surprise to be going there on this Sunday morning.

Our bus rattled along the Salt Lake heading west, taking one hour to make the twenty kilometres to our stop. We stepped off the rusty carriage straight into the villagers' Sunday market – a maelstrom of people and noise. The bus ground to a halt as it tried to squeeze through a street only just wide enough for it at the best of times, now cluttered with rickshaws, people and stalls.

In isolated places like this there was a strange but pleasant lack of attention directed towards us. I think the reason for this was that people just didn't believe their eyes and so ignored us.

Unfortunately we couldn't get into the temple; well, actually, we could get in, but only by paying the foreigners' price, which at fifteen *yuan* was fifteen times more expensive than the Chinese one *yuan*. This two-price policy is officially sanctioned by the government and extends to hotels, trains, museums and other sites of interest, and generally encourages the populace as a whole to try to rip off foreigners. As teachers we were entitled to the Chinese price, but unused to carrying our ID at all times, we had forgotten to bring the necessary documents to prove that we were Chinese residents, not tourists. We all tried and failed to convince the ticket seller, who stuck to her guns. '*Guiding shi guiding*,' she repeated – 'regulations are regulations.'

So, instead of visiting the temple we took a walk around the outside of it. A large area of what had been old houses had been cleared away along the outer wall for new flats to be built. A few of the old walls still stood, so we walked through the remains of the old courtyard houses with their wells now dangerously uncovered. At the far end of the rubble a line of old houses remained intact. An old lady, tall and gaunt, stood in her doorway, smoking a pipe. She smiled and ushered us into her house. Inside was a single room, surprisingly warm and dominated by a large bed. She gave us tea, which we drank quickly as she nodded approvingly at us. While we drank she showed us two kittens being kept warm in a box by the stove, then we left, thanking her profusely.

The streets outside were still vibrant, colourful and crowded. Street traders rolled out flat breads, cut cloth, and sat behind layers of fruit. We pushed our way to the edge of town and caught a passing bus.

DaiYu had a friend who lived half-way back to Yuncheng, so we stopped at one of the factories that dot the Salt Lake, processing the salt petre. It seemed a very deserted and depressing place to live: a long drive sloped downwards away from the road, at the bottom of which was her friend's factory work unit: a few blocks of flats, a factory block, a school, and chimneys that poured out black and yellow smoke that sank down and settled over the surrounding fields in a heavy cloud.

People spent their whole lives in places like this – but DaiYu's friends had gone off to Beijing, and I couldn't blame them, so we hitched a lift back to Yuncheng on the back of a tractor.

On the way back DaiYu said how pretty Spanish girls were. Mario answered, 'Some Spanish girls are pretty and some ugly, just like in China. The girls you saw at the Olympics were specially chosen to be pretty.'

She thought for a while and then turned to me and said, 'I've seen a few English films and, from these, I think English women are very serious.'

DaiYu continued to take us around Yuncheng and to visit our flat for quite some time. Then one day she came around looking very distressed, and we soon found out why.

'One of my teachers has told me not to come and see you,' she said.

'Why?'

'She didn't say why. She just shouted at me. She was very angry and she shouted at me. She said that I must not come here. I must not see you. I asked why I must not come, but she kept on saying, "No why – just don't." They made me promise that I would not tell you, they told me that I should not say anything to you – just stop coming here.'

'Well, we're glad you did tell us; and you must keep coming here if you want to,' I said.

'Oh – *tianle* – Heavens! Of course I want to come,' she said, brightening only a little.

A warning voice had told me that something like this would

happen, but still, that did not stop me from being angry. It was such an outrageous thing to try to ban us from seeing each other. That we were entirely blameless made me feel even more angry – like being the victim of a vicious slur.

But in China, the concept of struggling against temptation doesn't exist; the law doesn't even permit temptation to arise. The best solution to potential problems is to forbid young Chinese girls and young Western teachers to meet. Here we were with a two-year contract, and we wanted to build relationships, had begun a friendship, and immediately, because someone who didn't know us had decided it was bad, DaiYu had been warned off coming.

In Yuncheng the only time we met girls of anything approaching our own age was in the classroom with our students – otherwise not at all. We were starved of female company in a social setting, and DaiYu was our only friend at the time – male or female. It was a preposterous invasion of our private lives. Worst of all, we felt that with DaiYu we were at last beginning to break into Chinese society; it was DaiYu who had broken ranks by meeting us on a personal, not formal, level and everyone else was striving to remove her and all trace of the damage she'd done.

'Does this teacher think that we are trying to seduce you?' I asked.

'No. She is only trying to protect you,' DaiYu said.

'Aren't we even allowed to have friends that we choose inside the college?'

There was no answer.

The problem was what to do now – creating a fuss would no doubt clear the air and put us in a strong position with the college, but would it help DaiYu?

We were beginning to become confident in our position as the only Western teachers for hundreds of kilometres and I don't think we even considered our position to be in danger. If China has a Stasi-style secret police it doesn't exist in Yuncheng. There was no question of us being expelled over such a minor problem. The worst that would happen to us was that we would get a bad name, and that would certainly affect our welcome in the community. It was a tricky situation to deal with – so our immediate desire to go out and have a showdown with someone was quickly dismissed as being detrimental to us and even more so to DaiYu.

We had made such an effort to get to know everyone we met: in our work with our students, in learning the language, in getting out to the countryside schools to do model lessons and meet local teachers and see the conditions our students would teach in after graduation. Surely the college would not try and enforce their will in this matter?

In China, to achieve harmony is the ultimate goal in any relationship, so the college would never dare come to us directly. If we challenged *them* then it would result in a huge loss of face for the college, something that would be entirely detrimental to us throughout our remaining time in Yuncheng, and have even worse consequences for DaiYu.

We decided to do nothing – to carry on as if nothing had happened – and I think this was the best solution for everyone. From then on we were often followed when we went out, to see who we would meet. But as time went on the college began to have more confidence in us, and to see that our relationship with DaiYu had not turned romantic, so the pressures on her eased. She was no longer harangued for coming to see us, but for spending too much time learning English instead of studying electronics – that was an implicit backdown on the college's part.

Meeting Mr Cao, we attempted to clarify the appropriateness of students visiting our flat, and asked him, 'Is it all right for people to come and visit us? Do you have any objection to friends coming to see us?'

'No, of course they can come,' he said, and that was the final word on that.

CHAPTER EIGHT

XiaTian: Summer

Most people find a visit to the dentist a little stressful. A Chinese dentist would stretch the nerves of even the most resolute.

Just a glimpse through an open doorway would make my flesh crawl. Closer up they don't get any more reassuring. One window is usually full of grotesque close-up photos of mouth diseases: bleeding or swollen gums, concertinaed, chipped, twisted and rotting teeth in every shade between yellow and black, and inside, a few hand drills hanging perched over a large barber's chair, poised like the fangs of a praying mantis.

You can imagine my feelings when a tooth cracked, and, however much I put it off, I had to go to the dentist.

I told Dean Wu, who reassured me somewhat. 'I will tell Mr Cao that he must get the car and send you to a very good clinic in town.'

I turned up at the appointed time and had a sinking feeling when I saw no car, no Dean Wu – just two students waiting for me. One of the students couldn't speak English very well, and neither of them knew anything about the clinic in town.

'We will walk down the street. There will be a dentist,' one of the students told me. They whispered in Chinese and giggled as we walked. I tried to help them relate to how I was feeling by asking if they had ever been to a dentist.

'No. I've never been to the dentist. My teeth are too good.'

Just you wait, I thought.

We found a place. As grim as all the others. A little room with the door flung open to the street, and a huge chair which looked like I ought to be strapped into it – waiting for me.

'Whatever happens, I don't want my tooth pulled out,' I said.

It looked like the kind of place where they still used pliers. I didn't fancy my chances, once pinned down, to dictate what was or was not going to happen. I gave the students clear instructions which they said they understood. I repeated my instructions, and wasn't satisfied until they could explain back to me what it was I'd said. Then I took a deep breath and walked in.

A pleasant-faced old man greeted me and had a look into my mouth. So did my two students, his wife, and a curious peasant who had followed us in off the street. He took off his glasses and used them like a magnifying glass to focus in on my mouth. 'Oh God!' I thought, and showed him which particular tooth was broken.

He smiled confidently, and went off to rattle metal instruments in their tray.

My students began discussing my mouth and laughing.

'What's so funny?' I snapped. Then I tried to outstare the peasant who stood over the chair, looking down at me. I felt like a rat being dissected in a school laboratory.

The man returned with one of those little instruments that has a sharp hook on the end. I lay back, opened wide, and prayed that it wouldn't hurt.

It didn't. He removed the broken splinter, and then fitted a drill bit to his drill. I usually like to be injected up to the eyeballs before I let any drill past my lips, but he got it into my mouth before I could stop him. Thankfully he only used it to smooth off the broken tooth, then swabbed it down, and gave me the bill.

I was sweating and so relieved I'd have paid him double. I shook his hand vigorously and walked out, feeling like a condemned man who has been reprieved at the eleventh hour.

'Do you miss your family?' One of the students asked as we walked back.

'Not at the moment,' I replied.

'I think you are very cruel,' she said. 'If I left home, then I would miss my mother very much.'

'Have you never left home?' I asked.

'No,' she said.

I was woken early, by a heavy banging.

Only in China do people do DIY at six-fifteen on a Sunday morning, I told myself, until it slowly dawned on me that the battering was someone banging on my door. Despite my half-dreaming state it only took me a few moments to realize that whoever it was wasn't going away, and so I stormed out of bed, intent on giving some straight Western advice about coming to practise oral English at this time in the morning.

I flung on my dressing gown, stamped into my flip-flops, opened the door of my bedroom and – splash! – stepped into a layer of water. The sound of running water came from the bathroom, where I had a sinking feeling that something had gone wrong. I turned off the tap and took a deep breath before opening the door. I knew exactly who it was and why they had come, and didn't really feel up to it so early in the morning. It was, of course, Li DongPing's father, the party secretary of the History and Politics department (a very nice man, but he taught a very suspicious combination of subjects) who lived beneath us. With painful inevitability he told me that there was water coming through his ceiling. Apologizing profusely, I explained – I don't know what I explained – apart from the fact that I was terribly sorry – and he came in and helped me mop up the waves of lapping water that were washing through the hallway.

Finally the pools had gone and I apologized once more. Despite the fact this was the third time this had happened, he hushed me up and told me not to worry. The problem was that we still hadn't quite adapted to our sporadic water supply. On the top floor we had the least reliable pressure – we also, for no obvious reason, had a flat full of taps. You went into the bathroom, wanting to wash your hands, and no water, so, it was easy to forget to close the tap again, or not quite close it properly. Five the next morning the water pressure built back up.

After mopping up the water I went back to bed, trying to turn what had just happened into a dream. Lying there, face buried in my pillow, I told myself I needed a lie-in. Unfortunately, by 7.30 AM it was already so warm that the flies – dive-bombing ticklish areas – had got too irritating to permit further sleep. The month of May, and it was already hot, and marching inexorably on to midsummer. The change of temperature had been so sudden that it felt like only a few days ago that I'd been wearing sweaters. When it's this hot there's nothing for it but to lounge about in boxer shorts in the arc of the fan and wait for the afternoon to drip by.

Trying not to get too much sweat on my book, I enjoyed the rich silence after lunch, rare in China. No children, tractors, shouting, salesmen – everyone was asleep or, like me, too hot to move.

This calm lasted until dinnertime, and then, as the sun got lower, people went out and made up for their earlier restfulness. In the courtyard below, the retired ladies of the college started aerobics lessons, Chinese aerobics, ten steps of their formation dancing repeated over and over to the Communards' 'Don't Leave Me This Way.'

Formation dancing has been developed for people who want something more modern than ballroom dancing, but who aren't ready for disco. It also has the advantage that everyone does the same thing so that no-one stands out from the crowd. It is really very simple: walk forward two steps, then backwards, repeat this, clap, turn ninety degrees and then start again.

In another corner of the courtyard five women were doing hand exercises, and their children were playing between their legs, their high voices and laughter piercing even the loud music.

A student called round and enthused about a TV series he wanted to watch. The students had no access to their own TV, and anyway at this time they were supposed to be in self-study, but I let him in and we put it on, and he explained to me what was happening. There were two snake spirits that were dying and a poor villager took pity on one and saved it. It became a human and married him. After many years of happy marriage, a monk discovered what had happened and said that the marriage of the snake spirit to the human was a crime. He put the beautiful snake spirit under a mountain for five hundred years. Luckily her son defeated the monk, and came to save her.

Quite a simple story really, so I couldn't understand how we were getting so confused when Du GuoQiang tried to explain who was who. When he pointed out the husband, I said, 'But he looks like a girl.' Du GuoQiang said, 'But he *is* a girl!'

'So how can he be the husband?'

Eventually we got our wires uncrossed: 'Because the actors' parts involve kissing, the husband and the wife are both played by women so that people won't get angry.'

I found this very amusing – and had to explain the word 'kinky' to him. 'You see, in Britain I think people are more likely to get annoyed by two girls kissing on TV than an unmarried man and a woman kissing,' I told him.

He found that very funny too.

Apparently Yuncheng was living on borrowed time. Soon, and we didn't know when, the whole city could be in ruins. This was how the subject of Yuncheng's forthcoming earthquake was introduced to me by students.

They were surprised: didn't I already know?

'No,' I had to admit. 'I haven't been listening to Chinese radio recently. Nor do I watch Yuncheng television.' A one-hour slot after the national weather forecast, of limited interest to those not fluent in Chinese. Even if they'd given a three-minute warning, I probably wouldn't have understood it.

'There may be an earthquake this month. Has no-one in the college told you?'

I had to admit they hadn't.

The next group of students was slightly more adamant, 'It will be on the fourteenth or fifteenth of this month.'

At English Corner the physics lecturer, Mr Yang, who had recently spent six months in Brighton, turned up. When I could get a word in between their questions, I asked him about the earthquake.

'Ah. There is a famous man in China who predicts earthquake. He has predicted four earthquakes in China this year. The other three have already happened, to the exact time he said. There is only Yuncheng left.'

'Oh,' I said, not knowing really how to approach a conversation about earthquakes. 'Will it be big?'

'About seven on the Richter scale, and it will happen at the middle of this month.'

'Well, what do you do if there is an earthquake?' I asked. 'Climb under the bed?'

'You do nothing,' Yang RuiJun laughed.

He laughed at anything. Usually at subjects Westerners would treat with seriousness – beating up people in the Cultural Revolution when he was younger; how at school he did nothing but write political propaganda posters, and fight others saying, 'We are the true bodyguard of Mao'; how poor his village was; the prospect of war with Britain over Hong Kong.

'If there is an earthquake, then you must move to the corner of the room. That is the strongest part. Preferably an outside wall,' he laughed, implying that this was the exact opposite of what you should do. His laughter got on my nerves, but the Chinese do laugh for different reasons from Westerners, to cover up embarrassment, or for something that they cannot talk about, so I tried not to hold his cultural norms against him.

Once I had caught a student cheating in an exam. I sent her out and afterwards demanded to know why she had cheated. She laughed.

I quivered with fury. 'What is so funny?'

She laughed again. It goes completely against the Westerner's grain to be laughed at at moments like this, but it probably goes against the Chinese grain to be put on the spot in such a way. Nothing makes someone lose face so badly.

Today is 31 May – my birthday. It's one of those signposts like Christmas, Easter, and August bank holiday that normally mark the passage of time. Without any of the others in China, though, to wake up on the morning of 31 May and realize that I've just aged another year leaves me rather nonplussed.

Mario's birthday was a few weeks ago on 11 April, and at lunchtime we told Dean Wu, who got very excited.

'Birthday?! Ah! Your birthday – a very special day for you. Shall I speak to the President and say that he must buy a present for you on behalf of the college?'

Mario decided he'd rather not have any fuss about a day that no longer seemed a cause for celebration.

Dean Wu took me aside. Confidentially, holding my elbow with one hand and with a cigarette in the other, he said: 'You know, I wish you had told us – and I could have arranged a banquet for Mario – but now it's too late.'

He left me feeling like it was all my fault that Mario's birthday had gone without celebration, like I'd robbed him of the chance to show Mario his hospitality – and although I could see through this trick, it didn't quite remove the guilt. It did increase my affection for Dean Wu's crafty side.

Mario told Dean Wu about my birthday last week – so this time he has no excuse, and I feel a little apprehensive in case an enormous fuss is made. Being the centre of attention makes me feel rather inadequate and lame, such a fuss is made out of us on a daily basis that the thought of any more makes me feel exhausted. If the students find out, then they're bound to want to do something special – and that worries me even more. Their idea of a good treat and mine differ sharply.

I got up early – before six – and cycled off down to Hedong Square to do *taiqi*. I'd been really keen on learning some kind of martial art in China but our village kung fu training had dropped off a long time ago, so *taiqi* took its place.

What surprised me as the sun did a reverse action-replay of sunset – a red ball rolling up from the eastern horizon – was just how busy it was at this time in the morning. Housewives were already out haggling and nattering, buying vegetables and eggs, and kitchens rattled with the clatter of people preparing breakfasts.

Taiqi is very popular amongst the older Chinese. In fact I think I was the youngest pupil – and one of the only ones not capable of doing the splits or being able to kick in slow motion above my head. The style of learning was traditionally Chinese – a single master at the front went through the movements, while everyone else filed up behind in the big square and copied him. I was lucky as a foreigner to have one-to-one tuition with Bao LaoShi – a sixty-nine-year-old retired doctor who could do a slow-motion kick up to his nose, and did it repeatedly just to make me feel more inadequate.

'You have to force yourself,' he told me as I reached for my toes every morning. 'Only through pain can you become more supple. I started *taiqi* at the age of fifty-eight years – and every morning and night I used to stretch over and over – it hurt so much that sweat used to burst out on my forehead. It's the only way.'

I was sure he was right, but I wasn't up to pain at 6 AM – I liked to build up to it during the day. I was still reaching for my toes, hearing my muscles and tendons creak ominously, as he did the splits and lay along one leg just to illustrate the point.

I never thought that *taiqi* could be so tiring – but moving your body weight around in slow motion really does leave you invigorated and sweating. We went through our routines, had a chat about an upcoming competition in Taiyuan which one of the teams was training for – and then my time was up. I left people in small groups chatting or practising a movement, and Bao LaoShi relaxing with a fag.

Back at the college I approached my first lesson nervously, but nothing unusual happened – and no mention was made of my birthday.

After lunch the usual trickle of students wanting or returning library books arrived and amongst them was a deputation from class 9489 – with a large card. They presented it to me and left, a little shy.

It had been signed, and then put back into its plastic wrapping. Leaving the wrappers on is a common practice in China. Most people's sofas are still covered in their protective plastic. On the front of the card was a nauseating picture of a fluffy puppy dog. The popularity of kitsch in China is an unpleasant revelation, especially when you're expecting wash paintings of cloud-wreathed peaks, bamboo groves and swirls of calligraphy. But it's the thought that counts, as my mum always told me.

For the rest of the afternoon I half expected a phonecall from Dean Wu, summoning me to a banquet, but as the day went by as normal, I began to enjoy the fact that I had in some way escaped.

In bed at ten o'clock, I finished writing my diary, turned out the light and looked out of my bedroom window. The town was dark without streetlights – just the lights of individual rooms gleaming out. Most people seemed to be in bed already but in the block opposite I could see a group of friends sitting up playing cards. Stripped down to their underwear – vests and slips and baggy shorts – with the fan on, they had the air of people too hot to sleep, happy to spend the night up playing cards. I shut the curtains and lay back in the cooling blast from the fan. All in all it had been a very quiet and peaceful birthday – and I'd thoroughly enjoyed every minute of it.

This morning I walked into town to buy some vegetables. The sun burned mercilessly down, and although it was only ten o'clock my clothes were sticky with the heat. The fruit salesmen sprinkled their apples, oranges and pears with water to keep them fresh.

Fine weather like this usually filled everyone with a flush of vitality. This is not such a good thing if you are a foreigner in China. Because they were feeling particularly perky today, people who would not usually take any notice of me walking down the street looked up and shouted, 'Hallooo', 'LaoWai', 'How do you do?', 'Goodbye', 'ABCDEF ...' – it didn't really matter what they shouted, it was the tone that counted. Unfortunately, the tone was that which you would use to a performing monkey.

I had a rule: if someone spoke to me directly, or in a tone that was friendly, then I stopped to say hello. But this happened so infrequently I was usually speechless with surprise. The far,

far more common scenario was for someone to shout 'Hello' at me after I passed by, to the hilarity of their friends, who thought it was the wittiest thing.

Today it was people who were passing by at speed who shouted at me: people on bicycles or who were hanging out of car windows. A group of schoolchildren came cycling around the corner, and I winced because I knew exactly what they would do. They got quite excited when they spotted me, loudly pointing me out to their friends cycling next to them, then as we drew closer they went silent. As we passed, I just waited for it – and a few seconds later it came, all of the chorusing 'Hallooo! Halloooo! LaoWai! How do you do!'

Before I came to China I expected it, I knew that it would happen. But it didn't make it any easier.

The worst thing was that no one ever told children off for this behaviour. I was a LaoWai, so what was my problem? Most adults found it funny, and watched me curiously to see what I'd do when mobbed by shouting children.

I once brought this topic up with a student. 'You know, people often laugh at me because I look strange.'

He took this as an accusation, a smear upon his nation's honour, and immediately the conversation got a bit tense. This was now an issue of national pride.

'They are laughing to be friendly,' he told me, as if trying to protect me from information that would be to my detriment.

'I don't think so,' I said.

'They are laughing with embarrassment,' he said flatly.

'Really? Not laughing at me?'

'No, not at you,' he corrected me, '*with* you.'

I left it there. We would obviously not agree, and I didn't want to stir up that little thing called 'face'.

My students disappeared periodically during the summer – to help with the harvest or ploughing at home, or to go on teaching practice. During one of these group absences, I was asked to teach some middle-school teachers at a local town called LingYi.

They were a pleasant bunch whom I had taught before on

a few occasions. On the last of my four days' teaching, I was getting ready to say goodbye at the end of my lessons when the door opened.

'Excuse me,' an assistant said, and called me out. I was taken to the staff room where two policemen promptly arrested me. I had been spotted entering the town and the local constabulary had managed to track me down to the LingYi teachers' college. The LingYi head of police had been alerted and had come down personally to supervise my arrest.

He stood up to meet me, saluted and then rather surprised me by shaking hands with me.

'Do you have papers?' he asked.

'No, I'm sorry I don't,' I said, beginning to understand what had happened.

'I'm afraid LingYi is a closed area. Foreigners are not allowed here,' I was told.

I smiled – 'I'm very sorry.' I knew I sounded and looked amused about something they took very seriously, so I quickly did my best to show a suitable degree of horror, guilt and self-repugnance for breaking this law.

The policeman regarded me, then went off on a long speech. 'No foreigners allowed in LingYi county. We are not a licensed area for the reception of overseas visitors. If foreigners come through, they can't even get off the bus, but must go straight through to the next open area,' he said, giving me another stern look to indicate how heinous my behaviour had been. 'Not even stop to go to the toilet.'

It was all a grand farce, only possible in such a bureaucratic country as China. '*Guiding shi guiding*,' I was told at last – 'Regulations are regulations.'

China has always struck me as a country of stark contrasts – the vast dust-blown emptiness of the countryside, occasionally dotted with the figure of a peasant returning home, and the bustle of the city, where you cannot move without stepping on someone.

Now, at harvest time, those two Chinas meet, in Yuncheng. Today the streets of Hedong Donglu were paved with gold –

quite literally! It was only the first week in June, but the harvest had arrived at this stage of its journey northwards through China. When I got up at 5.30 AM, the gangs of peasants were already out, moving rapidly through the fields, cutting the wheat with sickles, backbreaking work. They finished early, when the sun burned down at mid-day, but then the wheat had to be threshed and dried. The peasants laid the cut corn over the road so the movement of cars, buses, cycles and feet over it would thresh it for them.

In the evening they returned with sacks and shovels and threw spadefuls of corn up into the light breeze, that became thick with the fine husks that stuck to my sweaty skin.

At last they carefully swept up all the grains of wheat from the Tarmac, into the sacks, and pulled the loads back to their village. At dawn the next morning, the whole process began again.

This evening it was DaiYu's birthday.

She phoned us at 7.30 AM to tell us.

'Hello, Big Brother,' she said. 'It is my birthday. Tonight we will have a party. Can you come?'

The day had passed quickly and as evening came the rain cleared. It gave the air a cool, damp feel, a respite from the sun.

We met DaiYu at the gateway of her work-unit compound, which was just a few compounds down the road from ours. The flat she used belonged to an uncle of hers who lived elsewhere, and so she had the rare privilege of a place to herself, when even most married couples had to live with their parents for the first years.

The gateman was openly suspicious of us, and refused to let us go into the compound to DaiYu's flat.

'Oh, Heavens! He is – you know – very old-fashioned. He wants to protect me. He doesn't think he should let foreign men in,' DaiYu explained.

When she came back out we cycled down to Hedong Square, which was the liveliest place in Yuncheng after dark.

A few tables and chairs had been put out and we sat at one and chatted. Mario's ponytail was a source of great interest to the people nearby. A man materialized out of the gloom and stood watching the three of us, soon joined by another two. They began to question DaiYu about us.

'Very funny!' laughed DaiYu suddenly. 'They want to know if you two are married. They think Mario is a woman because he has a ponytail; and because of your yellow hair, they think you are a very old man.'

Mario had a thick growth of black stubble on his chin, and it was beyond me how anyone could mistake him for a woman.

'He is wearing a red jumper. Red is a woman's colour,' she laughed. 'In China only women wear red.'

This morning the phone rang at 6 AM and then again at five minutes past. The third time was at about ten past.

It looked like I'd have to answer it just to stop whoever it was from phoning all morning.

'Hello.'

'Come and play table tennis,' the voice said enthusiastically.

'Don't ever phone me at six o'clock,' I said.

'Come and play table tennis,' the voice repeated a bit more uncertainly, then, 'I do not understand.'

Speaking simply and slowly is almost impossible when you are angry.

'Do – not – ever – phone me at six o'clock. And I don't want to play table tennis!' Click!

At seven o'clock someone knocked on the door. I stayed in bed. They came and went, and came again. After so many interruptions I was fully awake, but I had decided to have a lie-in and I refused to move.

At 7.50 there was more knocking. I had begun to despair of having a quiet morning so I decided to open the door. It was some students.

'Can we come in?' they said when they had already walked through the door. They wanted to carry on a conversation we had begun at English Corner about Karl Marx. I wanted them to leave as soon as possible.

'Do all English people look like you?' one of the students

asked, not believing that a country might not be full of Chinese faces.

I showed them a little pad of family photos that I kept for this very purpose. 'Here's one. This is my family. You see, my brother has dark hair, I have blond hair, my mother and sister have light brown hair, and my father has no hair. This is me with my family on Christmas day. This is me with my father on my last night in England. This is me with my mother. My mother was very sad to let me go,' I said, showing them a photo of my mother and me hugging in front of the camera.

It was at this point that one of the students burst into tears. 'You have such a beautiful family,' she struggled out. 'You must miss them very much.'

She continued crying, and I didn't really know how to reassure her – 'Don't worry, I don't really miss my family that much.' Not quite.

I took a stab at explaining how Western families work. 'You see, I love them and they love me. That is why we can leave each other. Because my parents love me, they are happy for me to leave and to make something of myself. If I stayed at home, then I would be unhappy. They want me to experience the world and grow up, because if I grow up they will become proud of me. In China you live with your parents even till old age. If I stayed with my parents until I am very old they would be very embarrassed by me. So we are all happy. But of course, we do miss each other sometimes.'

I wasn't doing very well and I didn't think she really understood me, but her tears faded into sniffles, and she left.

We'd taught many times at Yuncheng Middle School No 2, a local secondary school, and today they decided to thank us by 'banqueting' us.

On our first visit there we met a woman called Zhao. While the younger teachers had barely adequate English, and the English department dean could hardly pronounce, 'Hello', she could speak superb English, with the accent of an educated English lady of forty years ago.

'My father was a civil servant in Beijing, and I joined the

Red Army after my education in Shanghai. After Liberation, in 1953, I came here to help educate the people, and I am still here.'

Partly because of her accent and partly because of her familiarity with Westerners, she was very easy to relax with, and having finished our tour of the school we were pleased to accept an invitation to have a cup of tea at her son's house.

As we were chatting, for only the second time since we had arrived, it began to rain. Real rain, so that puddles filled the streets. The sudden damp freshness that the rain brought, the rich, earthy smells, made me feel suddenly homesick, chatting away, drinking tea as the rain dripped down the window. On an afternoon like this in England I would have curled up with a duvet and a pot of tea and watched a black-and-white matinée on BBC2. Instead outside the door lay deepest China, eight thousand miles away from home.

When we later mentioned to Mr Cao that we had met a retired teacher from the middle school, he told us a little more about her.

'Mrs Zhao. Yes, you know her grandfather was a very important man. He was a civil servant. A vice premier during the Qing Dynasty.'

'Was he a good man?'

Cao laughed. 'I don't think so.'

He didn't tell me, but from someone else I learned that it was this Mrs Zhao's grandfather who signed away Hong Kong to the British. The prototype of the kind of official blamed for bringing disgrace and dishonour to China.

Our two schools were very close and through our visits there we met Mrs Zhao's son, Song Wan, a teacher in the same school.

Today, as we arrived at the school gates Song Wan was there, waiting for us with his seven-year-old daughter, a thin, pretty girl with red ribbons tied in her glossy black hair – a very happy child, full of energy.

'She looks very lovely,' I said.

'She is not a good daughter,' he said with an exasperated

sigh. 'She is not clever, she doesn't do well at school. I think she has no staying power.'

We were taken to Beijing HuoGuoCheng – 'Beijing Hot Pot City' – for our banquet. The first course was a selection of delicious dishes – a meal in itself: roasted cashew nuts, sugar-fried walnuts, rabbit stomach, squid, green beans, boiled peanuts, sliced beef and lotus root with vinegar and spicy oil. It was a first course of ridiculous proportions: boiled chicken, seafood, fried white fungus – I was full by the time the hot pots arrived – plates of paper-thin slices of mutton, rabbit, chicken and fish, piled up in absurd portions. I dipped these in my pot of bubbling stock and munched away. Everyone else was drinking and chatting in Chinese as Mario and I sat together. When I was finished and beyond full, then came the *jiaozi*, and *mantou* (steamed bread), and *baozi* (steamed dumplings). I could hardly contemplate eating more, but somehow did.

After we'd finished, doggy bags were filled and Song Wan apologized for taking the left-overs home. 'It is a pity to waste it. I just want to let my daughter taste some, and my wife, you see,' he said. It was as if he thought we were too grand to witness such behaviour, though it was quite the contrary. I thought the amounts of food embarrassing and was glad to see it not being thrown away. I told him so, but he thanked me as if I, too, was just trying to be polite.

As the hot, dry summer went on, our water supply got saltier and saltier. Our winter supply was drawn from the county of XiaXian where they had warm fresh springs, but in the summer so much water was used for irrigation that the supply had to be drawn from the local underground reservoirs, which formed the same reserves as the Salt Lake.

Today the taps were producing a strongly-salted dark brown liquid, not so bad as long as you didn't look in the cup before you drank, and ignored the taste.

Even when the water supply was as rank as this it was better than nothing, for nothing was what we got most of the day as the water pressure dropped in the block, leaving the top floors high and dry. The water subsided to a drip, the taps croaked hoarsely and we could hear the water gurgle as it drained down the system far below.

To ensure that we had enough water each day, we took to using the red plastic bath that Mr Cao brought us as a mini-reservoir. As the water settled in this large tub we could see exactly what we were drinking: a layer of sludge covered the sides and bottom, and little things swam inside with jerky movements. But what can you do when you have no choice? The Chinese are very strict about boiling all water, and after looking into the bathtub – so was I. It wasn't pleasant, but after boiling then at least it was drinkable, and that was better than a lot of the world's population got.

Dean Wu finally formalized an invitation to his house for a banquet. It was not, of course, his first – he generously distributed those during our time here – mostly at school banquets when his superiors were present; strange fantasies where we discussed menus and he promised that he would get his wife to cook our favourite dishes. This, and other things, have taught us a lesson about the Chinese – they don't have the Westerner's zeal for truth, as they believe in harmony.

We were collected from our flat by Dean Wu's granddaughter, LiLi, a tall, spirited eight-year-old girl, wildly active, who had been one of the first people in the community to make us feel welcome. When other people stood back to stare at us as we passed by or shooed their children away from us, LiLi would come running up to give us a sweet, walk along holding our hands, or more often show us something she had caught – a bug-eyed cicada or huge hairy moth – before running off again.

At the sports field once, as we were warming up before basketball, she came over with some friends to play on the bars and talk to us as we stretched. When one of the little girls called us 'LaoWai' LiLi told her off, and taught her to call us 'WaiGuo Shushu' – 'Foreign Uncles.' Her mother – Dean Wu's daughter – was pleasant but didn't seem particularly modern, so I think she must have got this unusual sympathy with our situation from things Dean Wu had told her about his time abroad in Britain, Tanzania and Australia.

Dean Wu and LiLi seemed particularly close. We would often see them out together, especially on hot summer nights, gathering locusts in jamjars together to feed to their cat. Dean Wu, in a white vest and tracksuit bottoms, jumping about after the frightened hoppers with as much pleasure as his granddaughter. 'For the cat,' he would say, holding up a jamjar of long-legged creepy-crawlies that were struggling against the glass. So many Chinese like to exude an air of studied calm that it was delightful to catch him like this. He would look a little sheepish and not say much, but get back to chasing bugs as quickly as possible.

Dean Wu welcomed us in and sat us down at a table laid for five. His son – a large, unpromising youth of eighteen – was supposed to join us, but was late. So the four of us sat there – Mario, Dean Wu, LiLi and myself – and it was LiLi who started us off on the drinking. Dean Wu filled her tumbler to the brim with weak sweet Chinese red wine and she *ganbei*-ed it down in one gulp – and held it out to be refilled.

'Yes, yes – she can drink more than I can – surely!' he protested. Everyone knew that Dean Wu could drink more than anyone else in the college, despite his size. 'But her mother does not approve – she doesn't like her daughter to drink,' he continued, refilling her cup. 'Nor does her grandmother,' he added, with a mischievous look towards the kitchen.

After we had watched the eight-year-old girl finish six small glasses of red wine, Dean Wu got out a half-litre bottle of FenJiu. 'We must finish the first bottle before the *jiaozi* arrive – yes – surely!' he said, despite our protests.

The starters were delicious – pickled garlic, lotus root, shredded potatoes fried with chilli, prawn crackers, fried spinach leaves and cold beef sprinkled with chilli oil, coriander and spring onions.

The *jiaozi* arrived before we'd finished the wine – so Dean Wu speeded up the rounds of toasts – and soon we all joined in, proposing toasts which got increasingly random as the alcohol inhibited our brains.

Mario had told Dean Wu that he was a vegetarian – and he had promised to get his wife to make some delicious vegetarian *jiaozi* – but it became quickly very apparent that he had forgotten this minor detail. When he went out to get another bottle of FenJiu, Mario tipped his *jiaozi* onto my plate. 'I'm sorry, Jus,' he said, 'You'll have to eat these – I really can't.'

So it began.

Equipped with a bowl of *jiaozi* in each hand, and with extra supplies brought through on plates, there was a constant stream of slippery white dumplings going down my gullet. I picked at my bowl while trying to empty Mario's – and then got exhorted to eat more as my bowl was still full. Mrs Wu kept coming in and replacing the cooling *jiaozi* with steaming piles of fresh hot ones. She pleasantly, but firmly, instructed us to eat, leaving us in no doubt that we would have to finish *all* her *jiaozi*, or risk humiliating the entire family and their ancestors. Seeing that Mario wasn't eating much, they mistook this for misplaced politeness and began piling extra *jiaozi* up on his plate. I was doing my best to eat away the mountains as they arrived – a hopeless task. My surreptitious pilfering now became open gluttony, and I seemed to have at least three *jiaozi* in my mouth at any one time.

Eventually the flow slowed and I began to sense that the torrent was over. I thought I had managed to vacuum the table clear of them, when one last plate was brought in – just to fill us up.

Mario helped himself to a few, one of which he nibbled reluctantly. In my effort to save him from the horror of eating a fellow animal, I had nearly lost my own life due to over-consumption.

What Dean Wu made of it all I don't know – though I'm sure he couldn't have helped but notice.

Satisfied at last that we were both satisfied, Dean Wu had the bright idea of finishing up with melon and went off to cut one of his prize-winning watermelons into segments. If he supposed from the previous evidence that I was an insatiable guest and Mario a fussy eater, now he must have been extremely confused. I could barely contemplate the thought of putting another morsel inside my body and looked with horror at the size of my slice, while Mario slathered hungrily at slice after slice, trying desperately to fill up his stomach, which was sloshing emptily with FenJiu.

After a cup of tea we were finally released from their hospitality and at home I collapsed in physical pain. Mario, who had barely eaten a thing, was so pissed he found walking difficult. We both disappeared into our bedrooms – for very different reasons – and sweated the afternoon away.

Three hours later I felt well enough to walk and went to the toilet to rid myself of a little excess weight. I felt like a super-tanker jettisoning a few barrels of oil. Looking at my stomach I was surprised not to see stretch marks. Mario was in the lounge reading, in his dressing gown, sitting with his legs drawn up to his chest, looking very pale. He was listening to a Julio Iglesias tape a student had given him and looked as bad as I felt.

DaiYu took us to the zoo a few days ago. Set in a drab brown park, it was quite as bad as I had expected. Monkeys looked up from the bottom of their large concrete basin speckled with nut shells and monkey droppings; a bull meandered about its bare enclosure and we realized why it was in the zoo – because it had three hind legs, the mutated third leg dangling between the other two. There were two peacocks in a tiny cage; two Tibetan eagles the size of small children sitting upon their iron bar, regarding us from their perch with emphatic eyes as if we were the next meal; two wolves lay in a concrete enclosure, quite bored with life, looking forward to the time when it would no longer bother them. Two brown bears sprawled over the lip of a concrete bath and ignored us.

The last cage held two lionesses. 'Look, tigers,' said DaiYu. I explained the difference between lions and tigers as a lady peered over DaiYu's shoulder to gape at me. Me stealing the limelight from the animals.

I felt quite at sympathy with them. At least I was spared all the whistling, clicking, poked fingers and lobbed stones thrown to make them move.

A pair of chickens, the lucky ones in the animal world, marched cautiously round, eating the sunflower seeds that had been thrown to the lionesses. At the sight of food – the chicken that is, not the sunflower seeds – one of the lionesses perked up and gathered to spring, which sent the chickens off squawking with exaggerated consternation. I had a mesmerized crowd and suggested to DaiYu that she go round and sell them tickets. Eventually they got bored and left.

Animals in China definitely do not share the cosseted lifestyle of their Western cousins. Far from being put on a pedestal, they're more likely to end up on a plate. People here take an entirely practical view of their four-footed friends – they are either for work or food.

Today DaiYu came round after English Corner to help translate and explain a Chinese menu that we had borrowed from a restaurant. She was quite depressed and still receiving hassles for coming to see us. Depression was quite a new emotion for her, and in a certain way she explored its possibilities. She did have a lot to contend with.

'You know the time we went to the ice-cream bar?'

I did. We had discussed whether China was still communist or not as a traditional Chinese band in costumes and playing drums, cymbals and horns marched past, advertising Beijing beer. We had also talked about the future of China. I had suggested that the richer south and east might break away from the poorer hinterland. 'But we do not read this in our newspapers,' DaiYu had said by way of argument. 'The government gives them special privileges so that when they have developed, they can help us. They are also Han people. They have been educated so that they must help to build the country.'

I had felt a bit guilty for being so cynical. 'Maybe the people in the south of China think that they have worked for their money and that you are poor because you are lazy. Maybe they won't give you any money at all.'

DaiYu continued, 'Well, that time one of my teachers saw us and followed us after we had left. She knew everything we had done and where we had been. She was very angry with me, and went crazy. Oh, *tianla*!'

I remembered that after eating ice-cream we had gone looking for the material to have a padded-cotton winter coat made. However, it was little consolation that we had unwittingly led this busybody a long, tiring chase. I was furious. Such bigotry, suspicion and small-mindedness couldn't really exist. I tried to think what kind of woman could have spent her Saturday afternoon trailing us, expecting us to do – I don't know what?! It was an invasion of my right to privacy.

We have many phrases starting 'My right to ...' in the West, rights to privacy, religion, freedom of speech. But the Chinese have a very different view. Life does not bestow such God-given rights. As people entrust their fate to others, they do not focus on the individual as we do.

Another thing depressing DaiYu was that her eldest brother was getting divorced. He and his wife had not got on for four years, and now he had decided to finish the marriage.

'She will not agree unless he pays her 10,000 *yuan* and then 150 *yuan* a month. The court tried to dissuade them from divorcing; many friends and relatives have criticized them. The court told them to stay together for the child, as this is the best thing. But my brother was determined.'

A lot of effort is given over to persuading Chinese people to stay together 'for the good of the child'. This usually involves family pressure, work-unit representatives, and also the judge trying to persuade the couple to stay together. It is actually the judge's job to harangue the plaintiffs on their lack of filial duty, social responsibility or respect for the social institution of marriage.

'But ten thousand is an astronomical sum, considering that his wage can't be more than 400 *yuan* a month,' I said.

Where there is a child then it is usual for him or her to remain with the father's family. This sounds strange to those in the West, where the accepted view is that the mother is the best person to look after a child. But in China family rights supersede those of individuals. Just as a British marriage ceremony is all about God uniting two people, in China it is all about the woman leaving her family and joining her husband's clan. So it follows that any child born belongs to the father's family – even if the mother should then decide to leave.

'Yes, but she must give up the child, that is usual in China. Also, it turned out that she had been having an affair with an old boyfriend.'

So, by this roundabout route we came onto the topic of sex. Young Chinese people have little or no access to sex information. A friend told us that she was entirely ignorant of methods of birth control, until in hospital when she was recovering after the birth of her first child and a family planning nurse had come around and discussed the options available to her now that she had had her one child.

'Don't you talk about sex with your friends?' I asked DaiYu.

'No. None of my friends talk about sex, not even those who have got married. You know, I think they get married out of boredom. They get married straight after school, even though they are below the legal limit.'

'Your mother is a pharmacist, doesn't she talk to you about these things?'

DaiYu laughed with horror at this idea. 'Only the art students talk about sex. They talk, but they don't really know anything.'

'There are other things you can do with someone you love, that don't risk pregnancy,' I said. DaiYu sat down and looked attentive, like a front-row student. 'Yes,' she said knowledgeably, nodding. It was painfully obvious that she didn't have a clue what I was talking about.

'There are many things you can do together,' I started again.

This was not going to be easy.

The conversation that followed showed us that DaiYu viewed sex as a gift that a woman gives a man, not something that is shared.

My students worked especially hard this morning. I don't know what it was, maybe the weather – bright and sunny – or maybe it was the Friday feeling. Either way, they raced through their work and we were left with twenty minutes to spare.

'What shall we do now? What would you like to do?'

'Let's have an English Corner. Sit down and we can have a conversation.'

'Yes, let's have a chat.'

We did, but this time the usual roles were reversed. Normally, I talked and they listened, but now they interrogated me. It turned out to be a similar conversation to the one I'd had before about jobs in Britain. How had I found my job in China? How do students find jobs in England? Is it easy? Would the government assign me a job when I returned to England? That year was one month away from graduating, so it was a subject that was close to their hearts. When they graduated, most would be assigned jobs in schools for the rest of their lives. It was an apprehensive time as they waited to discover which education authority they would be sent to.

'Teaching is not a good job,' a student called Jia Yuan said. 'There is too much work and the pay is not very good. We don't want to be teachers, but there is no demand for translators or tour guides in Yuncheng. The only thing we can do is teach English.'

'We would like to do other jobs. In China if you work in the post office, railway, or in a bank, then that is a good job – there is little work to do, but still the pay is much better than teachers' pay. Getting a good job in China is very difficult. The college does not give us permission to go and look for jobs, so we must do it secretly. Advertised jobs are always very bad, they only advertise because people don't want to do them. Jobs advertised in newspapers and by the railway station are only for the peasants who come in from the countryside to get jobs. Getting a good job is by listening to word of mouth, if you know someone, they might tip you off. You see, getting the jobs depends on your *guanxi*.

'I do not know what I will do. My parents are looking for a job for me. If your parents have good *guanxi* with a leader, then they will send that person presents to get their child a job. But your parents must know the leaders of the work unit. Because of this, if your parents are peasants or workers it is impossible to get a good job.

'If I do find a good job then I must pay back the cost of my education to the education authority. It is very expensive. Maybe 5000 *yuan*, that's three or four years' wages, so it is very difficult.'

However, not long ago my students had come back from their six weeks' teaching practice, glowing with pleasure and satisfaction. 'Teaching is the greatest profession under the sun,' one told me. I don't think many believed it, but they had been taught to be patriotic and positive, and when they couldn't think of anything good to say it was easier to revert to slogans. But for a lot of the students the experience of being on the other side of the classroom *was* very special for them, a rite of passage. Having received the trust of their students, they talked about the pride of standing at the front of a class, the pupils' faces looking up full of learning, about marking homework, giving the students knowledge, tearful goodbyes with students when they had to leave. They spoke of the 'glorious profession of teaching' and how proud they were to be able to go back to the countryside to help the building of their Motherland. However, a student called Ji XiaoBin confided to me, 'It is all empty words. Of course we say teaching is a very good job. As most of my classmates have no choice but to become teachers, then we say what a good job teaching is. Otherwise they are very rude. Truthfully, teaching is a very dull job. Even waitresses and factory workers are better paid than teachers.' She had just come back from a secret job-hunting trip to Shanxi's capital city, having told the college that she was going to see an aunt. Unlike most of her classmates, Ji XiaoBin did have *guanxi*, an uncle in an engineering firm. Maybe he would get her a job.

The distress of my students was understandable: in China there is a growing gulf between town and country. The cities – especially in the south and east – are developing quickly, their populations becoming more affluent and sophisticated, while the countryside has fallen further and further behind. Agricultural liberalizations helped the peasants at first, and some became quite rich, but as ever the cities, with their swirling millions of consumers and businesses, have sucked all the wealth and money of China to themselves. So, being sent back to work in the countryside was like being sent into internal exile: exile from any chance of ever meeting another foreigner to use the skills they had studied; exile from a better standard of living, and from the exciting new changes in China. They saw their hopes of cashing in on China's modernization fading before their careers had even started. Deng XiaoPing told the people, 'To be rich is glorious,' but in modern-day China a teacher's job is anything but glorious.

Chen Yang, a young student only nineteen years old, told me about her teaching practice in one of the countryside schools. 'The students in the country are very simple and honest. They are also more diligent than students in the cities. In big cities, the children see that the people with money are not those with education. They are the businessmen. People with education end up poor, like teachers. So they think education is a waste of their time.

'All the students live at the school in large dormitories. After 9.20 PM there are no lights, so some of the students study by candlelight until 11 or 12 o'clock. The teachers were very kind to me but were very strict with the students. They have classes of about fifty students and their teaching method is very bad. I don't think they teach very well. Their pronunciation is especially very bad. If you put away the text book, then you would not know what they are saying.

'Where I was, in HeJin Province, it is very bad because everyone smokes opium. Yes, everyone does. It was on CCTV News, seventy per cent of the farmers smoke it. Even the policemen use it. I have a friend whose father uses it, he buys it for 50 *yuan* each *jin* (half kilo). There is lots of coal there, so although everyone is very dirty, they are also very rich. I didn't try it, but the teachers at my school offered it to me. They smoked it in the staffroom. It was very interesting.'

It was. I was astonished.

'Where does it come from?'

'From the south – Yunnan – The Golden Triangle.'

Dean Wu told us today that there would be a meeting to celebrate Teachers' Day. 'Some presents will be given,' he said confidently, 'and Mr Zhang has bought some presents for you.'

Having a special day for teachers is a good idea, I think, but in China it has fizzled out into an exercise where the leaders patronize the teachers, exhorting them up and onwards to greater efforts of self-sacrifice for their Motherland.

'Remember the youth are the future!' they say, then announce their half-blown plans that are supposed to rally a disappointed work force into action for the forthcoming year. But teachers in places like Yuncheng do not need more empty words, what they really need is a pay-rise and better work conditions.

There was a larger crowd of academic staff outside the hall than in it when we arrived. We had estimated that it would take one-and-a-half hours maximum for the speeches and prize-giving and decided that we should go in and get it over with.

The lecture hall, which sloped steeply down from the entrance high up at the back, was half-full of people, resigned to settling down to listen to a long session of platitudes. We looked for teachers we knew, but Mr Zhang spotted us, took the microphone and publicly invited us to the front row, where a special section had been reserved for 'foreign teachers'. We sat uncomfortably at the front – exhibits A and B. We were far too privileged to enjoy obscurity. The college was investing a lot of money in having us there, providing us with a furnished flat, salary and WaiBan, and they probably felt entitled to display us for our maximum publicity value.

The college bigwigs came out and sat in a row behind some desks on the stage. There was no applause. From right to left there were the two college vice-presidents, who nodded off early and slept through the whole proceedings; the retired Party secretary – who looked a mean, hard man, a true old guard with a wiry body and a neck so thin that the tendons stood out on it – then the present Party secretary, a pleasant plump man we had often met at banquets and with whom we got along quite well; the president, in a grey Mao suit, a man who couldn't smile if he wanted to (I know, because he once did try). He was one of the old-time communists, a peasant who seemed to like no-one and lived away from the college in an expensive private house in town from which he was chauffeur delivered daily; the vice-Party secretary, a young disgruntled looking man: then two more vice-presidents, one of whom was an old man with heavy jowls which gave his mouth a rather sad look, but with sparkling, bright eyes. The hierarchical complexities of Party secretaries and presidents was beyond me – presidents and vice-presidents could be Party members – but not necessarily. The two structures seemed to coexist, with presidents, deans etc. responsible for day-to-day affairs, and Party secretaries responsible for implementing and educating people about the new Party policies. During the Cultural Revolution, Party secretaries had been more important then their non-Party counterparts, but with the relative de-politicization of China, then presidents, deans etc. became more powerful.

The Party secretary began speaking, and forty minutes later he had finished, thanking the teachers and ending up with a bit about the Party's new anti-corruption drive.

Next came the president, who had sat entirely expressionless so far, an immovable bust in his suit with his top button undone. I gave him forty minutes maximum. He started by reading a pamphlet of which everyone present had a copy already and were using as fans in the heat. Two pages from the end we were doing quite well time-wise, but then he broke off and started ad-libbing. He got quite passionate (for him) saying that everyone must devote themselves to learning a foreign language, and promised all who passed the relevant exams a place abroad.

I began to see why we had been invited and displayed so prominently at the front. You want to learn a language – here are two foreign teachers.

As a British person it is my duty to sit alert and attentive in public, to keep up standards, no matter how bored I am. It's something we have all been trained to do since childhood. The Chinese have no such cultural norms. Behind me the babble of noise increased as people chatted to their neighbours and fanned themselves noisily.

The president roused himself in response to this behaviour –

and stopped in mid flow to tell them to shut up. They paused for breath then continued chatting as he continued talking. One hour later he had at last finished his ad-libbing and returned to the pamphlet. Each grunting sentence was finished off with an extra grunt to increase the impact.

It was at this point that I lost my patience. I could sit politely no longer. Time to show my frustration. I whispered to Mario, and then turned around.

I obviously had a lot to learn about audience patience. The Chinese members of the audience had lost it long ago, before they'd even entered the auditorium probably, and now two thirds of them lay asleep, open-mouthed and snoring gently, while the few still conscious rubbed eyes that were destined to fall shut very soon.

'Amazing!' I thought, surprised and exhilarated by such rudeness.

Two hours after starting, the president finished with an extra grunt of satisfaction, but nobody moved.

A teacher from the chemistry department, probably the only person except Mario and myself still awake, stood up and gave a short speech. He ended by shouting patriotically, 'It doesn't matter if teachers are paid badly because money shouldn't concern teachers.'

No applause, and we guessed that there was no pay-rise pending.

Then a student gave a speech. One of my students in fact, a lively alert girl who pronounced every syllable as perfectly as possible, concentrating hard on her lips and mouth shape. She wanted to join the Party, a privilege that means you're on the gravy train for life. Her speech probably got her half-way in: she thanked the teachers – our today was their tomorrow. Teachers must be assiduous as gardeners to ensure a healthy crop for the next generation. The generation that would lead the Motherland into the next century.

After her speech came the awards for the 'model teachers'. Then our awards that Dean Wu had promised us. Two photo frames, with pictures of Western women inside, mine blonde,

Mario's dark-haired. We were photographed by the press and then the meeting ended.

The insensitivity of dragging along two foreigners who can't understand a word of what's going on and parading them about, displaying us like a couple of carnival freaks for an entire afternoon, made me livid. If the present had been half-way decent then I might have forgiven them – but the two pictures were so naff as to be the crowning insult.

I felt sick at heart.

CHAPTER NINE

QiuTian: Autumn

Summer had been withdrawing imperceptibly for weeks. If I thought of the clothes I'd been wearing two weeks before, shorts and a T-shirt, then the change was obvious, as I sat in jeans and shirt clutching a cup of tea. People sat in their houses, reading or watching television, with a nagging feeling in their minds. Something wasn't quite right. Then it came back to them, of course ... After five months of blisteringly hot days, when sweat ran freely and sleep was begrudging because of the mosquitoes and the loud drone of the fan, they had forgotten what it felt like to be cold.

For the next couple of days their minds were alert, looking for signs that summer was over. Yes, the sun was definitely setting earlier, that was another fallen leaf, and the lady next door was already making bricks from coal dust for her winter's store. But what confirmed it for everyone was unexpectedly feeling cold.

I had been sitting reading as the afternoon shadows lengthened. It occurred to me, quite suddenly, that my feet were not warm. A pair of woolly socks stopped the creeping chill, but something had changed. We had taken for granted the luxury of endless hot days. People planned their lives, confident in the knowledge that perfect weather was assured for everything, but now the chain of hot weather was over.

Within no time at all we forgot the summer and adapted to autumn. The memory of long afternoons stretching into evenings became so distant that the idea of needing a fan to get to sleep was laughable. And so we were borne along with the gathering momentum towards winter.

For those who were unwilling to recognize the warning signs, there was the Mid-autumn Festival. One of my pupils, Zhu Gui, explained, 'In the Mid-autumn Festival there is the best full moon of the year, bigger and brighter than in any other month, and the moonlight is the most beautiful. After sunset everyone goes out to look at the moon shining overhead. The air smells of incense, and carried on the breeze is the sound of chattering and laughter.

'In China the full moon is the symbol of reunion. As the moon is full, so the family must also be gathered together around the table. If the circle is not complete, then it will mean bad luck in the next year. Then we eat lotus root and peanuts, and round pies filled with vegetables and meat. At the end we have a large moon cake filled with sugar and walnut paste. It is cut into slices equal to the number of people in the family, with one extra slice for the ancestors. It is always delicious.

'When I was young, my grandmother would tell more enchanting stories about the immortals who lived in the Moon Palace. Then our father would lift us onto his shoulders so that we could see the ripe moon, then at last we would be put to bed.'

After telling us about the festival, Zhu Gui gave us a bag of mooncakes, and then left.

Thousands of years ago, their tribal ancestors would have celebrated the harvest on a moonlit night. By the time of the Song Dynasty, in the tenth to thirteenth centuries, it had become a people's festival. Tables of people in the streets were served from public wine shops, and everyone ate seasonal fruits, under decorated lanterns. Above them rose the pale full moon.

At the turn of the century on festival night, the Empress Dowager would distribute the most delicious foods to her palace servants. Then she would paddle out onto Kunming Lake. Water-lily lanterns floated on the water, delicacies were served on board, and the surface of the lake was iridescent as the fireworks burst overhead.

It was easy to fall for the romantic image of the Mid-autumn

Festival. The family meal, the scent of acacia blossom on the cool air, stirred by distant flute music.

Wang QiaoQiao, a student from a peasant family in JiShan county, had given me a more realistic idea of what the Mid-autumn Festival means to the majority of Chinese people. When she answered my question, 'What will you do over the holiday?' I felt that it had been a silly thing to ask.

'We have a brief celebration at breakfast, eating moon cakes, then we start the usual day's labour in the fields. The ground has to be ploughed, and the spring wheat sown, and the cotton picked. I don't like picking the cotton; we go around with baskets on our backs, and stoop and pick all day. That is very tiring.'

Of course, for most of the students, holiday just meant work of a different sort.

We were up early on the morning of the Mid-autumn Festival, early enough to see the sun rise over the smoke stacks. We grabbed our bags and started walking down Hedong Donglu to the long-distance bus station. All the students who had not left the previous afternoon after lessons were now on the move, carrying clothes and holiday homework. We joined the trail and walked. An hour later we were on the bus, which was full of migrant workers heading home for the holiday. As the town was coming to life, and we were falling back to sleep, the bus set off.

We rumbled slowly through country villages where strings of yellow corncobs and red chillies were hung to dry from the eaves of houses; piles of firewood were stacked against the walls and old ladies with bound feet sat washing vegetables in doorways.

Between the villages there was the occasional factory – a cluster of chimneys under a plume of dark smoke – but other than that, there were only fields being cleared for spring wheat. Ditches were filled with the husks and stalks of old sweetcorn now ready for the bonfire. Oxen and mules dragged the plough, goaded on by shouts and whistles. A few fields were walled off, the walls of rammed earth protecting the orchards from theft.

The bus stopped at one of the villages, and was loaded up with live chickens. Tied in bundles of eight by their legs they were unceremoniously thrown up on the roof, then laid across the top of the bus and tied down, a quivering carpet of feathers and blinking eyes, squawking timorously. Then we were on the move again, the bus's slipstream a swirl of feathers.

We crossed the Yellow River by ferry. Inert lorries piled high with Shanxi coal stood waiting for space. There was another coach on the crossing, an air-conditioned affair that only tourists or China's new rich could afford to travel in. This one was full of Chinese people. Children wearing baseball caps and eating moon cakes pressed their faces against the glass, while their parents smiled politely and ignored them. I went outside to have a look at the chickens. They had had the down on their stomachs and chests plucked and the skin there was bright pink. Some looked dead as their long necks hung limply down the side of the bus. Others watched with their reptilian eyes, blinking occasionally.

The Yellow River is always an enormous mud flow, and today it was bursting with summer rains. The strong current made the ferry overshoot the landing platform. The other coach got off all right, but ours got stuck in the mud of the river bank. Everyone disembarked, and we dug and scratched and pushed for an hour; eventually the bus surged forward, the engine screaming in defiance, and we continued on to Luoyang.

We stopped only to unload the chickens. Whilst we were moving they had been silent with fear. As they were lowered to the street, however, they scratched and clawed down the side of the bus, struggling against the string that held them before they dropped down in a mess of excrement and feathers.

By the evening we had safely arrived at Luoyang Teachers' College, and were drinking beers from the fridge in two VSOs' – Heather's and Rebecca's – flat. The room full of people, Chinese and foreign, was so animated that everyone forgot to go outside to look at the moon. Dancing, chatting, drinking and singing – us taking the rare opportunity to be unashamedly Western, while the Chinese guests enjoyed a night abroad, an evening's holiday in an English pub.

We swapped stories and caught up with news of friends spread throughout China. An old Scottish teacher, Liz, had a funny tale about her new bathroom, where the college had replaced her squat toilet with a Western one as a kind gesture. Rather ignorant of the way Westerners relieve themselves, the height of the toilet had confused them somewhat. To solve the problem they had buried the toilet one foot into the floor of the bathroom, so now the seat sat a hand's breadth above the tiles. A reasonable height in their eyes for people to perform their bodily functions. James chipped in with a tale of how he once found a Chinese guest actually squatting with his feet on top of the seat.

If anyone had gone out they would have stepped into an evening choked with pollution: the fumes of cars and lorries clogged the air; in the nearby fields peasants were gathering their rubbish – torn sacks too old to be mended, fallen leaves and the cuttings of trees, dried stalks of maize – and were burning the lot. The thick tendrils of smoke brought tears to the eyes, but up through the mustard fog you could still see the moon. The yellow hue of the pollution and its natural black spots gave it a slightly rotten look, like a windfall apple in an orchard.

Whenever we met Song Jiang, our entrepreneurial friend, he seemed to be undertaking new ventures. Walking home from town today, he insisted that we join him at his house for corn-on-the-cob.

'My wife has just bought a load of sweet-corn for a good price. So we have plenty to spare.'

'Tell me,' he said, when we sat down in his living room. 'Have you heard of this book? It's called *Deserted Capital*. It's a new release and has caused quite a sensation. It's written by an author from Xian and it's supposedly about Xian, and the fact that it is no longer the capital of the country. But really, it is a criticism against the Chinese arrogance about their past greatnesses. It says we must modernize our attitudes and ways. The authorities wanted to censor it, but instead of removing the censored material the author has just left large parts of his book blank.'

'Why did they want to censor it?'

'The story is centred on an artist in Xian who is having an affair with three women at the same time. He cannot decide which one he needs. The censored bits are sexually graphic. I thought I would translate this book into English. Would you like to help me? We will have to act quickly or someone in Hong Kong or Taiwan will have done it before us.'

Unfortunately, we could not contact the author in time, and this idea was shelved.

Next time we called around, Song Jiang was very excited to see us. He opened his door in anticipation and put out his hand, but instead of shaking ours he pulled us in.

'Hi, Mario! Hi, Justin! Good to see you! I am all alone here because my wife is at work and my son is at school. Would you like coffee?' he asked as he went into the kitchen.

The table was laid out with sweets, tangerines, peanuts and cakes. Song Jiang poured us coffee and sat down. It suddenly occurred to me what I had been missing for the last while, a friendly person with whom I could be at ease. With whom I could sit back as the jewels of information spilled out.

'So how are your shares doing, Song Jiang?'

'Very well, they are now trading at over seven *yuan* each. Excuse me, I've got a cold and am taking an infusion of opium, it's very soothing for my chest.'

'Opium?'

'Yeah – from the flowers – here, what do you call these flowers?' he asked, showing us a small bundle of poppy pods wrapped in newspaper.

'Is that legal?' I asked.

Song Jiang laughed. 'No – illegal. My mother grows them. Now my father has died she lives in a retirement home near Ping Yao where nobody takes any notice of her. In her back yard she can grow these poppies. You see, you break a bit off and boil it. There's some more in the kettle if you want some.'

We talked about what he had been doing since we last saw him, but soon he returned to 1989. 'You know, I think we treat our people like slaves. When I was in Canada, I was very proud of my country. I thought things were getting much better. Things like human rights. But when I watched those TV pictures – the bloodshed – and when I came home and listened to some of the teachers who were there, I was disgusted with China.

'After Tiananmen the government cracked down on the colleges and universities. They created lots of new jobs for "Instructional Staff" and changed the coursework that the students studied. The feeling we had in colleges before 1989 has gone. You just don't have it any more.

'You know, these meetings that we have, nobody speaks their minds. They all pretend and everyone knows that nobody believes a word of what is said. All they do is read the newspapers line by line. I don't go, so they fine me. I do not care. They are twisted people. If anyone criticizes the Communist Party then people say, "You are making a stranger of yourself in your own home." ' Song Jiang laughed. 'They like fines. The college have started a new system. I teach reading to class 9212, and Duan Yu teaches reading to 9211. When we hand in our marks for the final examinations, the marks will be compared, and whoever gets the better will be given more money. They will reduce the pay of one teacher, and give it to the other. Nobody knows if it will work. The government tells everyone to use the free market and so they try and apply it to teaching. This is the New China – socialism by capitalism. It is so degrading.'

We sat in silence for a few moments.

'Hey, why don't you both stay for dinner? Stay here, I'll just go and buy some things.'

While Song Jiang was out, his eleven-year-old son, XiaoShan, returned home from school and went straight into his bedroom to do his homework.

Song Jiang returned. 'I don't think XiaoShan's teachers are very good,' he said. 'They work the children too hard. My son must be at school before seven-thirty, but he doesn't get home until six o'clock. Then he has two hours' homework. It's too much, he's only eleven. He's still only in junior school.

'The teachers and students are under a lot of pressure for good results. The teachers need to get high marks, and so they push the students very hard. Each thinks that his subject is the most important, and so they give the students more and more extra work to do. Recently, one of my son's teachers told me that my son must work harder. The teacher said that my son was spoiling his marks spread, he needed to do better. The teacher wants his class average to be over eighty-five per cent. So he asked me to help him make my son work harder. I told my son that I would give him a hundred *yuan* if he improved his marks.'

'That's a lot of money, isn't it?'

'I think he'll spend that in a week. You know, my son likes kebabs and video games. In one evening out, paying for his friends, I think he spends twenty *yuan*.'

The dishes arrived: sliced pork tongue topped with spring onions, a soup of meat chunks, fried eggs, tomato and a salad of celery mixed with mayonnaise.

Problems with the post – and consequently the Chinese attitude to work – seemed to be destined to plague my time in China. Not only did the post office staff take a uniquely bureaucratic delight in hindering my outgoing letters – but now Mario and I were experiencing difficulty in even getting our incoming mail.

At our college – the departments full of students and teachers, the administration offices, the other residents and family members – we all had the one postal address. All our mail is delivered to a college office, who were then responsible for sorting out the day's mail and then delivering it to the departments, offices, or keeping it for residents, like us. The man in charge of this was a certain Mr Wang.

He took the sack of mail and then quickly sorted it out into its relevant groups, with most mail going into pigeon holes in the teaching building. A select few were kept in a desk drawer in the office. Parcels, recorded deliveries, and our mail, were kept locked up in a cupboard for especially safe keeping. This task, and the sorting of newspapers and magazines, constituted

Mr Wang's full-time job. To supplement his wage – and probably fill up his spare time – Mr Wang sold old stamps, cards and envelopes, and all in all he seemed to have quite a relaxed life.

Mr Wang's hobby – like that of so many Chinese people – was stamp collecting. By giving him our English and Spanish stamps (rarer than golddust in places like Yuncheng) we developed good *guanxi* with Mr Wang, who then telephoned to tell us of the arrival of any letter for the foreign guests.

Mr Wang never seemed to me to be the busiest of bees upon God's earth, so it was a surprise for Mario and I to find that he had been relieved of part of his duties, even more surprised when it turned out that his job has now been split into two, to provide a certain 'Comrade Jiao' with a job. Who exactly Comrade Jiao was, or where she had come from, I couldn't tell you. What I do know was that she had enough *guanxi* with the college that they had to give her a job. What they came up with was – wait for it – to put her in charge of the locked mail cupboard. Her full-time job was to look after a locked cupboard which never had more than five items of mail in it.

Comrade Jiao was in her early twenties and was highly uncertain about communicating with us in any way. Even for her to look us in the eye was rare. When she would see us coming, she'd unlock her cupboard and pass us our mail without speaking. That was when she was there, of course – we soon found out that Comrade Jiao didn't have the most rigorous work ethic.

Any fool can see that the job of guarding a locked cupboard lacks career prospects, and so we could hardly blame Comrade Jiao for not spending every minute of her working day at work – but when we were trying to collect our mail it could be highly frustrating.

Mr Wang was still pleased to tell us when we had mail, but he no longer had the key to the cupboard, so he was unable to give it to us.

'Any mail today?'

'Yes – three letters – one for Mario and two for Justin,' he'd say.

'Can we have them?'

'No. That's not possible. Comrade Jiao is not here. She's gone home.'

That time it took us three days to get our letters. Three days of frustration knowing that in that cupboard we had mail from home, but we couldn't get at it.

I complained to Mr Wang, 'Why did the college employ Comrade Jiao? There was no problem with you – you were fine. Can't she give you a copy of the cupboard key?'

He seemed surprised by the logic behind this question, and very suddenly I could sense a gulf beginning to open up between our respective cultures.

'It's not my job any more. It's Comrade Jiao's, but she's not here,' he said, smiling tolerantly at the demanding foreigners, as we passed him another handful of Western stamps.

At four o'clock today we met up, as arranged, with the owners of our local shop, Da Xiong and his wife, Ma Sha, an endearing pair of semi-peasants whose children all worked in the shop with them. Da Xiong was an efficient man who, next to his wife, seemed quiet. She was short, loud, unashamed and always seemed to be eating. When we went around to their shop, which sold everything from clothes, film and lightbulbs to food, beer and children's sweets, she would have her lunch on the counter, a few bowls of soup and noodles which she'd munch using a *mantou* (bun of steamed bread) as a plate.

'*Chi guo le ma?*' Ma Sha would say. 'Have you eaten?' and then offer up whatever she had dangling from the end of her chopsticks. They were very generous, often giving us free bags of whatever was to hand, without asking for anything in return. Uneducated, unsophisticated, they were peasants through and through.

They kept a cat, a ginger Persian, that prowled the shelves and the counter. Pets are rare in China, and although this was a professional rat-catcher, it was nice to play a little with it. The last time I'd gone round she'd watched me wasting my time with the stupid animal and she began to bubble over with amusement.

'What's the cat called?' I'd asked her.

'Cat!' Ma Sha'd said, grinning.

'No. What's its name?' I asked.

'Cat!' Ma Sha shouted, then laughed at the absurdity of my question – naming a cat!

When her laughter had subsided she took me aside and asked me if I liked apples. I said yes, so she told me to come back at four o'clock the next day for apple picking.

So today we were off.

Pushing our bicycles through the piles of litter that marked the end of Hedong Donglu, we followed the mud path that led through the fields to the village about half a mile distant. Like the door into the Secret Garden, crossing the threshold of Yuncheng led us immediately out into another country, which could have been a hundred miles distant or a hundred years gone. No road, no cars, no tractors, no people – just fields of harvested maize on either side.

Da Xiong pointed to the brow of the rise to our right, behind which was the Salt Lake.

'That's my land. I've planted one hundred and sixty apple trees there, but they are still too young to bear fruit. In a few years though . . .'

We cycled on, and soon reached a mud wall of beaten earth, with a large wooden gateway in the middle. Each portal hung crookedly on its hinges, and a large rusty chain secured them. This reminded me of some nineteenth-century barn. Ma Sha shouted through the crack and we waited. Soon the doors were unlocked and dragged open.

The gateway opened into a small yard. A derelict house was used to store the farm implements, and a small tractor in front sat rusting. Next to the tractor was a small brick-lined pit formerly used for collecting rainwater, now dry and smothered with weeds that burst through the mortar. In the mud-walled field were rows and rows of trees, bending under the weight of their apples. There were piles of rotting apples on the ground, thick with wasps that buzzed angrily around. There was a smell of cider, and through the tall grass, which gave the place a neglected feel, a few chickens clucked, pacing underneath an old cart.

'Sweet or sour apples?' we were asked, and then led between the rows to where the sweet ones were.

Ma Sha picked the largest apples she could find and gave us the best two and munched on the third. They were tart and sweet together, crisp, juicy, with bright white flesh inside.

We began to fill our sack, and they theirs. Ma Sha spent more time helping us than picking her own, taking apples she didn't like the look of out of our sack and throwing them away to bounce through the grasses, and then replacing them with bigger and better ones. As is always the case with fruit picking, we ate as much as we picked. Our sack came to sixteen kilograms, and with it secured to the back of my bicycle, we returned to Yuncheng along the dirt track.

They had picked twice as much as us, and Ma Sha, as she munched on a supply of apples hidden in her pockets, laughed and cackled and told us that at that price, we were stupid to have picked so few.

'You're stupid,' she laughed, and handed us each another apple from her pocket – and laughed again.

One day DaiYu mentioned that she had visited the home of an old classmate. 'He was not there, but his mother – an editor – was a very kind woman. If you met her, I think you would like her. I told her all about you and she seemed very interested.'

We said that we should like to meet her and find out. We met up with DaiYu away from the college as she was frightened of what would happen to her if she was seen with us, and then cycled the rest of the way together.

The lady – Xu Ting – even looked like a writer: well-built, but not overly large, wearing over her slightly masculine body, a long, grey woollen suit and a drab knitted jumper. Her face was quite broad with full lips and large white teeth. The parts of it seemed too large when viewed individually, but together they looked somehow right. With her imposing and confident face, she was neither pretty nor ugly, but some third characteristic, something that was quite compelling.

She lived in a single room, which was almost entirely taken up by a double bed, with her husband and two sons. One was an art student at Linfen University, the other was still studying at school. At the time, I presumed that they had another room somewhere for their children, but this need not necessarily have been true. The bed could have fitted four at a squeeze, or the floor space could have fitted two.

A neighbour came over to do the job of entertaining us – leaving Xu Ting free to talk – a pretty girl of nineteen with minimal English and an unnaturally long neck, which kept on drawing my attention. The Chinese believe that a long neck is the sign of long life, and if so, this girl had many more years coming to her. After giving us tea she squatted on the floor and smashed walnuts with a hammer, and then picked through the nuts for us to eat. Straight after she began peeling apples faster than we could eat them. We chatted with Xu Ting as the girl kept up a steady supply of food.

Xu Ting was a writer mainly of stories about women, usually ordinary Chinese women. She also edited a magazine called *Hedong Story Magazine*. Hedong – east of the river – was the literary name for the Yuncheng area, dating back to when the capital of China had been Xian rather than Beijing. She had written a few novels too, which she published herself, paying the publishers and then letting them sell the books.

After about two hours her husband returned home from work. His factory was one of the ones that lined the Salt Lake and made industrial-grade salt. A small man, he appeared quite insignificant next to his wife. A rather plain and vague person, whatever personality he had was simmering well below the surface.

A week later we returned to her room to meet her son, the artist. He was in his last year and hoped to become a professional painter. He showed us a few of his paintings. They were all oils, not the ink-wash of traditional Chinese painting. Popular themes in Chinese art are the peoples of China's minorities – here in the north the nomadic Tibetans and Mongolians – and the son had his fair share of these. But looking through his paintings they were refreshingly different from the standard, moodier, studies in the art of emotion.

We left and she gave us a few back copies of *Hedong Magazine*, which we were very grateful for even though we couldn't understand a word.

Writing was generally looked down upon by the Chinese people I knew. Entertaining common people was seen as a common skill, almost like prostituting your education, and the popular view was that there were so many writers in China, it was very easy to earn a living from it.

Last night at 4.30 AM, there was a crack of thunder. It was so loud that it rocked the building and woke me up with a start. I thought that the long-awaited earthquake had arrived, then the rain started. A long heavy curtain of water, and I could feel the suddenly cool fresh air rush in over me from outside.

Mario and I went out for lunch today, and last night's rain had washed away all the mud that had been used to fill in the potholes, so now the road was a pock-marked strip. Our little restaurant was usually quiet at lunchtime. The female owner always seemed a little worried as if her food was slightly rotten and she hoped we wouldn't notice. It never was though, and her chefs did the most delicious dish of fried aubergines that I know.

She was knitting when we arrived and welcomed us, wringing her hands nervously while her little daughter played with the remains of a kite that was wrapped about her body and which refused to fly.

Her husband and all the kitchen staff came out to say, 'Hello,' and listen to our order. The weather has suddenly turned cold after last night's rain, so our bodies needed a substantial bowl of noodles to keep out the chill.

We had four weeks until the heating came on, on 15 November. Four weeks in which it would get swiftly colder. 15 November is an arbitrary date set by the government for the official beginning of winter. Until then it's forbidden for work-units to put on heating, in order to conserve the country's coal stocks. The coldest spell the previous year, when it had snowed heavily and the Mongolian winds blew so that the daytime maximum had been minus fifteen degrees, came the week before 15 November.

Today there were two other customers at the restaurant, a man and his wife or girlfriend – they were both so young that it could have been either. He was obviously drunk, and almost fell off his chair when we walked in. He was fixated by us, and started trying to get his girlfriend to turn and look at us. She did, and they both collapsed into giggles, and then started whispering 'Hello,' to each other, and laughing all the more.

Eventually I could see him decide to come over and talk to us. It took a while for him to realize what he had decided, then a bit longer to establish control over his legs. Suddenly he lurched over and sat down opposite us. We ignored him, and carried on talking and eating, as he sat swaying gently and getting red in the face.

He reached out to grab Mario's arm. Mario stopped and looked at him, removed his hand and told him, 'You are drunk. Go away.'

He didn't. We finished our meal and he sidled over to watch us pay.

'Ten *yuan*,' the owner told us, looking more worried than ever.

'Ten dollars!' He told her. 'Make them pay dollars. They're rich, they're foreign.'

She gave us an embarrassed and apologetic look as she handed us our change.

CHAPTER TEN

PuJu Opera Night

歌 劇

It was the last night of *Li Xi Yen*, a modern opera about a village and its struggle in the new China. Operas, that most Chinese of art forms, are usually rowdy affairs, lacking the polite silences of their Western counterparts. People offer round cigarettes, chatter and laugh throughout the performances, commenting and elaborating on the action.

We had arrived early, me carrying one of our students, Chao Xia, on the back of my bicycle, to be in time to get a ticket. Luckily, we were ahead of the rush. The queue was only two or three people long, but as we got to the front and pushed up against the little round hole, two people behind us forced their hands in front of ours. At first, this kind of behaviour – English to the heart as I am about queuing – made me very uptight, but it's hard to survive in China, where pushing and queue-jumping are normal, if it always makes your blood boil.

Now, I'd learnt that all this situation needed was a certain degree of physical force: a push and a shove in the right direction and the problem was solved. The hands fell away and they both apologized. You see, only a Chinese person with power would act like I did, and so despite the clothes in which I was muffled they sensed that I was a powerful person who might get them into trouble. We got our tickets and as we left the two pushers-in and the next person in the queue scrambled and mauled for the narrow opening.

'*Ayaa!*' Chao Xia exclaimed. 'One of our tickets is separate from the others. We have been given tickets in two different rows. I think we can change them.'

'Isn't your father a worker here, don't you have any *guanxi?*'

'No. My father works for the company, but not the art group. And I am frightened of seeing my father. He is very strict with me. He will be very angry if he sees me with you. He will say that I should be studying.'

Guanxi or no *guanxi*, she went through the doorway at the rear of the ticket office, a little room where a man and two women were sitting around a coal heater keeping warm and chatting, balancing their cups of tea on the cast-iron stove to keep them hot.

Chao Xia explained our predicament to them while we waited outside.

Despite the dim light and although we were wearing the standard army-surplus greatcoats, our height, build, white skin and long red noses immediately betrayed us as foreigners. The ticket lady took us in at a glance. If she helped us, in return we would be bound to help her in some way. She got up and took Chao Xia off to change our tickets. We returned to the theatre foyer, where a few glass cabinets had been lined up with food displayed inside. It was dim and dirty in the stone-floored hall, and the single working bulb cast a very yellowed light: I felt that I was inside a sepia photo.

Despite the gloom, a crowd had followed us inside, and now, as we looked at the nibbles for sale – prawn crackers in crisp packets, Donald Duck bubble gum, salted peanuts, water-melon seeds – they began to hem us in.

Those closest up to us were the old, rude and near-blind, come to get a clear focus, less than one arm's length away. Further off people were squinting to see us clearly, and others stared vacantly at us, chewing on melon seeds, cracking open the shell, taking the seed, and dribbling the husks off their lower lips with practised movements of their jaw and tongue. Each one like a dull-eyed cow chewing the cud.

Chao Xia returned. 'Very funny,' she told us. 'That lady thought I was your *WaiBan* (foreign affairs officer). She told me that she might come to ask me for a return favour soon. She asked if she could find me at the *WaiShiBan's* Office in the college. I told her that I was only your student. She didn't think that I could help her then.'

The double doors – padded with foam that now showed through the holes in their black plastic covering – opened, and a young audience of youths in baggy suits and open shirt-collars, and girls in black leggings and bright frilly tops that lit up the room like neon, all poured out from a previous performance. A noisy tide of smokers and shouters who stood laughing on the steps outside.

Now it was our turn. The audience for the opera, in Mao suits and traditional side-fastening tunics with cotton clasps, all hobbled in, the women on the stumps of their feet and the men bent well over their crooked walking sticks. Chao Xia found our seats, which was not easy as the numbers of each were written on the back of the chair and we walked down behind our row and then climbed forward into them.

Not being able to read Chinese characters very well, I missed much that was happening in Yuncheng that was clearly written and displayed for everyone else to see. I never knew how popular opera was until I started going in an attempt to find an evening social life, but it seemed a new opera was on every few weeks as touring companies came through. Nor – until I got more into it – did I realize how many different styles of opera there were. The one we know in the West, Peking opera, is quite a new style, certainly younger than our local style that was called *PuJu. PuJu* is a very traditional style. I thought I could just about hear a difference in the sound, but to the average Westerner it's just like Peking opera.

The Chinese have an astounding inability to live up to their reputation of being an organized society. They're not. In fact I think that sometimes they go out of their way to create bureaucratic chaos as it's the only way of employing a billion peoples' time. At the opera, if you make people fight in queues, then number only half the seats (and then on their reverse side), it stops people thinking about more important things. This thought occurred to me as I saw the geriatric audience all around me arguing and fighting over their seats. A major problem was that everyone headed straight away for the best seats regardless of whether they were theirs, taking them in the hope that the ticket owner would not turn up.

'Give me one hundred of the best British queuers and I could sort this country out.' I muttered to myself.

As the arguing and shouting continued, the displaced people moved around looking for seats with their correct number on, and in their turn displaced the people who hadn't got a ticket at all, but who had pushed through in the hope that their rightful owner would not claim them. One of these people was in front of me. I knew this, because he looked nervous as an old man in a blue Mao suit and moth-eaten fur hat came along, bent double and squinting to find his seat number.

'That's my seat,' the old man snapped at the intruder, who tried to look relaxed and confident.

'No, it isn't, it's mine,' he replied, bluffing convincingly.

'That's my seat,' the man repeated, raising his voice and shaking his stick.

'Let me see your ticket!' the younger man said.

The old man refused and started making aggressive swings with his stick that threatened to unbalance him. A crowd gathered to watch, which was nice because for once it wasn't me they were staring at; for once I was part of the audience.

Such fuss permeates every aspect of life: from coming in to people's houses, sitting down, having a cup of tea, leaving, buying a ticket, and finding a seat. Sometimes I think it all part of a sinister plot by Deng and his Long Marchers up in Beijing to keep the people down. Of course it isn't really sinister, just, as the students are fond of telling me 'Our Chinese Way.' I found all the shouting and arguing and hassle left me exhausted, but for all these people the jostling and trying it on was all part of the fun of an evening out, combining the pleasures of rugby, intimidation, debating – and of course opera.

In many ways Chinese and Western societies are at opposite ends of the scale of social organisation. Many of these contrasts can be explained in terms of the difference between a modern society and one that is still rooted in the peasant traditions, like China. Westerners like to talk about feelings and emotions – the Chinese about facts. We say, 'How are you feeling today?' to start a conversation; a Chinese will say, 'How much money do you earn?' Get a Chinese person to introduce his country and he'll say, 'China is the third largest country in the world with 1.2 billion people and a long and glorious history over six thousand years old ...' Western societies are highly individualistic, but also show a degree of conformity that allows us to operate without too much fuss. We couldn't live in a modern society without being highly organised and that's probably why whole industries are devoted to making us feel like we're still individuals. Because we're only cogs in the wheel we devote all our efforts to disguising that fact. Dress, style, tastes, beliefs, how we spend our free time, there are so many ways we express our individuality – and yet, put us together and we co-operate in an almost mechanical way. Far more like a 'faceless mass' than we see ourselves.

In China, everyone professes to be the same and have the same opinions, and even blurs his or her own identity by using phrases like, 'Our Chinese People ...' But this is coupled with a complete dislike of acting together on a larger scale. Compare the organized traffic systems of the Western world to a Yuncheng highstreet, where pedestrians, cyclists, motorbikes, cars and buses combine in a perfect living example of Chaos theory. This certainly not the termite-like uniformity with which we like to characterize the Chinese.

The noise and hubbub diminished slightly as everyone relaxed. The lights went down and the curtains opened – onto a delicately lit stage of loess cliffs and mountains, with a few peasant huts sheltering amidst bamboo groves. In front of this a single man, dressed in a Mao suit sang with all the characteristics of Chinese opera: facial expressions, posturing, and movements, punctuated by the clok! from the orchestra.

Chao Xia lifted her glasses and squinted to read the words that were projected onto a vertical screen at the right-hand side of the stage. She began to translate in a vague sort of way.

'A kind of flower – somebody is coming to visit them.'

'Them,' was the villagers, and the man singing was the village leader, who was joined by a bunch of ever-so-bouncy peasants whose dress was a mix of country and poor-city styles. Two girls stood demurely at the back with long pigtails trailing down their red jumpers and they held up a red banner, which said: MANY HAPPINESS AND JOY AT YOUR ARRIVAL! WELCOME.

The local peasant, with a white cloth around his shaven pate, spade in hand, came on to find out what was happening, and then our star 'somebody' arrived, coming down the earthen path that led from the mountain. 'Somebody' was the new government head of the area. He was welcomed in a quick burst of song, and then a crude palanquin consisting of two bamboo poles supporting a modern red plastic chair was brought in, onto which he was put and carried along like a bride, to the amusement of the audience.

'The village is short of money. They want to build a road to town to get more money – get rich. When the Master of the county comes, the villagers are very happy to welcome him,' Chao Xia said.

After a quick spin around the stage, the Master demanded to be put down, and after a struggle was allowed to stand, and after another struggle regained his luggage (carried, rather unconvincingly, in a sack.) All the officials I had ever seen had lackeys to carry their leather satchels for them.

'He doesn't like to be carried, because he is a good master,' Chao Xia told me as they continued to argue on stage about whether he would walk to the village or not. 'He wants to go through the hardships with the people. So he even carries his own luggage.'

Scene one ended as they marched off the right-hand side of the stage, taking the path to the village.

The curtains opened again and took us inside a cave dwelling, the straight hole in the hillside which is the poorest kind of house. A peasant with padded cotton jacket, calf-length trousers and a blue bandana sang of his hard life: he sang about his lazy wife – still in bed and hidden under a blanket – about how the government gave nothing to the people; how in this poor remote village they were ignored by the government; how no official had come here for years. Taking up his hoe he strode off to work, determined to fight against his poor lot.

As he left, the shape on the bed began to move, and out popped the young wife, unkempt and bleary-eyed.

A chuckle of amusement washed through the audience. 'She is very lazy,' Chao Xia explained.

As the Lazy Wife got up, the Master arrived after his long walk, and he stopped outside her house to share a cigarette with the village leader. The Lazy Wife was about to take her chamber pot to throw it outside, but when she saw the two men on her doorstep, was too embarrassed to go out. She tried to hide, but the village leader saw her and ordered her to come out.

The crowd laughed as she spat on her hands to clean them, and then spat on her comb to smooth her hair into place.

Meanwhile the Master and village leader were inspecting the yard, very disapprovingly, and with a nosiness that offended my notions of privacy. Kicking an old reed basket away and tossing a broken spade into the dirt, they were still inspecting this 'social problem' as the wife came out.

'She has five children, and is pregnant again. She is lazy, dirty, and poor. She takes bad care of her family,' Chao Xia told me.

The Chinese are very hard on the unfortunate. It is unlucky to help them – people are poor because they are lazy. Once I showed a picture of a blind beggar to a student and she said, 'He is a very lazy person. He is playing tricks. He is not blind, he is only fooling. If I saw him I would go up and kick him! Bad man.'

Women are also seen as the centre of the family, so any problems in the family must necessarily stem from the mother. The Lazy Wife was now being criticized: she was making herself poorer with each child and adding to China's population problem. She ought to be ashamed of herself! A bit harsh on the poor woman, I thought, as in reality, it is often the father who is keen to have more children in order to have as many sons as possible to help him in his old age.

The woman's husband returned and invited the two men into his house. He sat them down and went to pour them water from a thermos flask. But with such a lazy wife, what could you expect? There was no boiled water, and no water for boiling in the buckets. He shouted at his wife and sent her off, grumbling, to the well. He cleaned two small cups with his grubby shirt and poured them both a measure of spirits. Then he asked them for some money for himself, not realizing who they were. The Master was very angry and told him, 'You make yourself poor. You are lazy and dirty. All you do is depend on the government.'

The peasant was beside himself with anger, so when his wife returned with water for their tea, he took both buckets and threw them out the doorway.

'Correct your bad thinking. If you want the government to build a road, then you must work harder yourself,' the Master told him.

In reply the peasant, ignorant of the real identity of this man, began to complain about the government. 'I have such a large family, I need more money. If you won't give me more money, then I will die of anger.'

Scene three opened in the yard of a more substantial peasant house. Mud-brick walls, whitewashed and hung with clumps of yellow maize and red chillies. In the yard was a low table, of knee-height, with accompanying stools. There were two figures: an old woman in traditional clothing, walking with the tip-toe steps of once-bound feet, and her husband, an aged and bearded peasant.

'He is the retired Communist Party leader of the village,' Chao Xia told me. 'His wife wants him to change his clothes to receive the Master, but he refuses to. He complains. He isn't satisfied with what the government does. They pay no attention. They let these people be poor. That is why he goes into the shed – he will not come out and meet the Master.'

The old peasant sat in the barn amongst the cows and sacks and straw, repairing a rope. The Master arrived and the old lady welcomed him. She poured him tea, served in bowls, country style, and served him fresh dates. The old man in the barn grumbled to himself, 'People used to come and have their photos taken with me. I was in the Eighth Route Army.' 'He listens to see if the new Master is good or bad.' Chao Xia translated.

'Is he good?' I asked her.

'Of course he is good,' she answered. 'He is very kind. When he talks to the old lady, he doesn't call her "country woman" but uses her name. He is not over-proud with the people.'

Although not entirely convinced, the old man came out of the shed to welcome his guest. He couldn't believe that the Master understood country people as well as he did. Wasn't he a city slicker in his new suit? What did he know?

But our Master had more to him than an ability to be understanding and concerned. He inspected the old couple's apple tree that had never borne fruit, and taught them how to prune it properly so that next year they would have apples. The old man was still not convinced and tried to resign from the Communist Party. He gave his letter of resignation to the Master and then began to sing.

Chao Xia translated: 'He has gone through hardships in following the Communist Party, so he is disappointed. In the period of Chairman Mao, the Party shared the hardships with the people. Now some of the new Party let the people be poor. So he is angry.' Chao Xia stopped, while the old man continued singing.

A sudden burst of fierce applause broke out. 'Why is everyone clapping?'

The Master says that, "The Communist Party is like a fish in water. The Communist Party cannot live without the people." This is why they clap.'

There were more bursts of applause demonstrating the audience's strength of feeling against corruption in the Communist Party.

'He wrote to the government many times, as village leader, to ask for help but they don't give him any. He went to the City to see them but the government leaders were having a very delicious banquet. When they came out, he saw that none of them were peasants.'

The good Master leapt up at the end of the song with a look of outrage and shock, as if he had never heard such things before. But before he could say anything, the old lady started to sing too.

'She says in the old days that the women cared for the wounded soldiers in their homes. Their relations with the Communist Party were very good. She reminds the Master of this time.'

Scene three ended with the Master snatching up a bowl, filling it to the top with strong spirits and gulping it down.

'He is drinking the people's bitterness,' Chao Xia told me.

'Bad Party members are like a sickness in the body of China!' he shouted, before leaping off to face another challenge. The old couple, who had stolen the show really, looked on.

The next challenge our new-style Communist Party official had to face was in scene four.

The curtains opened onto the scene of a village fishing business: a net, a pool and a rock where a young man sat with his head in his hands, watched by the Master. The Master, whose knowledge extended from apple-tree pruning to fish-farming, took a ladle of water up and explained to the boy why his fish were all dying.

'The Master knows much science. He knows many knowledge of apple trees and fish. The young man doesn't have the knowledge how to keep fish, so most of them die. He has lost most of his money. He says that he has asked the village leaders for help, but they will not help him.'

The village leader, the policeman and a city businessman arrived.

'They want to take the fish without paying. They are cruel, they threaten the young man. We have an old Chinese proverb – he is like a man standing between his mother and his wife, or a mouse between two lumps of *dofu* – he doesn't know which way to turn.'

*

Scene five. A few villagers were gathered around a noticeboard with a long list of names on it. Bouncy young peasants were laughing and joking. An old peasant with a bent back came up and asked them what the notice said, as he could not read.

'They tell him it is a list of names of people that will be given money by the government. The old peasant asks if his name is on the list, and they tell him, "Yes, here at the bottom!" and so he sits and waits to get his money.'

The old peasant lit his pipe, waiting for whoever was going to bring his hand-out. He had been tricked however, as the list was of people who had to give money to help build the new road. When he found this out, he spluttered in anger, and attacked the sign with his spade.

Scene six.

A widow was lamenting her dead husband in her white-washed house.

'Her husband has died and her daughter is ill,' I was told.

A rich man came to lend her money, but he was drunk and made her drink too. Then he sat at the table and asked her to sing for him, then, after closing the curtains and checking outside the door, he chased the frightened woman into bed.

The Master arrived in the nick of time, and struck him to the ground, where he curled up like a dog. To pay for his crimes the rich man had to pay money to the Master before he could leave.

'Her husband died because he was ill and there was no road to send him to the hospital. The road was the problem.'

The widow kow-towed in appreciation, tried to sing for him, offered him wine, and then, as he'd refused all else, took a deep breath and lay back on the bed. Our kind official refused her offer and gave her all the money he had to save her daughter.

In the final scene, we returned to the house of the Lazy Wife. A doctor – a young pretty girl in high heels and a pink suit – arrived to abort her baby. Unfortunately, the Lazy Wife – after being criticized – had tried to abort the baby herself by hitting herself with a stick. She was carried to the bed seriously ill, and the Master rolled up his sleeve to give blood to save her.

Everyone gathered round to help him, and the spotlight illuminated him giving blood as a woman in the background sang a plaintive melody, bringing a murmur of approval from the audience. The Lazy Wife was saved.

As everyone was celebrating her survival, the government truck arrived carrying the dynamite needed to build the road, and surprisingly, the Master's wife.

'She is not happy with their relationship. The problem is his work,' Chao Xia told me. 'He works too hard. Everyone has their own domestic problems, (ie all countries) and he promises that he will look after his family as well as do his work.'

At this point no-one seemed to know if the opera had ended or not. Half the audience were up, a noisy crowd surging towards the doors.

'Is it over?'

'I don't know,' she said, squinting to read the characters.

It was not over. There was one further scene: the Master, weak from giving so much blood, was carried off on his crude palanquin and all the villagers, young and old, came together to help carry him. Even the old village leader arrived and tore up his letter of resignation, while the new village leader held up the bag of intravenous fluid which would help the master recover.

They all struck a pose, like a revolutionary statue, as the lights dimmed and the rumble of dynamiting began.

The few people in the audience still sitting, joined in the impatient shoving at the doors, which guaranteed that no-one got out quickly. I was nearly knocked off my feet by a grey-haired man half my height, as we struggled out into the icy night air.

CHAPTER ELEVEN

DongTian: Winter

The weather quickly got colder, and all the signs of summer –
old people in the streets, badminton being played, young people
promenading – had gone. Out came the cotton-padded trousers
and jackets – quite simply clothes stuffed full of raw cotton
that was stiff and heavy, but incredibly warm. Everyone looked
as if they'd put on stones overnight and now the streets were
full of little Chinese Michelin Men.

1 November and we still had no heating so getting undressed
at night was like being dipped into icy water. Climbing into
bed was worse. The sheets were so cold that they felt wet, but
all that was as nothing compared to climbing out of bed in the
morning, leaving the heavy, cosseting warmth of four cotton
quilts to face another day of cold.

To try to reduce the draughts in my room I taped up all the
joins and cracks in the window. Over this I tacked a large sheet
of plastic and sellotaped it to the wall. The first time I put it
up it had been ripped off within half an hour by the draughts.
Now, with further modification, ie lots more sellotape and
tacks, it stayed in place, pulsating in and out with the gusts of
wind, breathing like a giant lung.

In the dark my alarm went off. It was one of those wind-up
clocks that had the same high pitch as shattering glass. I lay
in bed, and enjoyed my last moments of warmth. Between
getting up and going to bed, I'd never feel warm. The cold
seeped in through my skin like dampness, and once it was in
your marrow it didn't leave.

Clear blue skies like this in England would mean a fine day. Here, in Yuncheng, it meant north winds and Siberian temperatures. I dashed over to lessons. A wind, just arrived from the Mongolian Steppes, had frozen everything in an instant. The puddles were frozen into ripples, and the fine snow blasting against my bare skin made me feel like I was being showered with fine shards of glass.

If the conditions in our flats were bad, then the only consolation for me was that they were not as bad as the classrooms and student dormitories: gaping and smashed windows, and when it arrived, even more ineffectual heating. The students sat shivering through the lessons, barely moving, wrapped up like a classroom of snowmen.

Exercise was the only way of fighting the cold, and jogging through the south of Yuncheng tonight, in the old city, we passed a funeral procession.

In an unlit street, its dirt surface turned liquid by the rains, there was a file of musicians beating drums and cymbals, blowing on little Chinese horns and trumpets. Behind them came the mourners dressed in white rags, with white bands around their heads, and carrying staves with white cloth tied onto the end, which they dragged behind them.

At the back two men carried a large, brightly coloured memorial flower of cane and paper, arranged like a giant carnation. They all looked very tired, as if they had been walking for a long time.

The hired musicians were already out of sight, and the rest of the procession of white clothed mourners passed like ghosts in the dark.

Fine snow fell this morning, drifting aimlessly like white blossom. Last night, I was walking back from town and as the sun set, the temperature plummeted to minus 15°C, and my muscles began to seize up with the cold, so that I ended up limping home.

Today the central heating arrived, although it didn't mean the house was warm. There was just enough heat, I think, to ensure that no-one could freeze to death, but only just. I left my curtains closed all day, shut the door and left all the lights on as an extra source of heat. When it was this cold every little bit helped.

There was an old people's club near to the college and I offered to give them a talk about old people in England this morning. They had one hundred and seventy members, who learned history, literature, drawing, health care, and how to raise the standards of their grandchildren. It was hard to know what to say to them; what did I know about being old?

We arrived at the club (which was for retired *cadres* – officials – only) during a quiz. We sat down and waited at the back until they were finished. They were much livelier than I'd imagined. I think I'd expected a cobweb-filled room of ancient withered bodies close to death. Instead they were teasing each other, shouting and running about; in fact they were a lot more active than my students. It was really good to see. This lot had been through more than most people's grandparents: Liberation, the Great Leap Forwards and, as *cadres*, had been ideal targets of 'criticism' in the Cultural Revolution.

When I got to the front and began my talk, they listened very politely as I talked about the position of old people in Britain. I appreciated this even more when I remembered the teacher's-day audience. I must admit I kind of forgot my theme with all the stop-starts while what I said was translated, and rambled a bit, and then decided to make myself stop before they all fell asleep.

'Any questions?' I asked.

Silence.

Oh dear, I thought, I've bored them solid.

Song Wan, who was translating, told them that foreigners liked to have questions at the end of a talk. Immediately up went the hands, and they shouted out their questions.

'Why do you let your old people live alone?'

'Do peasants get pensions like other people?'

'If you haven't worked during your life, then do you get a pension?'

'If a son doesn't look after his parents, then does he inherit any money?'

I liked the rationale behind the last question, in China it seemed very logical.

A lady from Shanghai stood up. Her lower jaw seemed to hang loosely down, and even wobbled from side to side, as if she were already half a skeleton. It gave her voice a quavering quality as she asked if she could sing a song with me. She had learnt it as a child in a missionary school in Shanghai.

I said, 'Sure. Fine, let's go!' while I cringed inside.

We started singing, or rather she did. I had no idea what song she was singing, or if indeed it was in English. Humming along and making noises that seemed to fit – I managed to catch a few words at the end and joined in the final chorus.

'My friends are your friends, your friends are my friends – true friends!'

We had been invited around to Dean Wu's again – for another *jiaozi*-fest. Mario phoned up Dean Wu's wife during the morning to check that she knew that he was a vegetarian. Dean Wu hadn't told her, and I think it threw her into a minor panic. Dean Wu was very apologetic to both of us, saying it was his fault for not remembering to tell his wife – and she was suitably stern with him.

Of course we were required to drink FenJiu, but at a slightly less frantic rate than last time, and today Dean Wu seemed more inclined to chat. We asked him about the piece of land next to the sports field that had been bought by the college.

'The college has bought the land to build houses,' he said. 'But they are quite expensive – for eight square metres it costs 30,000 *yuan*; a hundred it is 40,000 *yuan*; and a hundred and twenty it's 50,000 *yuan*.'

'Will you buy one?'

'No – they're mainly for young people. They do not have houses, but the older people like me have a flat provided by the work unit. My daughter wants one, but we cannot get enough money.'

'How much do you have saved up?'

'About 20,000 *yuan* – but it will cost me that much to send my son to Beijing to study. You know, I am lucky to have three daughters who will help me out with the costs of his wedding. They have told me not to worry. You see – my mother – when she dies her funeral expenses will cost me 7,000 *yuan* – and then for my son to get married will cost about 20,000 *yuan*. He'll need a TV, washing machine, fridge, motorbike – that's a new one – and maybe a house of their choice. Surely! Living away from the home is much more popular now. Not for me – I still live with my mother and she still tells me what to do. If I'm out late, she will stay up late and wait for me – and she often tells me off, surely!'

Dean Wu's mother was advanced into her eighties – a relic from a past age of China. Hobbling about on bound feet she was a cheerful and pleasant old lady and looking into her wrinkled old face was like looking into living history. One of the last generation of women to grow up with the ritual of bound feet, she'd been born just after China lost its Emperor and took its first lurching step towards the modern world. It only really found a sense of direction when she was nearly forty and the Communists under Mao took power. It was strange to think of a fifty-two-year-old man still living with his mother and doing what she told him – in England any such would be a misfit. Here it was the traditional, filial duty, the proper way for a son to behave.

Just then there was a telephone call – which seemed serious from the way Dean Wu sobered up – he talked away in confidential tones and then put the phone down.

'That was Vice-Dean Wang's husband. He is a top official with the police and he was trying to catch some gamblers. You see, there was lots of gambling during a recent festival – and he was asking me if I knew any names. I told him that the only gambling done was within the family,' then he said seriously, 'I don't like that kind of thing.'

I couldn't tell if he meant gambling or informing.

In the West, where we have so much of everything and can afford it if we haven't got it, it's hard to appreciate the difficulties of developing countries. An example of this was this afternoon, when we were graced with the presence of Yuncheng's head of foreign affairs, an obviously really important man judging by his size, suit, and lackey, who carries a handbad-sized briefcase. It takes a lot of money, *guanxi* and banquets to get that fat.

Dean Wu came into our flat first, and then acted as host to the man, a Mr Xu. Even thought it was our home we were obviously not to be trusted as hosts to such an important guest, as Chinese etiquette involves quite complicated rituals. Well, actually not that complicated, just difficult for Westerners, who, like me, get bored of repeating everything three times, and punctuating all the ceremonies with forceful prods, pushes, shoves and lots more. But Dean Wu was a past master, and he was in his prime.

We watched, forgotten and quite redundant, as Dean Wu went through the formalities: Mr Xu was welcomed in, struggled with when he tried to take off his shoes, pushed through the lounge door, herded away from the poky seat in the corner, politely instructed to sit on the sofa, and after three refusals finally allowed himself, with more than a little resistance, to be grappled into it. It was a pleasure to watch theatrics that are as crucial to social interaction as talking about the weather is in England.

At last we were all seated.

Mr Xu was given an A3-size pad from his briefcase by his assistant, and Dean Wu explained the problem.

'Mr Xu, he is the Head – yes! – Head of the Foreign Affairs Bureau. He has had, what we call "exploratory talks" with the Chinese ambassador and a Spanish company.' Dean Wu was obviously relishing the chance to show off his English skills, and said 'Foreign Affairs Bureau' and 'exploratory talks' with real delight.

'Now, I think Mario, you will understand this,' he said passing over the document to him. 'It is in Spanish. It is the plans for building a chicken farm. You translate it into English, and I will translate it into Chinese. We will be – a partnership! – no?'

Dean Wu had done very well so far, using us as the final check on any translations he had, so I wasn't really sure what we could ask for to get back some *guanxi*. We all laughed and chatted, with jokes about our new 'partnership' for the correct length of time. Then Dean Wu, as tactfully as he had brought Mr Xu into the room, ushered him out again.

In the break between lessons today, I was so down that I enjoyed chatting to Deep Throat, our Rebel Without a Hope. He had started off on another of his blockbusters, this one a dictionary that aimed to prove a link between Chinese characters and the Bible stories. I smiled and listened – but could barely believe I was here in China putting up with all this, was it really better than nine to five in an office in Britain?

'You see this character – it is the character for "greed." The top two are the *mu* radical – symbolizing trees – while beneath is the radical for female, so altogether this character symbolises the two trees in the Garden of Eden with Eve underneath.'

'This is all I need,' I thought, 'Some crackpot trying to prove that Chinese characters are divinely inspired.'

Deep Throat was encouraged by my lack of reaction. 'Yes, it is very interesting. And there are many more – I will show you.'

Tonight was a bitter winter's night, with the sky scoured of clouds by the icy winds. We stood in the stream of people leaving the cinema, waiting for the six students who had been our chaperones to catch us up as they filtered through the crowd. Tonight we were taken to see *Raise the Red Lantern* starring GongLi, China's best-known actress, who plays a woman sent to be the youngest of a rich landlord's four wives. She witnesses the hanging of the third wife as a punishment for her adultery.

Once together we started to walk home, the wind slicing through our clothes and cutting us to the bone.

'What did you think of the film?' I asked Wang Yong, one of the students.

'It has a very good message.'

'What message do you think it was?' I asked.

'I think it shows how bad the Old China was before Liberation. It is good that nothing in this film is in Modern China.'

I tried to agree. 'Yes. The hanging of the third wife was very cruel,' I said, but he missed my meaning.

'Yes,' he said. 'We no longer hang people in China. We shoot them instead.'

Wang Yong, like the other students was very proud of this film and other films that have been successful in the West. That Zhang YiMo, the director, was constantly criticized by the authorities wasn't something they seemed to know about: China isn't really a good place to find out about things like that.

The walk back to the college wasn't too long. We said thank you, goodnight, and we all went our separate ways. Inside the flat it wasn't much warmer than outside and straight away the phone rang.

'Hello,' said a girl's voice. 'My friends and I wanted to talk to you tonight, but you left too quickly.'

'I'm sorry. But did you enjoy the film?'

'I did, did you?'

The conversation with the mystery caller continued in a similar vein as with Wang Yong but she thought the film showed how 'bright and beautiful' the New China was.

'Do you like the weather in China?' she asked me. Could I use chopsticks? What was England like? Why had Mr Mario got long hair?'

I told her it was a ponytail.

'How do you spell "ponytail"? What is the difference between "ponytail" and "pigtail"?'

I explained the difference between 'must' and 'have to' and immediately put the phone down and went gratefully to bed.

One of the teachers in the Chinese department was a simple, uncomplicated, and apparently open woman called XiaoPu. Tall with a ready smile – unfortunate considering the state of her teeth – she decided to like us at some point, and since then

I'd found it hard to work out if she really did like us or was after something.

Like all Chinese she'd heard that Westerners turf their children and parents out into the gutter at the first available opportunity, then enjoy their privacy alone. When she first came round we told her that our grandparents did not live alone or in a home, but with aunts and uncles. She clapped her hands – almost in gratitude – saying we were '*ting hao*' – 'very good'. Our chat continued along family lines: she was scandalized that unmarried people could live together, and sniggered at the very idea, saying in Chinese '*bu xing*' – 'not here.'

She thought all English people had yellow hair and was shocked and confused by my family photo where there was every shade between blond and black. It took some persuading for her to believe that they were really my family.

Today she'd come around for one of our 'chats'.

'You have a good name in the college,' she told us. 'If you get a good name, then everyone accepts this and follows suit. If you get a bad name, then everyone thinks you are bad. We have a saying, "If someone speaks one bad word of you, then you are finished." The last foreign teacher, he got a bad name. On Sundays he would go out for the day with female students. He was very arrogant. They were only girls.

'I will cook for you,' she offered suddenly. 'I want to cook for you. I will be your mother,' she said clapping her hands in excitement. 'I will be your Big Sister. I will mend your clothes and cook. You can prepare lessons and when you have finished, I'll have a meal ready. I only have a husband and son. That's not enough for me. I have time to help you too. I can come over whenever you need me.'

This was one side of her. I saw another one morning when she caught me at home.

'Oh, I haven't seen you for fifty days. I am so happy!'

I had wanted to relax and enjoy a quiet morning off lessons, but she wanted something, anything in fact. I was a bit nervous that she was trying to make a move on me because she was brushing up close and touching my forearm, which is very un-Chinese.

'What's this?' she said, pointing at a bottle of whiskey, kept only for moments of despair or exultation. She insisted I give her some, then spat it out in disgust.

I had to act, and tried to bustle her out.

'Can I just stay five more minutes?' she asked.

'No,' I said.

'Let me see something Western!' she said.

She went through the flat: the living room, my bedroom, the kitchen, the bathroom examining everything. I gave her a handful of English stamps and she left, skipping with gratitude and saying goodbye over and over. I was worried that she might try to kiss me, so I apologized again for having to make her leave, and hurriedly shut the door.

This morning the students were determined not to do anything, and as their teacher I felt unable to motivate them. They sat with their heads in their books, unwilling to co-operate with anything I was doing, and I didn't have the energy to encourage them – so I just stood disillusioned and waited for them to answer.

Twenty-week terms drag on interminably, and what with the cold weather, power-cuts, and worst of all, lack of letters from people at home, my mood had been darkening for a while now.

I looked through my tapes this morning and the thought of having to listen to another one of them again filled me with an intense feeling of boredom. I picked them up one by one and just looked at them. I felt like I was trapped in time, cursed to go on repeating each day over and over interminably with no hope of even the most minor change to bring some relief. I was still listening to the same music I brought out with me so long ago.

It was coming up to Christmas and it was hard to think that Spring Festival, and the winter holidays, was five weeks away. Christmas has no place in Chinese culture, so it was odd not to have the consumer build-up as winter deepened, not to hear any carols or adverts, nothing.

But tonight it was our 'Christmas' party. The Communist Party criticized colleges who were having Christmas parties this year, as it was the One Hundredth Anniversary of Mao's birth the day after. A date of far more relevance to China.

Our Christmas party was a Mao's One Hundredth Anniversary party combined with a surprise appearance by Father Christmas. Father Christmas was me.

I was being hidden in the Department office while down the corridor in the largest classroom, the two hundred-odd English department students were squeezed in for tonight's party. All the desks had been moved to the edges of the classroom, and all the students were packed in behind them, with a space in the middle of the room for performances. They were very excited, and the babble of noise that echoed down the dark corridor to my hiding place only made me feel more apprehensive. I had my beard – a straggly thing made of cotton wool – on already, and I was only awaiting the arrival of my red coat. XiaoPu had a lot of difficulty finding any coat big enough to fit me.

Dean Wu was filling up my sack with sweets, melon seeds and peanuts. We'd just come, with him, from a Christmas banquet, where we three got drunk while the President and a few other leaders looked at their watches until it was alright for them to leave.

'You must go in and throw the sweets to everyone. Yes, surely! All of them. And be jolly, ha!' he told me through a cloud of cigarette smoke. My coat arrived; it was pink, and skintight, but the students had never seen a Santa before so I didn't think they'd mind. My eyebrows were stuck on and my little red cap pulled down firmly.

'Father Christmas!' Dean Wu laughed.

I moved out behind Mario, XiaoPu and Dean Wu. I felt like a pop star about to walk on stage at a concert. We walked down the dark corridor to the lights and expectant and excited students beyond.

Suddenly I was in the bright room, and the students exploded into cheers. My 'Ho, ho, hos were drowned out in the explosion of noise. The students screamed and clapped and waved – and screamed again. I started throwing handfuls of nuts and sweets and they were all imploring me at the top of their voices to throw that sweet to them. Surrounded by a wall of faces, arms, and noise, I'd never been so popular, and I began to feel embarrassed for them. I didn't feel comfortable being the focus of such adoration. But China was always full of surprises, and I never knew that my students had so much life in them. They certainly didn't in my class, but this was their first and, for many, last chance to see Father Christmas, and it was something that none of them could forget.

Everything was grey. The sky was grey, the air was grey, the plants were grey, people's expressions were grey: all the colours had been reduced to shades of grey.

Oh God, not another day in China. Got up, taught; in the afternoon played basketball and twisted my ankle; bought two *binzi* (flat breads) to make sandwiches for dinner and as I queued two students giggled at all the hairs on my legs that they could see in the gap between my jeans and socks.

On a day like this only a letter from home could cheer me up – but people at home seemed to spend more energy apologizing for not writing than actually doing it. I went to check if there were any letters at the little office at the college gates, but good old Comrade Jiao, the lady whose job it was to lock our letters in a cupboard and then disappear with the key – wasn't in at 10.30 AM. Nor was she in at 4.30 PM, because she'd gone to the cinema and hadn't come back. It was no consolation to me to know that I might have letters, but until this rather vacant girl turned up, I wouldn't know.

Last week we were invited to the English department Christmas banquet. The department had been awarded 2,000 *yuan* for getting two students into the university at Linfen. Instead of deciding to spend the money on anything useful, an impromptu meeting of the English department decided to take itself out for a banquet. It was announced as being in honour of the two foreigners, to celebrate Christmas. When we arrived it was soon apparent that we were not the guests of honour, however. The department had managed to kill two birds with one stone and had invited the Party secretary of the Chinese department over as well. We could tell he was the guest of honour because everyone was trying to get him drunk. He was tricked, deceived, cajoled and blatantly lied to to make him drink more. As the table was full of English department teachers no one tried to help him, but all conspired against him. When he was red-faced from the spirits he had already drunk, they started in earnest. His chief tormentor was one of the form teachers, a large fearsome lady, schooled no doubt in the tactics of the Red Guards and who could back up her sharp tongue with a heavy thwack! She was the welfare worker, responsible for the everyday behaviour of the students. Quite a Victorian matron she was, lambasting the students regularly for missing their morning exercises, or evening self-study. It was she who criticized any girls who came regularly to see us. Despite this, she had taken a liking to us, and in between drinking bouts with the Chinese department Party secretary, she demanded I guess her age.

I said, 'Twenty-eight.'

'No. Guess again.'

'More than thirty?'

'Yes.'

'More than forty?'

'Yes.'

She was forty-nine.

By now she was making this poor man, maybe half her size, drink multiple shots. He knocked back his drink with loud bluster while she spat hers out or surreptitiously poured it away. He was too drunk to notice.

Usually Mario and I were at the centre of attention, so a respite from this meant I could relax a little and chat to Song Jiang, who was sitting next to me.

'I hear you've earned a few thousand lecturing in the local schools,' I said.

'Yeah. I did two weeks. It is good money,' he told me. 'Some friends and I have started buying shares in the new Taiyuan stock market. It costs 2,000 *yuan* to buy a place, and then we bought shares in FenJiu for 3.5 *yuan* each share. I bought 7,000 *yuan* worth of shares. I think the trading will start sometime in the New Year. These shares will start at about twice what we bought them for.'

'So how did you find out about this deal?'

'Oh, my friends,' he said matter of factly, 'they are in the know.'

Tonight I've had quite a stimulating lesson with QunXia, my Chinese teacher, where we spent about an hour and a half discussing various topics. I had prepared a piece about summer in Yuncheng and I talked about people coming out and playing badminton, and wearing bright clothes and being very happy. I thought I had included pretty much everything. She read it but was not impressed.

'Wrong!' she said. 'Not good. Your writing is not good. There is nothing about flowers or trees. If you write about summer, then you must mention flowers.'

This was typical of QunXia, who was quite outspoken for a Chinese woman. After saying 'Wrong!' she liked to tease me for my barbarity.

'How old is your Britain?' she asked today.

It's hard to be precise about such an arbitrary date. Unification with Scotland, the Norman Conquest, when? About nine hundred years old,' I said.

This answer reduced her to fits of laughter. 'Our China is five thousand years old.'

'But China in its present form is not five thousand years old. Most of China was only added to the state at later dates,' I said, but she refused to listen. China does have a recorded history much older than that of the English-speaking peoples, but they also seem to be a bit vague about dates. A good guide to dates in Chinese history seems to be, take a number and double it.

But maybe more than any other people, the Chinese define

themselves by their history, which has been written down for much longer than that of other countries. They have believed that they are the only civilized people in a world of barbarians for so long that this idea is still strong in their national ethos. The Chinese have a similar opinion of themselves as the European nineteenth-century colonists did, who believed that they were racially superior to all other peoples. This can be seen in their attitude towards China's minorities in Tibet, Xinjiang, Inner Mongolia and throughout the south-west provinces.

I liked QunXia, and so could let her off most things – but I hate smugness in anyone. If I wasn't a Westerner I'm sure I'd hate the West for its self-satisfied smugness and self-serving politics. And as for the English with their Island Race, Mother of All Parliaments and those words that seem to trip off the tongue of any politician: 'Our ... is the pride/envy/best in the world,' they make me see red.

But living with this national conceit in China, which is so excluding, was seductive – there's something almost magnetic about it. Despite all the glaring faults of modern China, I couldn't help wanting to be included.

For Christmas we were meeting up with some other foreigners in Taiyuan, the provincial capital. Our bus left early in the morning so it was very cold at first with a thick layer of ice covering the windows. In my Chinese army greatcoat my body was warm, but a draught down by my feet made me feel extremely cold. After two hours we stopped at a layby to pick up more passengers and I got off to walk around stiffly, just to get the circulation going. As the sun began to shed some warmth then it became quite a pleasant journey – until the sun set again – when the temperature plummeted. We sat and shivered for two hours as the kilometres passed slowly by.

When at last we arrived and stepped off the bus, my legs had stopped working properly and I limped to the flat.

I didn't have much choice of foreign friends in China, there were so few foreigners in this area, so when we all met up we seemed a rather incongruous group. Of the forty foreign teachers in Shanxi province, most were Evangelical missionaries from the USA. They were a serious bunch who discussed the problem of World Bank funding at breakfast, did baptisms in the bath, flew home every holiday, and generally embarrassed the five or six normal American teachers here. You will understand me when I say we didn't much mix. The rest were roughly split into VSO teachers from Britain, Behais from the US and a few more independents.

We did have one mass party once, when we all danced and drank cool beer, while our religious brothers and sisters, who were tee-total, left to have a Bible reading. We did mix a bit of course, but when a pretty girl from the Deep South came up and started a conversation with 'I wonder if you'd mind if I asked, but what does Jesus mean to you in your life?' I had a feeling that we didn't have much more in common than our white skin and the English language. For me not foundation enough for a friendship.

So here we were on Christmas Day, a small group of six non-evangelical people: three English – Marsha, Phil and I; two New Zealanders – Norrie and Neville; and one Spaniard – Mario. The Christmas glitz, the excuse to spend money, had made an appearance in Taiyuan in the form of blow-up Santa Clauses that were being flogged on the streets, but other than that Christmas didn't feature in the Chinese calendar. Our feelings were also a little confused. Mario, as an atheist, didn't want to celebrate Christmas in any way, whereas I wanted the works – turkey, a tree, decorations. Unfortunately for me the decorations amounted to a few strips of coloured paper hung from the ceiling and as to the meal the vegetarians won the day: we sat eating vegetarian *jiaozi* in a cold street-restaurant in Taiyuan. I think foreigners of any nationality in any country must talk about similar things: a bit of griping about the locals, a bit of cultural knowledge recently learnt, a bit of, a funny thing happened to me last week and I would die for a Mac-Donalds or bit of roast lamb – and we weren't so different. The afternoon went by in a friend's flat as we sat and watched *Roger Rabbit* and *Casablanca* on a video borrowed from a Chinese teacher, and in the evening we put on some music and danced.

It felt so good to be a Westerner again, doing things Westerners were supposed to do, in a crowd of people where I was as 'normal' as I could be. I always got a strange feeling when meeting other Westerners – at first I felt uncomfortable in their presence, talking at normal speed again, and trying to remember all the unspoken intricacies of social etiquette which I had forgotten from lack of use.

But now we were back in Yuncheng and the three days of excitement had been and gone – like it never happened. International New Year we celebrated with DaiYu in a restaurant where by 7.30 PM everyone except the manager and a chef had left – and we ate in a dark room, counting the rats that were heading for the kitchens.

I wasn't used to working over these festivals; we'd been teaching for seventeen weeks non-stop and still the Spring Festival holidays were three weeks away.

Professor Bao was the big fat jolly man who lived on the fourth floor opposite us. He never really spoke to us, but chortled, nodded, grunted and chuckled all at once, a cocktail of sounds resonating from deep within his stomach, making him wobble all over with satisfaction.

A professor of Chinese, he had an international reputation, and recently had been to Japan to attend a conference. Unfortunately he did not have the knack of talking to us in simplified Chinese, but embellished his language with literary flourishes and with obscure references which made all but his most simple grunts unintelligible.

We had lived happily on the same floor for some time – him chuckling hello, while his wife spied on us from her doorway, watching our comings and goings – occasionally visiting each other. Once he came to ask us to fill in the information sheet for an international *Who's Who* of scholars. We were sitting there helping him when from the corner of my eye I saw a shadow cross the doorway. I went out into the hall to investigate and found that his wife had followed him across the landing into our flat and was now going from room to room, having a good look at everything. I intercepted her in the kitchen and she only had time for a few mental notes before I snared her in conversation and used it to lure her away. I could see her eyes flicker over the room – the click as each item was registered before she followed me out. I knew the next topic of gossip in the neighbourhood would be the dreadful state of the foreigners' flat.

One day in early January we had a pleasant surprise. We had already celebrated Christmas and New Year, and were still hanging on for the Spring Festival holiday, when we were invited to the Baos' son's wedding. The invite came three days beforehand – ample warning for China.

On the special day the staircase was decorated with lots of small 'Double Happiness' character paper cuts, a trail leading up to the Baos' door. The end of the trail was marked by a large red 'Double Happiness' on the door itself.

People had been arriving all morning, bearing little packets of red paper – envelopes containing gifts of money. We came back from our morning's teaching and found our isolated top-floor stairway now thronged with noisy and excited Chinese people. The groom had already collected the bride from her house, and taken her to the restaurant to get married, the usual venue for weddings. We followed them, cycling into town with Dean Wu, who was quite lucky to always be invited to these kind of events as our translator.

When we arrived we found that the first restaurant was already full of wedding guests so we were sent across the road to another, where a back room with extra tables had been set up for the overflow guests.

Nobody here seemed to mind the fact that we were missing the wedding ceremony that was being held over the road in the other restaurant. They had given their gifts and were now more interested in getting their money's worth. After the three toasts of FenJiu we all tucked in, heads down, feeding from the trough. Half-way through the meal Bao senior and his wife came in. Both Professor Bao's cheeks were smeared with red paint according to custom, and his wife carried a tray full of small spirit cups. He was going around toasting with each table. That he had already visited a number of tables was obvious in his extra resonance and wobbling. We took the drinks, raised our cups to each other then drank them down with loud slurps. With more cheerful bobs, Bao thanked us and moved on to the next table.

Soon after Bao, the bride and groom and a few of their male friends arrived. They too had their cheeks smeared with red. As we had missed the wedding ceremony, I couldn't really be sure which was the groom and which was the best man. We drank again and they moved off, very unsteady on their feet.

Cycling back with Dean Wu we were all quite jolly. Full of delicious food and a pleasant amount of alcohol, we found that Dean Wu was quite forthcoming, as was usual after a meal and a drink or two.

'Ah, you know in 1959, Bao – he was a teacher in Beijing. But he criticized Mao during the One Hundred Flowers campaign. He was sent to Lingyi county to be re-educated through labour and to learn from the peasants.'

The Hundred Flowers Campaign is the name for a rather unpleasant period in Mao's reign: in a precarious position, as leadership struggles began to ease him out of power, he called for the public – and especially the intellectuals in the 'democratic parties' – to speak out in criticism of the Communist Party. 'Let a Hundred Flowers bloom together; let a hundred schools of thought contend. The more you love the Party, the more you will speak out in criticism.' Understandably, people were not very forthcoming at first, but eventually they did speak out, increasingly criticizing Mao and even calling for power-sharing and democracy. Mao allowed this situation to continue, 'to coax the snakes out of their holes', and then subjected everyone who had spoken out against him to a severe dose of punishment euphemistically referred to as 'criticism' and 'self-criticism', then sent them off to the countryside.

Dean Wu was still talking. 'He married in the countryside, but was severely criticized again during the Cultural Revolution. In 1980 he was rehabilitated and allowed to leave Lingyi and come to Yuncheng.'

'Did he never want to return to Beijing?' I asked, but Dean Wu did not answer.

From that I took it to mean that he could never return. Bao had also married, had children and put down roots, so now Yuncheng was probably more home than Beijing. But rehabilitation only goes so far. Even after his death, Mao still haunts people's lives in China.

Today the weather was very clear. I could see the South Mountains from my window, the whole curve of them as they curled around either end of the lake, and at the far east there was a peak that I'd not seen before. They were all dappled with snow, all the gullies and ravines stark in shades of light and dark.

For the past week I'd been in bed by eight o'clock at night, as the electricity had been turned off in our quarter of town to keep the factories working. Each night it was cold and dark as I sat by candlelight, wondering what to do. But there's not much you can do by the flickering flame of a candle – reading and writing aren't practical, and there's no point sitting doing nothing when it's as cold as this. Your mind keeps on returning to one thing – how cold you are.

So, there was nothing for it but to give up on the day and wait for the sun to rise again.

Earlier this morning I walked into town to buy some food for the flat, as we had run out. It was too cold to cycle – going at speed just meant letting stronger and colder draughts in through the openings in my clothes.

The few vegetable salesmen in the street were a muffled group whose contours were disguised in coats and scarves and whose weather-stained faces were stuck as far into their hats as they would go. They could have been either men or women.

Like them I was smothered up in my army greatcoat, Russian hat with flaps down over my ears, and a scarf over it all.

In town, some Uigers and Khazaks stood forlornly selling furs and fur-lined coats from far off Xingjiang. They were culturally closer to me than to the Chinese. Far away from their mountains, steppes and yurts they seemed very vulnerable in the cold streets of Yuncheng.

I watched one Han Chinese – stiff with winter clothing – finish off a deal with a Uiger. The Uiger was old and short, with a thin face elongated by a pointed beard, who looked as though he'd just been robbed, his stance and expression both hopeless, while she was a stocky, confident woman who snatched the pelt from him and walked off smugly with it.

I joined a crowd looking at some fleece-lined coats and hats. One coat was lined with a fine, tightly curled kind of wool.

'What kind of sheep is this?' one of the local Chinese men asked me.

'I don't know,' I replied.

'Come on. You must know. What is it?' he demanded again.

'I really don't know,' I said again.

'But don't you have lots of sheep where you are?' he asked.

'Yes. Quite a few. But still I don't know what kind of sheep it is,' I said.

'Are you from Xingjiang or not?' he demanded.

'No,' I said. 'I'm from England.'

There was a burst of embarrassed laughter, as everyone joked about such a ridiculous thing – mistaking a foreigner for a Chinese man!

He tried speaking to me in Russian.

'Sorry, I don't speak Russian.'

'Your Chinese is very good,' he said, shaking his head. 'You fooled me!'

'No, no, it's not very good,' I said as we shook hands and parted, he laughing to himself, and me thinking that, just for an instant, and just for a few people, I had actually been accepted as a native. With hat down low and my scarf pulled up I walked home, an undercover LaoWai.

CHAPTER TWELVE

Free Enterprise

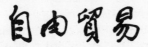

This evening Deep Throat and the physics teachers, Mr Yang, came around for a chat. First Deep Throat, inhaling trails of smoke that enveloped his mouth and nose, as he pushed through the half-open door and stood for the polite formalities of welcoming a guest in China to begin.

'Come and sit down!' I said.

He did and then launched into a conversation. 'You know, the English department is full of factions,' he told us, 'and we all conflict. Dean Wu is not popular. Most teachers and leaders mistrust him. He still does business the old way. Duan Yu, he is the enemy of Dean Wu, you know, everyone says Duan Yu, Li JianQiang and I, we are good friends – we are a gang. Duan Yu has left on sick leave to do business.'

He relaxed after having got this off his chest, and soon his mind returned, naturally, to 'sordid details.'

'You know, my friend, Shen Zong, he used to be very sexually unsatisfied. His wife does not enjoy it. He used to go around and tell everyone how he is unsatisfied. He turned to philosophy, you know, that is why he began researching *Journey to the West* – the book in which the Monkey King travels in search of enlightenment. He is very interested in Buddhism. He has written a book containing his ideas about life. He has become a Buddhist.'

This marked only a short interlude before he returned to the subject of the corruption and sordid behaviour of Communist Party officials.

'I am a member of the Democratic Association, one of the six or seven political parties in China,' he said proudly. 'There are maybe five members in the college. Mr Bao (the Chinese teacher), he is a member. We meet occasionally to smoke together. It is not very serious. You know we are not free. The first line in the Democratic Party's constitution is, "We accept the authority and leadership of the Communist Party." All parties must accept the leadership of the Communist Party – otherwise you cannot exist.'

It was at this moment Mr Yang arrived. Just as strong a personality as Deep Throat, but very different. He had spent six months in Brighton, kept up to date with world events, and was a newly enrolled member of the Communist Party.

'What do you think of John Major?' he chuckled. 'What do you think of Hong Kong? Why is Chris Patten trying to ruin Hong Kong before it is returned to China?'

I told him that most British people were not interested in Hong Kong and, in any case, I didn't think the democratic reforms were designed to damage China, but to help the Hong Kong people.

'Then why don't you have democracy in Hong Kong for the past hundred years?'

'I wish we had done,' I said, and I do – but still, he's got a very good point.

'What about foreign businessmen exploiting Chinese workers?' he said.

'Foreign companies do exploit the workers,' I said, 'but the environment for this has been created by the Chinese government. I think the government is quite happy to exploit people so that they can get rich: corrupt officials misuse their power and neglect to enforce Chinese law.'

Bribery, corruption, it's all endemic in the Communist Party, which, like all organisms, is primarily concerned with its own survival. The current Open-door Policy seems to be a repeat of the last great opening-up of China in the late eighteenth century, when corrupt officials and foreign businessmen came together to exploit the Chinese workers.

In China, under a Communist government, the labour force

has probably the fewest rights in the world. No independent unions are allowed and the people responsible for the enforcement of labour laws are also those making the money.

'In fifty years' time, everyone in China will blame the foreign businessmen for exploiting the workers of today,' I said. 'But now the Party and newspapers all support this foreign investment, saying it's helping China to modernize. The problem lies with the Chinese officials – they're too corrupt to protect the workers.'

'Did you see the BBC *Mao's Personal Life* documentary when you were in Britain?' Mario asked Mr Yang.

'Yes,' he said.

'The Chinese authorities were very angry about the programme, weren't they? Did you see anything bad in it? For example, about his sexual life?'

'Oh – ha, ha!' Mr Yang laughed. 'Everyone knows that Mao had many women. That is not a problem.'

'Then why was it banned?'

Mr Yang laughed nervously, which showed that we were being too direct, and were making him feel very uncomfortable. If we pushed him much further then he might lose face, so we let it drop.

Deep Throat and Mr Yang were quite a unique combination this evening, contradicting each other constantly.

Deep Throat accused Mr Yang of only joining the Party after having being forced to, having been declared a model teacher, a title which I doubted had much significance than maybe a little more pay, and was more hot air than anything else.

'That's not true,' Mr Yang replied. 'Anyway, I don't go to meetings.'

'Then why join the party?' Deep Throat asked in his resonant voice.

It was fun seeing Deep Throat taunt Mr Yang – but whatever the moral or conscientious objections, joining the Party is a wise career move. Only forty million or so people are members, so it's quite a cosy little club and refusing an invitation to join might have repercussions. If invited, then best join, despite any personal objections. Turning a blind eye to its faults won't be too hard, like opposing war but working in a naval shipyard.

I personally preferred Mr Yang to Deep Throat and found it hard to condemn him – in the same position I wonder if I would have joined or not. Now, Mr Yang tried to get off the subject of his joining the Party, and, as if trying to prove he wasn't a Party stooge, launched into another story of corruption.

'You know, when I returned from England I flew via Moscow. In the airport a Russian policeman begged me for a cigarette. I was very surprised – a Russian begging a Chinese for a cigarette! When I was young, Russia was much more developed than China, and here he was begging me for such a little thing. I gave him the packet. There were also some Chinese men who were smuggling puppy dogs through customs. They had bags full of puppies and their greatcoat pockets were full of more dogs. I asked them how they could carry so many dogs through customs. They told me that they had 300 dollars to bribe the Russian customs men and at Beijing they had *guanxi* with someone in charge. They told me that they could sell each puppy for 10,000 *yuan* – more than 1,200 dollars for each puppy! Very interesting.'

It might seem strange that puppy dogs can fetch such prices in China – more than two years' wages for a lecturer in the college – strange, that is, until you start to understand the new China.

The majority of people see an animal as a functional beast there to guard, pull the plough, eat rats or be eaten. Pets for pleasure aren't luxuries that even cross their minds. But these smuggled puppy dogs weren't for the majority, they were for the rich wives of the élite in cities like Beijing, Shanghai and Tianjing. This group maybe amount to a fraction of one single per cent of the population, but in China that's still a few million people.

How do rich people in China behave? They show off their wealth. But the problem is that there isn't a wide enough range of consumer goods for them to be able to do this, so enter these toy breeds, little yappy dogs that make you want to drop-kick them under a passing steam roller. Fluffed up, carried on the arm – ostentatiously exhibited as the new status symbol of an élite who after forty years trying to prove themselves loyal members of the proletariat, are now rediscovering the pleasure of unashamedly flaunting their wealth and status.

Mario and I went down to Hedong Square the other evening for noodles. A warm, calm evening in spring, with lots of people out, eating mutton kebabs and noodles and bowls of Eight Treasure soup.

As we were eating, Ling Zhen, an old friend of DaiYu's, came to join us. Tall, good-looking and confident, he was an ex-art student and now worked for one of the state-owned cinemas in town, a poor job where he got barely as much as teachers, but at least he could stay in Yuncheng and not have to teach in a village school.

We had visited his room several times, a small space, with oil paintings and calligraphy covering the walls. There was just enough room for his hardboard bed and easel. A tape recorder was playing Madonna. It was a prehistoric machine and churned out the music at such a slow speed that the songs were nearly unrecognizable. No-one seemed to notice, it was all foreign anyway.

Now we soon got chatting and he told us how much our Chinese had improved since he'd last seen us.

'Before, we could say nothing, but now we can have a conversation! I have opened up a shop. Come and see,' he said, and we followed him to the other side of the square, where he had set up a small Western-style bar, serving ice-cream, milkshakes (with no milk) and coffee.

'In the summer it's too hot inside the houses so everyone comes out onto the streets. I open up and sell very well. But today, it's not warm enough. What I really need to make money is food. What is good Western food? How about hamburgers, can you teach me how to make hamburgers?'

He came around a couple of nights later to learn. I mixed mincemeat, onions and egg together while he stood in the doorway and watched, along with Mario.

'That's *yancai*,' he said. 'Onion. "*Yan*" means foreign, better than Chinese. Everything's *yan* now.' He laughed.

I flattened out some very basic burgers and he looked at them with disgust. 'Is that it?' he said.

'Well, you've got to cook them,' I told him.

We cooked them, then sat down to eat. Yuncheng Television was broadcasting MTV and we watched as Ling Zhen tried his burger. A female rock star – now past middle age, but squeezed into tight jeans and tiny top – was grinding her hips and thrusting her pelvis forward to the rhythm of the music. I was surprised to find myself embarrassed by the music and images – after so long in China the sexuality that oozed from the screen seemed so gratuitous as to be almost bestial; but in England it would be nothing special at all. I was amazed how prudish and Victorian my reaction to it was, but all in all it seemed such a sad interpretation of the culture and country I missed so much.

I watched Ling Zhen, wondering what ideas he'd get about Britain from this display of near-naked female sexuality. It would have horrified my students, but Ling Zhen was more modern.

'Do all women in your country have such large breasts?' he asked in mock horror.

'No – much bigger!' said Mario.

'Are they gay?' Ling Zhen asked about two men in another music video. 'There were two lesbians where I used to live in the south of town. One was like a man and one was like a woman. They were very funny. There was always shouting at their house. Their families would come and criticize them and all the children would shout at them. In the end the woman-woman left. The man-woman was lost without her. She just couldn't do anything, she was incapable without the other.'

His burger remained half-eaten. 'Don't you like the burger?' I asked.

'O! It is too meaty. It is *bu hao chi*,' he said, looking ill, 'not very delicious. If I sell this at my shop, then no-one will ever come back!'

Today we went to visit LingYi, one of the local towns near

Yuncheng. I had already been acquainted with the police there, but today with our 'Alien Travel Permits' we hoped for a more law-abiding visit. In the morning, we met some middle-school teachers, sixty of them, crammed in to a single room, covered with a roof of plaited reeds which dulled the noise that came in through the open doors and windows, through which the sunlight was streaming.

There was a banquet lunch for us, and then we were taken to visit a middle school that had been built from local contributions, at a cost of over three million *yuan*. Number Two Middle School was quite a plush affair, the best that this richer-than-average county could afford. A thousand students – mainly weekly boarders from the surrounding villages – studied in classes of sixty or more and lived in identical rooms whose floors were covered by mattresses that could be rolled up during the day.

It was strange as we walked through the entire school not to see a single pupil. We could hear their hubbub all around, and sometimes catch a glimpse of one of them peering round a doorway. But if we ever caught them out in the open, then they turned and fled away from us. They were of course both tremendously excited and terrified by us, their first foreigners.

Our tour completed, we walked down the stairs and out of the main doors. As we stood outside having our photos taken with the teachers, a great clamour rose behind us. Every window in the great block was full of faces, all pointing and shouting and waving down at us.

At English Corner today we had a fierce discussion about Eastern Europe. We were talking about China's economic reforms, which are designed to build a Socialist Market Economy, something as near to capitalism as you can get without actually calling it that.

I said, 'China had no choice but to drop communism, because it didn't work. Look at Eastern Europe – the people gave up communism in favour of capitalism.'

'What do you mean?' a student interrupted, determined to

find me out on a statement that I considered plainly obvious, but which she saw as a subversive untruth.

'Communism is a nice idea, but it doesn't work. Compare East and West Germany. Capitalism in the West produced a much better life than Communism in the East.'

The student shook her head. Poor Mr Hill – so badly misinformed, her laughter seemed to say. 'No, Eastern Europe fell because it was undermined by Western capitalists. Now only China is left to defend communism.'

It was my time to smile. In the past I had doubted what I was saying, but not now. Although neither of us had been to either Germany, and all our knowledge was based on the images we saw on our TVs, or what our media had decided to show us, in this case I was more confident that the British press had an interest in giving a better picture. The collapse of communism in Eastern Europe came at a rather difficult time for the Chinese government, just six months after they'd used tanks to suppress dissent in Tiananmen Square.

As a result, my students and colleagues had a haphazard knowledge of what had really happened. In the case of Czechoslovakia, the Chinese press neglected to mention the fact that the Czech communist government was no longer ruling the country as it reported the Party's internal talks and official communiqués. The first ever mention of Vaclav Havel's name came on the day he was actually elected President, but with no mention of his previous role as a dissident or his imprisonment, just some biographical details.

In this case I was determined I was right; but so were they, and we agreed to differ.

DaiYu brought me out to buy some meat today.

'You know we should not buy pork,' she told me as we mounted our bicycles and started to cycle down Hedong Donglu. 'It is diseased. The authorities have announced on TV that people should not buy it until they have discovered the cause. Didn't you know! Oh, heavens!' she laughed. 'Maybe you will die tomorrow, and then who will do English Corner this week? Poor Mario will have to go alone!'

Never mind, the pork we saw was much too fatty to buy.

The markets in Yuncheng were full of quite extraordinary sights: a cage full of snakes, alert and poised; buckets full of squid – dead; bowls of seaweed; plucked chickens lined up on a wall with their long necks hanging limply down, crawling with flies; not to mention all the people milling around, shouting, chatting, cursing, picking through piles of vegetables and enjoying a noisy morning shopping.

We found beef almost immediately, in a grubby little shack in the busy market. Cooked beef pieces sat in a glass cabinet in front, and in the doorway two youths stood with cigarettes jammed into their grins. An old lady, leaning on a hand-powered meat grinder, stood beneath an old hunk of beef hanging from a hook. We went inside, into the darker shades of the room, across a walkway of concrete slabs raised above a floor that was awash with blood. A beef carcus hung on one side, on the other a high wooden table, its surface deeply scored by the cleaver and crumbly with damp blood. Upon it was piled mounds of fresh red flesh.

I pointed to one bit and the lady carved a muscle off the mound and put it in a bag for me.

DaiYu had to go off to see a friend and as I cycled back I noticed large crowds of people cycling the opposite way, towards Hedong Square. Near the college, I passed lots of students, and as it was lesson time I stopped to ask them why they weren't in class.

'We have been given the morning off to go to Hedong Square to see a public sentencing of criminals. Fifteen were sentenced to death, fourteen men and one woman,' said one.

'Really? Did they shoot them in Hedong Square?' I asked, a little horrified.

'No, the criminals were then driven out of town and shot.'

My students were quite animated, and had enjoyed the spectacle as a break from lessons. Their morning off had been a real treat.

'In China, public executions happen mainly before New Year as it is considered to be bad luck to have condemned criminals alive afterwards,' I was told, and the whole episode, and especially my students' reaction to it, left me feeling a bit uneasy.

Mario had the flu last week – which meant everything was very quiet inside the flat.

Attitudes to illness is one of those areas where Chinese and Western viewpoints come into direct conflict. I spent most of my time turning away great crowds of students who came noisily tramping up our stairs. 'But Chinese custom says that it is polite to visit people if they are ill, to show our concern,' a group told me today, determined to go in and show their respect.

I was equally determined not to let them. 'But in the West when we are ill, then we really prefer to be alone. When Mario's better then you can come and visit him.'

At last they went away, unhappy, feeling that I had prevented them from doing the proper thing.

Song Wan came too – alone – bearing a large bag of fruit.

'How is Mario? Can I see him?' he asked.

I said, 'I think it would be better if he was left alone as he is sleeping at the moment.'

'OK – yeah. Is fruit OK?' he said, opening up the bag. 'In the West you give flowers, but in China we give fruit.'

Song Wan decided that he should go, so as not to disturb Mario, and I saw him out. In China, turfing people out of the house like this is actually very rude, but I hoped that Song Wan would be understanding.

'I think I must go?' he said.

'Yes, I'm very sorry, come again when he's a little better and I'm sure he'd be happy to see you.'

It always surprised me that Song Wan – whose English was actually of a very high level – only worked at the middle school. Maybe his ancestor – the illustrious mandarin who signed away Hong Kong – didn't do him any favours for the days after the Cultural Revolution.

A while ago we had helped him fill in a CV for a new international school in Canton where all the teaching was bilingual. He got the job – at 2,000 *yuan* a month, five times his present wage – but he could not move the *hukou* (registration document, enabling its owner to get subsidized education and health care) of his wife and daughter and so would have had to leave them behind. Because of this he didn't take the job, but stayed in Yuncheng.

Since then Song Wan seemed to be getting increasingly depressed. A skilled man with no future or opportunities. His sister managed to go to America with her husband to study and his mother had been staying with them for just over a year now. But Song Wan was no nearer to going abroad than he was when he'd begun his career.

'So will your mother come back from the USA?' I asked.

'I think she must come back, because my father's here,' he said, but his words had a hollow ring.

'Does she like it there, do you think?'

'Yes, she like it very much. Much cleaner, newer – many freedoms as well. She has been in Indianapolis for a year. She told me in her letter that she will stay an extra six months. You know, I think her English is very good now – I think she is fully fluent.

'You know, my mother's family are very numerous and quite rich. They were quite important before Liberation – now many of them live abroad, but during the Cultural Revolution we suffered very badly, and we could not admit to having foreign relatives. We have now lost touch with them.'

'Do you think you will ever get to go abroad?'

'Ah, yes. You know – it is very difficult to go abroad, but I think – I think someday I will go abroad. I can only hope.'

'So, why is it so difficult?'

'Well, I think the government doesn't like too many people to leave and get new ideas, they want everyone to stay at home and stay poor.'

'So tell me, Song Wan, do you think your future is good?'

'I don't know. You know, prices are going up very quickly. Also there are the Four Great Problems in China – Corruption, Inflation – and I forget what the other two are. Corruption is very bad. The people who join the Communist Party are very corrupt. They have no ideas, they only want power so that they can get rich. They do not believe any of the stuff they tell us. You know, my mother is also a member of the Communist Party, but things were different then; they worked to make things better. Not now. Everyone wants power, because power is money. Even the lower officials become rich.'

'But tell me, if you became an official tomorrow, would you become corrupt?'

He thought for a few seconds. 'Yes, I think I would,' he laughed, shaking his head. 'It would be very difficult not to. We say, "If you are a good official then you are finished." People will put pressure on you.'

Overcoming corruption is, I think, the biggest problem for China today. But that's easy for me to say – I don't have to live here and risk my future by trying to make a stand.

Corruption has always been endemic in China. *Guanxi* seems so integral to everyday life now, I can't believe it's suddenly appeared from nowhere. Within the traditional hierarchical structure in Imperial China everyone knew the rich could do what they wanted and the poor were weak anyway. During the long collapse of the Qing Dynasty around the turn of the century, corruption became even more rife – and with the Warlords things only deteriorated further. Chiang KaiShek and the KuoMingTang were strongly linked with the Shanghai mafia.

It was only the Communists who managed to instil some higher moral character into China's administration. But the Cultural Revolution opened the floodgates again as the Maoists, who emerged at the top of the heap, believed their loyalty to Maoist Thought entitled them to privileges, power and illicit luxuries. Now, with the economic reforms it's been the Communist Party leadership and their relatives who have been in the best positions to take advantage – and have wasted no time in doing so.

Anger about rampant corruption, not a push for democracy was the catalyst for the Tiananmen Square demonstrations in 1989, but the democratic movement was so thoroughly crushed that now, for the young in China, political reform is a closed avenue for their energy and idealism. The only cause for which the government will let them struggle is that of making themselves rich. And hopefully in the frenzy, nobody will realize how well-off their masters are.

One of our ex-students, Da Xiong, came back to see us last night. An intelligent and pretty girl, whose family were from Yuncheng itself, and not the surrounding villages.

She was one of six students from the entire province who had managed to upgrade in mid-course to the university at Linfen. She was an open-minded girl, and I remembered that at English Corner she had spoken out against the One-Child Policy.

'So have you got a boyfriend?' we joked with her.

'No, I have not, I am too young, and I don't really like Chinese boys. None of them interest me. If I get a boyfriend, then I must get married. You see, I want to leave Shanxi, and maybe do postgraduate study in law or something. You know, I was very happy when I was your student,' she said, and while she spoke she nervously twiddled her fingers. 'When I was a student here, there was gossip, you know. Our form teacher would shout and criticize us for coming to see you. Now it's all right, I can come whenever I want.'

She asked us then about how we spent our free time. 'I have much free time now,' she told us, a little bemused. 'I don't know what to do with it. Here my life was studying. Now I don't have to study so hard, I don't know what to do.'

'Well, what are your hobbies?' I asked.

'I don't have any really,' she said. 'I have always studied hard.'

This is quite a sad but common predicament. When Chinese children reach the age of about ten they no longer play outside like the younger ones. They are pushed so hard at school that there is no time for irrelevant activities that do not bring in marks or money.

It was a shame to see a bright and lively girl who simply did not know how to amuse or enjoy herself in her spare time. Spare time was a phenomenon she couldn't remember having.

At this stage in their lives many students got married – the next step after school or college.

Da Xiong told us about one of her classmates who had taken the English name Anthony. He had graduated from Yuncheng at the same time as she had gone to Linfen. He was full of confidence and pride, with his career as a teacher ahead of him.

'He came from a very poor village and thought it was a great honour to return to his school and become a teacher there. For him, teaching was "The Most Glorious Profession Under the Sun". But not so now. He is very disappointed. The school is very rural, the conditions are very bad and the children do not want to learn. There is a conflict between the headmaster and the deputy head. Sometimes they fight each other with fists in front of the children. He was very ashamed.'

She left us then, promising to come and see us when she was visiting her parents again. She never did.

With true Chinese practicality, the college authorities announced today that DaiYu was a 'Model Student.'

She came around to our flat to tell us the good news – an act that for the last year-and-a-half had earned her severe criticism.

'*Tianle* – heavens! It is very funny. I was so surprised. Oh! I am so happy!'

This unusual switch in the college's attitude came about because last week DaiYu, one of two students representing our college, came eighth in a provincial English speech competition. She was the only contestant who wasn't studying English, many of the others coming from universities rather than colleges. This presented the college with a problem; they were vilifying a girl who obviously had excelled in learning a foreign language in her spare time (which the president had recently become keen on) whilst studying electronics as well. She had even beaten the other contestant from the college who studied English full-time, and was thus the best English-speaking student in the college. Such a student was to be held up as a shining example to her comrades.

'The college said I was a glorious example of what a student should be!'

'Well done, DaiYu!' I said, laughing. Then a thought occurred to me: 'I hope that doesn't mean all the girls in the college will think they can come visiting now, "to improve their oral English"!'

Yesterday we had a phone call from Ling Zhen. He had come around last week to introduce us to his fiancée, a pretty girl who seemed unable to speak so overcome was she to be in the presence of two foreigners.

'Come and visit my bar,' he said. 'Now I have a new one. It is not as near to Hedong Square, but the rent is cheaper. It's opposite the post office on Liberation Road – you'll know it when you see it.'

We did – a shop with the doors standing open and the light from within spilling out into the warm evening over the pavement where some garden furniture had been set out. We sat at one of these tables and were soon joined by Ling Zhen with three glasses of beer.

'So, is business here better than in the square?'

'I don't know really – I've only been open a week. But at the moment the weather isn't hot enough. It has to be really hot so that people can't sleep at night and have to walk the streets to cool down – and walk into my shop!' he laughed.

'There certainly seem to be a lot of people around here,' I said.

'Yes,' Ling Zhen said, looking from side to side. 'You see the buildings to either side of mine, they join up over the top, to make one big brothel.'

At that moment two girls came out of what appeared to be a karaoke bar to the right and went into his shop. The front one looked well-to-do, in skirt and high heels and more than a few *yuan*'s worth of make-up. She bought some drinks and returned inside, after giving us a long look.

'She's the matron,' Ling Zhen told us, sitting down again. 'She's the one in charge of the girls. They come from all the nearby countryside. All of them "worn-out shoes", easily used and thrown away.'

'So who works the shop during the day?'

'I do.'

'But don't you work at the unit still?'

'Yes, but there's never really anything to do. Every once in a while we have to work very hard, but not at the moment.'

'So are you going to sell hamburgers?'

He gave me a serious look. 'You want to put me out of business?'

Where else would you expect to have afternoon tea than in deepest China? It was something I had never had before, but so far from home I was determined to enjoy it.

Li DongPing, the department teacher who had invited us, spread out some dates, local sweets and cakes, and then put on a tape of classical music, 'To create a good environment,' she said, and sat down.

'So where are your husband and son?' Mario asked.

'My son is at his kindergarten all day now, a special private kindergarten that is better than the college one. The teachers there are specially trained to teach children. These teachers have much knowledge, they're really nice. The kindergarten is appended to a teachers' college so they are all well trained.'

'So, what's wrong with the college kindergarten?'

'Oh yeah. The teachers are really bad. If the children are inside, they want them outside. If they are outside, then they want them in the classroom. They often scold the children – "What are you doing? Stop it, that's bad!" – this kindergarten is good, they have parents' meetings often,' she laughed.

'So how much do you pay?' Mario asked, choosing one of the favourite Chinese topics – money.

'Oh. Very expensive. Just to get an invite for my child I must pay five hundred *yuan* and then each month I must pay fifty *yuan* extra.'

That's a lot, as she only gets 400 *yuan* a month. 'So, what do they teach your child?'

'Calculations. Chinese characters. How to say – morals –

230

moral education. They can also say simple English words, "hand, nose, eyes", and paper cutting. But it's mainly play. I had fun at kindergarten when I was a child. Mine was a factory kindergarten, so it was much richer than others. Kindergartens in the countryside maybe not so good.'

Private kindergartens? What would Chairman Mao think of this? I'd heard of a German lady setting up a private infant school in the capital of Shanxi – Taiyuan – but I was surprised how quickly these things spread. Private education is not priced to be widely available – half its appeal to Chinese society is its exclusivity, but it's here to stay.

'How is your clinic going?' Li DongPing also ran a clinic specializing in herbal medicine.

'Just so-so. Better in the winter. You see, people's illnesses are seasonal, we call it *danji*. But it's a kind of income.'

'Are you making a profit or not?'

'Yes, though the position of the clinic is not so good. No traffic. In the city would be better. Our customers are students, and students are not so rich, so we must make it very cheap for them. You know, there are eleven other clinics between here and the first crossroads, so we must be very competitive, very cheap.'

'Have some tea,' she told us.

'Thank you,' I said.

'You're welcome,' she replied awkwardly.

'Could I have a top-up as well?' asked Mario.

'Top-up – what's a top-up? Ah, top-up – finish it? No? Oh – fill-up, yeah, I know. Now, my husband is thinking of doing some simple operations at the clinic, as he is a surgeon. He works very hard, you know. He is quite good, he doesn't go off drinking or playing *mahjong* and losing money. He stays at the clinic all the time. I only see him at night and at mealtimes. His dream is to have his own hospital. It is only a dream, when we will be rich.'

'You know, during my last holiday in the places that foreign backpackers visit, now they also have a few ultra-rich Chinese couples there,' I said, and told her a little about the young, rich mainland Chinese tourists that I had witnessed on my travels.

'Yeah, if you are an official, then I think you can be bribed. Bribery is very, very – you can't imagine, I think. Just as in January the head of the Education Bureau died. Before he died, his son got married, and people promised him 110,000 *yuan* because his father was the Head of the Education Bureau. But just days after the wedding, his father died and so people only gave him 30,000 *yuan*. It was bribery. When he is alive, then the son is useful, so he is promised 110,000 *yuan*. Then days later he dies, and the son only gets 30,000 *yuan*.'

'Was this the head of Shanxi Provincial Education Bureau?'

'No – Yuncheng! Just Yuncheng! You see, there is a great difference between the officials. If you always live like the people, then you will never become rich. If we get a hospital, then our dreams will come true – and we will become rich.' She laughed a short, bitter laugh at hearing her dream spoken aloud.

CHAPTER THIRTEEN

Marriage, Chinese Style

中國傳統婚姻

DaiYu came around today with her new boyfriend – a good-looking young student who is deadly serious about being an artist. We were leaving for our summer holidays the next day – a long-awaited spell away from the constant attention, to meet up with friends who came out to China with me, explore the more beautiful nooks of the country, eat in Westernised cafés in towns on the backpacker trails – just to get away from it all.

DaiYu had now graduated, and as a goodbye present, she bought some plain T-shirts on which her boyfriend would paint a design of our choosing for us. Mario chose a familiar symbol from Chinese *chop* (personal seals used on documents), an antlered deer on a red background. And what should I choose? For me it could only be the character '*Kè.*'

Mario had persevered at his Chinese character learning; he had been ensnared by the beauty and composition of the strokes, but I'd never been hooked. In fact, at my present rate of learning I would have died before I could read a newspaper. But one character did enchant me – *Kè*. It's hard to describe why to people unfamiliar with Chinese characters, but it has something to do with the order, style and composition of strokes that build towards the final character. However '*Kè*' means 'a quarter of an hour', which isn't particularly deep, so I searched my dictionary for a more inspiring meaning – something more esoteric. But it doesn't really have any such depth – so, a quarter of an hour it'd have to be.

DaiYu's boyfriend studiously painted on the composite strokes – each in a certain order and in a delicate style. He had had an offer from another Yuncheng graduate to go up to Beijing to copy pictures to sell to tourists, but he didn't want to do this – it wasn't real art, he told us. There were so many vague opportunities for them both now, but nothing tangible. The only definite thing they could do would be to go off to their local middle schools and become teachers for the rest of their lives, which they refused to do. Anything else was uncertain.

It was a choice that faced all my students too, but I felt more for DaiYu. For someone like her to spend her life in a rural backwater would be a terrible waste, it would be like burying her alive. For centuries China's population has been her greatest strength, but with 1.2 billion now, China can afford to waste the lives of many DaiYus. I felt she couldn't afford to waste a single one.

We went out for a meal and treated them to a mini-banquet. Walking back to the college we stopped at the top of Hedong Donglu. There was a sad moment as we said goodbye – until next time – then headed our separate ways.

It was a warm evening and Dean Wu was sitting on the pavement with some older members of the college – all in vests and shorts, debating something passionately. They didn't see us in the warm evening gloom, and we slipped back to the flat.

I couldn't imagine how any of my students must have been feeling as they readied to leave Yuncheng to return to their insular communities, far from the opportunities of the economic powerhouses of eastern China. But DaiYu had been so central to our lives here, I wondered what it would be like without her, her calls, her ready supply of friends and her patient willingness to help us with our life here. I felt almost that we had come of age now – our Chinese was good and we could handle ourselves suitably in Chinese life, so our keeper was no longer required. But we were never short of keepers here – it was her friendship I'd miss.

*

I'd been back from my spring holidays a month and, as I began my final term here, I found that the routine of life hadn't altered much. Students told me about their holidays: a few went to visit relatives in Taiyuan or ShangHai – one even had a brother who was a pilot for China Airways and so flew for the first time – but for most of them it had been a holiday of working in the fields. One mature student told me how he spent every night sleeping in his family's fields because as the summer heat intensified water became increasingly scarce and access to the irrigation channels had to be severely rationed. Each farmer in their village had two hours a day and his two hours came in the early hours of the morning. He seemed quite satisfied though, so I presume it wasn't a disastrous harvest for his family.

Although life seemed to have continued in pretty much the same way over the holidays, every time I left Yuncheng and then came back, I was always struck by the changes that had taken place. Now, stepping onto the rickshaw that would take me from the station to the college, I noticed that something quite extraordinary had happened. Usually, there was a new shop here or there with a sign in neon lights, a piece of land cleared for development, or a new building seemingly grown out of the ground in a fortnight, but this time it was a bit more fundamental. All the shacks, shops and houses that had grown up along the roadside had been demolished. Flattened.

'What's happened?' I asked my rickshaw driver.

'Road-widening,' he said as he panted up the long, slow incline to the college. 'Modern road.'

It was difficult to get anything more out of him, but a mature student did give me more information.

'It's a road-widening scheme – the authorities want to give the city modern roads. They tell us that it is important for the image of the city if we want to attract modern investment. But now they have run out of money.'

There were people at the end of Hedong Donglu who were still moving the rubble away brick by brick to rebuild their homes someplace else.

'But what about the people who had shacks there?' I asked.

'Most of the homes were illegal. People from the countryside came and built them,' she said.

'I do not agree with it,' a friend told me. 'It is just another expensive scheme – a waste of money. All those shops destroyed, and now nothing happens. It is just like the Communist Party headquarters – why do they need such a large building? They are greedy men who are just making themselves rich.'

This all seemed very reasonable, but another student told me something different, so I didn't know the truth – and nor, I think, did they. I was quite intrigued as to what might happen to all these itinerant shops and traders when they were moved on, but they seemed to have recovered well, just relocating around the city, and new traders took their places on the broad pavements – in tents this time, but very much there nonetheless.

One thing we had to do now we were back was to congratulate QunXia, our Chinese teacher. Over the holiday, she had taken the plunge and got married. Marriages seem to take place at very short notice in China – just before we'd left she'd announced her wedding, to take place four weeks later.

She'd met her husband – her first boyfriend – when she was twenty-four years old. He was one year older than her, and we would see them occasionally on a Saturday evening, going off to a dancehall with a few friends, he cycling and she sitting on the back of the bicycle.

For a long time she didn't know if they would get married or not, as he had never mentioned the subject, and obviously it was not something that a girl could bring up. Before he did, eventually, they had been dating for a year and a half – which is a long time to be involved with someone and not get married in China.

She had stopped teaching us now, but last night we went round to their flat, which is in a block near the sports field normally reserved for unmarried teachers. Single people slept three to a room, so QunXia and her husband were lucky to get one of the rooms to themselves.

The block itself was a decrepit affair, dirty, dusty, with

blocked toilets and no working lighting. There were four floors, with long, draughty corridors running the whole length of the building, and off these forty or so rooms. The corridors were dark and littered with all kinds of refuse, but in the private rooms everything was spotlessly clean.

In QunXia's room there was a large double bed, a pair of brand new wardrobes, a dressing table, a sofa and a TV. All the upholstery was red, red cushions, curtains and bedsheets. The walls were adorned with red paper cuts that would give good luck and fertility to the couple.

Married life seemed to be suiting QunXia very well. She had assumed the role of hostess and wife so effortlessly that it appeared her life up to this moment had merely been a preparation for it. She invited us in and sat us down. We asked her about the wedding and she told us all about it and showed us the video.

The noise from the TV, which was put on the minute we appeared, made it difficult to make conversation. This evening NBA basketball, very popular in China and shown every night on prime-time TV, was on.

'Black men,' QunXia said. '*Aiyyya!* They're so big. Black men are good at sports, but are not very intelligent. They're always having wars, aren't they? Dark skin is not good. In China we have a saying – A good wife must have three things: she must be faithful, she must be hard-working, she must have white skin. If she doesn't have white skin, then she's no good, if she does then the other two don't matter,' QunXia continued.

I sensed a slight change in her now she was in charge of a household. Before, she had been interested in life outside China, but now that she was a wife, and hopefully soon a mother, her attitudes had shifted. Now she was a Chinese matron – prejudiced against things and people not in her family or circle of friends. She was the centre of the family and thinking was her husband's job. It is always a shame to listen to a friend saying things not worthy of them – and I wished QunXia had not spoken.

I'd heard nothing about Song Jiang since returning, except

that, like Duan Yu, who was in Taiyuan, he was in Xian on 'business'. That was unofficial, of course; officially both were on sick leave. It really meant that they were off making money while they were supposed to be here teaching – I think having good *guanxi* with someone high up must have helped.

Li DongPing speculated about what would happen to Song Jiang. 'The college will have to tell him to come back and teach. If he refuses to teach, then they will have to offer him another job. But they cannot sack him as he is in the work unit.'

They seemed to be the only two people I knew making any money from entrepreneurial activities.

This afternoon I had a surprise visit from an old student, Jia MeSi, who had been in her last year when we arrived. She was dressed in quite modern clothes, and her powdered face, bobbed black hair and scarlet lipstick gave her a glamorous look. As I remembered, she had good English and was quite an extrovert.

'So how are you doing?' I asked, getting her a cup of tea.

'So-so,' she said. 'I teach in a village near Yuncheng – but I do not like it. The students are not very clever. Everyone there are peasants.'

'Have you kept in touch with any of your classmates?' I asked.

'No.' She gave me a long look. 'No. I am too ashamed of my position. I do not want them to know I am badly off.

'Do you remember Li Yun?' she asked suddenly. 'I have heard that she now has a foreign boyfriend. It is very common at her university.' She gave me a very direct look. After a pause she continued. 'Mario tells me you have a girlfriend,' she said.

'Yes, she's a teacher in Taiyuan,' I said.

She chewed something over in her mind, but remained silent.

'Do you have a boyfriend?' I asked.

'No,' she said. There was a long pause as I felt her eyes bore into me. 'You know – we always used to think you were very

238

handsome,' she said. 'Are you interested in having a Chinese girlfriend?'

'No, not really. Thank you,' I said, appalled.

She left soon after, and I went in to have a talk with Mario.

'You know, I have a feeling that she just offered herself to me,' I said, still stunned.

'Yes, she did the same with me – all that stuff about foreigners and Chinese girls, how handsome you are – poor girl.'

Without DaiYu, we had been taking ourselves out alone, and now we seemed to be meeting new friends quite often. One of them was Shi Jin.

We'd first met him two weeks ago at Dean Wu's daughter's wedding. He was part of the groom's entourage who had come to pick up the bride from her house and take her to the wedding ceremony. We were Dean Wu's photographers and Shi Jin was the groom's. In fact everyone with the groom seemed to have some kind of device for recording the wedding day. The groom worked at YCTV Station, and so one of his friends, a cameraman, came, together with sound recordist, director and Shi Jin.

Before they could come to get the bride, however, the dowry had to be collected, and this Dean Wu's son did, bringing back the requisite bedsheets, suitcases, TV and washing machine on the back of a van.

The Party secretary – Li ShuJi – wrote the names of everyone who came, and alongside them how much each person gave, in a red wedding book. He and another man cross-checked the money in a cloud of cigarette smoke.

The flat soon filled up with relatives, children, friends of the bride, and neighbours, all waiting for the groom.

When the groom's party did arrive they were taken to a side room and fed according to local custom, while the bride, who had been casually chatting to the guests in jeans and a T-shirt, went to change into a red bridal jacket and skirt. After she was dressed and photographed eating *jiaozi* – the last meal she would take at her home – she was then locked in the room with her friends and mother.

The groom had to rescue her, paying money at each stage of the proceedings: to unlock the door, to open it, to enter, and to get out again. This was not a nice formal ceremony, but involved pushing, shoving, trapped fingers and hard bargaining. The amount of money he paid reflected how much he valued his bride. It took him forty minutes to get his bride and get out of the flat. Forty minutes and 470 *yuan*. The best part of a month's wages for him, to be given to the bride's family.

It was generally agreed that he had been very tight with his money, but to have given too much might mean that the bride's family would try and get more off him in future.

It was during this long débâcle that we chatted to one of the bride's friends. An old classmate of hers, now an English teacher in a countryside school.

'So when will you get married?' I asked her.

'I am twenty-four now. My marriage was arranged for me when I was twelve. I will marry this year,' she told us.

'Do you know how the happy couple met?'

'They were introduced to each other by a matchmaker. It is always a matchmaker. Even in love marriages, they are first introduced to each other by matchmakers. This is still the only way young people can meet.'

A Chinese friend who was already thirty and still unmarried explained the problems he had in meeting suitable girls. 'If I see a girl and I like her, and she likes me, still there is a problem. If I go up and introduce myself and ask her to talk to me, she will think I am too forward. Maybe she will think I am a bad man. Instead, I must find someone to introduce her to me. That's the only way we can meet. The problem is, I don't like the girls my family knows, or they don't like me.'

He was quite well off so he shouldn't really have had a problem at all. For poorer men it is more difficult – and bound to get increasingly so, as the One-Child Policy created a huge shortfall in female babies. Experts reckon that there will soon be a thirty million deficit of brides in China – the entire female population of Britain. In the richer parts of China, a woman from a poorer province can be purchased more cheaply than a local girl, so the slave trade in young girls is becoming a problem.

As we were talking, Shi Jin introduced himself. He came up and said, 'Hello.' Then, 'Can I be your friend?'

For Westerners this would, of course, be seen as quite a ridiculous way for adults to begin a friendship. We believe that friendships should develop over time, but in China things are done with more formality; friendships and business blur, friends are *guanxi* – they can incur costs as well as giving benefits. So it doesn't do to mix with people less powerful than yourself; they won't be able to help you, but will want more favours.

It seemed a callous attitude at the time – and it's something I still don't fully understand. Older Chinese people complain that young people don't know how to make close friends – not as close as they made – but then old people everywhere say that kind of thing. Other people have told me that it's because of the Cultural Revolution, when everyone betrayed everyone else, so people aren't seen as trustworthy any more; some say it's because of the strength of the family structure; others have blamed the economic reforms, saying that each person is out for himself. I don't think I will ever really understand – my view of the Chinese and friendship has been entirely skewed by the fact I am a foreigner – but I have a feeling the situation isn't as bad as the moaners make out.

Not being Chinese and not being used to this kind of question, though, I was at a bit of a loss – I mean, how can you answer a question like 'Can I be your friend?' A straight 'no' was out of the question so I smiled and said, 'Yes, of course.'

Despite its inauspicious beginnings our new friendship turned out to be everything we hadn't expected. Quiet, calm, Shi Jin was quite the nineteenth-century Chinese gentleman.

Not long after we'd first met, Shi Jin telephoned us and invited us around to his house. Once inside, and after the initial questions and drinks, he showed us his calligraphy. He was in an international *Who's Who* of the art. He and his teacher both studied CaoShu calligraphy – a flowing style of writing started by a Ming dynasty scholar four hundred years ago.

He had two pieces on the wall, thin strips of paper each with a descending swirl of Chinese characters. He told us what they meant, reading the characters in *putonghua*, the clear punchy singsong sounds of literary Chinese.

Then he showed us how he painted, his brushes, his *chops* – seals made from jade with all the different inscriptions on them – explaining everything in measured tones.

Next he got out his *erhu* for us, a two-stringed violin-sized instrument that is cradled in the lap, and played a piece from Mongolia. The piercing high notes tumbling down in melancholy scales made me feel that I could almost be on the bleak, windswept steppes.

Zhu Gui was a very able student who graduated a year ago now. Tall and good-looking, he was a fluent English conversationalist and was quite unlucky to have the classmates he did. With interested fellows he could have become even better. His father was an educated peasant, and with the help of his extended family he was paying 2,000 *yuan* a year to go to the college. Although his English was by far the best in his year he had failed politics in his college entrance exams. As college entrance requirements in China require students to pass all their exams, and then they decide which subject each student will study, Zhu Gui was unable to continue in state education, and had to pay for his further education privately. He was quite unusual in that he had paired up with a female student called Li XiYan as self-chosen *duixiang* – formal boyfriend and girlfriend. They were together almost always outside lesson time. I hardly ever spoke to Li XiYan, though; outside class she was a peasant girl through and through, deferential and quiet. Although a shade paler than me she was quite adamant: 'I am yellow, you are white. White is beautiful, I am ugly.' Whenever I met Zhu Gui, Li XiYan would drop five paces behind and follow at a polite distance.

We had high hopes for Zhu Gui, so when I met him after he had disappeared for a while I said to him, 'I haven't seen you for a long time, what have you been doing?'

He said nothing.

'Are you alright?'

'No. I have lost all my ambitions. I have no aims. Can I come and see Mario and you, can you give me an aim in life?'

I said, 'Yes, you must.'

He didn't, but after graduation Zhu Gui did indeed do well, getting a good job in Tianjing, translating. One night, quite out of the blue, he telephoned us.

'I saw the sea for the first time. My heart was in my mouth. It was so big and grey. So beautiful, but unfortunately Li XiYan's parents said that I must return home or I could not marry her, so I returned home and now we are married.'

'It's a shame about the job, but congratulations on your marriage! So what are you doing with yourself now?' I asked, down the crackly local phone line.

'Oh – I do nothing.'

'How is your wife? You must be very happy together!'

'Ah, yeah. I don't see her too often. She is working at a middle school near her home. She really enjoys teaching. I think she is a good teacher. She is very kind, you know, and she loves her students.'

I was very pleased that he had gone to the rich east and managed to get a good job, but it was so frustrating that he had had to give it up in order to get married and was now doing nothing.

Towards the end of our time in China, Song Wan, our friend from Middle School No 2, came round to give us a leaving present, a set of Chinese opera masks – bearded faces painted in bold colours with extravagant expressions. He explained the meanings of the colours.

'The faces with a majority of black,' he said, 'show the character is principled. This one – mainly white – is CaoCao, a crafty man not to be trusted. Green means loyal and honest, blue means valiant and irritable.

'Those with horns are warriors, without are civilians. The beards also have a meaning, white beards represent old people, and red or black means they are fighters.'

I thanked him, and I asked him if his school would be

following the new government ruling that China was to have a five-day working week, not six, as before.

It was a long-standing joke amongst the foreign teachers that what a Western worker could do in five days, it took at least six for a Chinese worker. Though I think that was being generous to some of the Chinese workers that I knew. I had asked Dean Wu the same question a while before.

'Oh, yes, surely!' he'd said, getting quite excited at the idea.

'Will that mean doing more lessons during the week to make up?' I asked.

'No. No,' he said, looking a little unnerved by the suggestion. Later it was decided to wait until a fresh term started rather than to disrupt the present one.

A similar decision had been taken at Song Wan's school.

'So what will you do with yourself when you do get a full weekend?'

'I want to travel. There are many places around this area that are disappearing. There were some marshes near Yuncheng that were very beautiful. They have been developed. I think I would like to go to YongJi. There there are trees, scenery, mountains and a waterfall.'

'So things are getting better for you, do you think?'

'I hope so. This year we have had many worries, but I hope life will get better.'

This morning we had a surprise phonecall from DaiYu, all the way down in GuanZhou – Canton. The last time I had seen her was when she graduated without a job, or without any idea of what she'd do with herself.

'Hello, Big Brother, it's me – DaiYu! Oh, yes, I'm having such a good time; there are so many foreigners here – English, French, Americans. There are parties here every night, and music – such good music! Why did you never tell me about your country's popular bands? Queen, Beatles, The Clash – Oh! I have learnt so much here.

'I have a friend, he is Jewish, and he is called Esra Jones. You know, he is not very happy, but he is very funny. He is teaching me about human rights, it is very interesting.

'You know – I am learning French too. The Frenchmen here are very romantic – and last week I earned 500 *yuan* interpreting for them at a trade fair. We drove through town with loud music, and they were all singing – it was just crazy! They are so wild! They gave me money, and I said no but they gave it to me anyway. It is nothing, they said, and gave me 500 *yuan* for just one day. Crazy!'

'So what else are you doing down there?'

'I have started working for a translating firm – they give me 1,200 *yuan* each month, but it isn't very interesting. At first I didn't like it here – the people are very rude and they're only interested in money. I can't understand what they're saying, you know, I think they sound like they're always cursing each other.

'Hello? Big Brother – you know, I think I must go now, my boss is here. Give Mario my love. Bye!'

The line went dead, and I went to get some water for a cup of tea, feeling more than a little envious of DaiYu and her exciting life of parties and foreigners; and, I being catacombed here in Yuncheng, feeling more isolated than ever.

I had a letter from Zhu Gui this morning, to say how pleased he had been to talk to me on the phone – and that his wife has had a baby.

He wrote:

Life has been more hectic since our great gift. Everything made by him seems so fresh and exciting. But I got busier than before. Although I'm busy, I still spend time to learn English and listen to the BBC every day, in order to catch more chances of high-paid work. Now, I feel the burden of feeding the family on my shoulders. Maybe my dream will come true in 1997? [I found it difficult to know how to react to such a letter – it's capacity for hope was phenomenal and made me feel old and cynical.] There's another thing that we are very sorry for – we didn't invite you nor Mario to attend our marriage ceremony. But actually, we only had five days to prepare for our marriage in a typical Chinese way after XiYan's mother stopped opposing us. Now XiYan calls it 'All-in-Rush Marriage', 'And Full-of-Pity One', I add.

Now, I become very interested in the people from different countries –
the way they think, the way they live ... What I'm longing for is to
continue learning in some famous university abroad. But it seems not so
easy to go abroad now in China. How can I get to go abroad to a
university to learn? Is it so difficult to go abroad as people say? Would
you give me some pieces of advice? I'm longing for your answer.

Yours sincerely,

Zhu Gui & Xi Yan

*

Shi Jin, our new friend, managed to look both surprised and
pleased to see us, then ushered us in. There was a little fumbling
over the scarves, hats and gloves but, thankfully, no excessive
physical force. Nor did he pester us to our seats but gently
asked us to be seated.

Tonight, as I relaxed, I found that I'd been missing this quiet
little man over the last few weeks. He had a diminutive body,
that looked like that of a six-year-old sitting in his father's
armchair, his slight frame carefully positioned in the middle of
a seat whose back and sides seemed to tower up around him.

We nodded and smiled at each other, and then the evening
began with him questioning us about our travels during the
holidays.

'We Chinese, we do not like travel,' he said firmly. 'People
say that they have neither the money nor opportunity, which
is true, but when China was much richer than your Western
countries, we didn't like travel either.'

'Tell me,' he said, turning to the TV – while we had been
talking he had been flicking through the channels, studying
our reactions to see which we found most pleasing – 'How
many channels do you have in your countries?'

I told him four. This pleased him, as China, though a
developing country, had more than Britain. He said, 'In the
daytime we have three. In the evening we have thirteen. We
have four national channels, and also each province has their
own channel. This is our Yuncheng Television.'

Yuncheng TV came on for about one hour a night, just after
the seven PM news and weather, showing us local news and
adverts. At the moment an official was reading from the newly

released *Collected Works of Deng XiaoPing*. The cameraman panned in and out to make this – a man sitting behind a desk, reading badly, with stops to cough up phlegm and reread bits – more interesting. It didn't really work, although I was glued to the TV to see whether the man would spit or not.

'Oh. Have you seen these pictures before? I think you will like these,' Shi Jin said, flicking through the channels and handing over a wad of 3-D pictures. 'Here, this is the most beautiful,' he said, giving me a picture which, with the most unfocused look I could manage, turned into two wolves howling at the moon. After we had exhausted his supply of 3-D pictures, he asked us if we could sing. I hated being asked to sing – not only was it embarrassing, but it was made worse when someone cracked up at my Chinese, or because English sounded silly to them. But the Chinese loved to perform when they went out, and karaoke was becoming increasingly popular.

'No.'

'No.'

'I can,' he said, as he shut the front door so that the lock clicked, then he sat down and plugged his microphone into his midi system and switched it to karaoke mode.

Was this the learned Chinese gentleman I knew? I'd expected a pleasant evening as Shi Jin uncovered pearls of Chinese wisdom before our eyes. Instead, he'd turned into a gadget monster.

Mario and I didn't know what to do as Shi Jin, calm as anything, selected his favourite backing tracks on a tape of keyboard music, and then serenaded us with the lights down low.

I tried acting like a Chinese audience. I ignored him and ate some sweets and peanuts from the coffee table in front of me, but it didn't work – whether he cared or not I felt guilty for being so rude. But try as I might, I couldn't look a man in the eye who was singing love songs to me. I watched the speakers instead, and pretended it was a normal tape I was listening to. But the speakers were gruesome in their own way. They had concentric rings of LEDs that pulsed in and out with the strength of the music. The flashing circles exploding from the

247

centre, like starbursts, with each consonant were unpleasantly compelling and even hypnotic. Only a truly deviant mind could have designed this monstrosity.

He sang us two songs, but then couldn't put the microphone down and started talking to us through it. It was like sitting in your living room chatting to a PA system. We were eventually persuaded to sing, or rather Mario said, 'Yes, Justin likes singing . . .' and I returned the favour.

'Thank you. Very good,' Shi Jin announced into the mike, before at last putting it down. Then he rewound the tape and listened to our singing, which he had recorded. I knew our dreadful efforts would soon be circulated throughout his wide circle of friends and relatives, and any foreigners who ever came to Yuncheng would have to disprove the idea that English and Spanish people cannot sing. Having caught us on tape he seemed happy to put the thing away, and he sat back.

'If I went to England what could I do as a job?' he asked.

'I think you would have to learn English, then maybe you could teach calligraphy. You see, very few people in England can speak *putonghua* – standard Chinese. Even the Chinese immigrants in England can only speak Cantonese,' I told him.

'I think when you can understand this TV,' he said, flicking channels again, 'then your Chinese would be perfect. To learn Chinese properly, though, I think you must start learning with children and work upwards with them. That way, in maybe six years, your Chinese would be quite good. See, can you understand this?' he asked, passing over his daughter's comic book, age range four to six.

I didn't, although Mario could understand most of it.

Mario and he carried on chatting about something I didn't really understand, so I looked through his coffee table magazines. Some Singapore Airlines magazines were laid out ostentatiously for everyone to see. Travelling abroad is a real achievement in a country where getting a passport can take years, with no guarantee of success. Shi Jin had never been abroad, but his father had visited Taiwan and Singapore for what he described as 'cultural meetings'. There was an arts magazine from Taiwan, a place that looked much more exciting than mainland China, and a book entitled *Fifty Historical Cities of China*. I found all the ones that were in Shanxi province, but got a little bored and turned to watch the TV.

Yuncheng TV had gone off the air after its hour, and one of the four national channels was now broadcasting a drama about some youths sent to the countryside during the Cultural Revolution. One boy happened to chance upon a girl washing in the river. A topless girl – viewed from the rear, soft focus, with the glare of the sun upon the water as she romantically splashed diamonds of water into the air. This was quite a risky shot for China, and was quite the sauciest thing I'd seen for two years.

Unfortunately, the storyline was a little more banal – *Swallows and Amazons* in the Cultural Revolution. The two love birds ended up getting stranded in the woods overnight, he saving her from shivering to death and she forgiving him for being a peeping Tom. They had fallen passionately in love by the morning, and after a quick snog there was a joyous celebration amongst all their friends when they were found.

'I have a collection of badges from the Cultural Revolution,' Shi Jin interrupted, and took out an old brown envelope and emptied it out onto the table. Thirty badges of assorted sizes appeared, all bearing the profile of Chairman Mao on a red background. Some had details such as a peasant hut, a space rocket, or factory in silver added along the bottom, but otherwise they were fairly identical.

'Whoever made these must have made a lot of money,' I said.

'They weren't sold, they were given to the work units, who gave them to their people. Everyone had three or four pinned onto them, and at home they would keep a bigger one for looking at in the morning.'

We inspected them. Most had been made in Yuncheng, and on the reverse side behind the head of Mao they had a joined character meaning 'Chairman Mao in the middle of our hearts'.

Next came Shi Jin's coin collection, varying from a Han dynasty coin made in 220 BC, to a 1994 Mao Centenary coin.

I had always believed that old coins had a hole in them to allow them to be strung around the neck. But Shi Jin explained, 'This shows the relationship between earth and sky. The sky is square, so the hole in the middle is square; the earth is round so the coin is round.'

He collected lots of little things, money ration books for food, bicycles and TVs, and showed us them all until it was time to leave. He walked us to the compound gates, which at ten-thirty had been shut, and as we cycled off down the road he stood and lit our way between the houses with his torch.

Tonight, we had a pleasant surprise: Song Jiang phoned us.

'Hi. Justin? How are you? Are you busy? Come over for a coffee!'

We were there within ten minutes, and Song Jiang was standing on his balcony waiting for us.

'So will you be teaching here or not?' I asked. Song Jiang had been offered a teaching job in a private school in Taiyuan, but the authorities had, thus far, refused to let him go.

'Ah. You know, I will see the president tonight to discuss things.' Song Jiang smiled.

'And what will he say? Will he let you go?'

'I will give him – bribe. I think a few hundred *yuan* should be enough. A friend has told me that the president is quite friendly towards me and won't give me too much trouble. I went to see him last night at his house but he wasn't in. You see, the college gives me a flat, salary, pension, my whole life, so I cannot leave it. I would be giving up too much.'

'So what are you going to do now?'

'Last November my friends in Taiyuan telephoned me. Their school was expecting a visit from the principal of an American school, so I disappeared from here and reappeared in Taiyuan. My job was to arrange everything and translate, and all that kind of work. My friends kept getting in touch with me, and they found me very useful.

'The school is a private school. It is called South Pacific International School. This is our first term. We have five hundred students, and next term we will expect to have one thousand. Ninety per cent of our students come from very rich families – like managers in the coal industry and top *cadres* (ranks). They all have opportunities to make extra money by corruption. We don't care where their money comes from, we will educate their children to be better than them.'

'So how much does it cost them?'

'They must pay 100,000 *yuan* for their children to stay for however long. The school is a fully boarding school, and everything is paid for – clothes, books, holidays around China and holidays abroad. Our largest class is thirty-six, while in public schools there are fifty or sixty students. The school is owned by the South Pacific Corporation, and that is owned by a Hainan millionaire. He also owns a steel plant in HeJin town near Yuncheng, and many plantations on Hainan Island.'

'A hundred thousand is an astronomical figure! Most people only earn 300 *yuan* a month. This school is pandering to the ultra rich only, isn't it?' I asked. 'And will the trips abroad be free too?'

'No. Families who want to send their children to work abroad must pay 5,000 dollars contact fee. Then they must pay for the flights themselves.'

'That's all very expensive, isn't it?'

'Yes. We are going to make their children Erudite, Bilingual, Self-Improved and Modern.'

'Bilingual?' I said.

'Yes. I teach all our teachers English. Those who don't learn English very well, they do not have such a bright future with us!' he laughed. 'I must go in and check the teachers' quality. So they are all very frightened of me.'

'So will you move up there to live permanently?'

'Yes. The school is not yet quite finished, but when it is I will have a bigger unit than this flat. The school's headmistress is the same age as me. She has had very similar experiences as I have had. In the Cultural Revolution, in teaching.'

'So how are your shares doing?'

'It is said that the Taiyuan Share Index has been superficially boosted by some Taiwanese businessmen. They boosted the Index to over 1,000, then sold everything and the prices dropped. The Index is now only 600. You see, we have no experience, we are fresh to all these things. We must learn the hard way.'

'I notice you have a large cage in the next room. Have you started keeping pets?' I asked.

'Oh, yeah. I have two dogs. They are at my parents-in-law at the moment. I bought them at the height of the Beijing prices at 28,000 *yuan* for two. But now the Beijing government has banned pets in the city and so the price has collapsed. The female is expecting little ones, and I think I will sell them.'

'So is your future bright, Song Jiang?' I asked.

He smiled. 'This year has not been easy. My shares have not done well, we can only wait for them to go up in value. Also, you see, my wife is pregnant.'

'Really! But you already have a son. Won't you lose your job if you have another child?' I asked. Work units were responsible for the number of babies their workers had, and had to keep to strict quotas, and so were very hard on the irresponsible people who went over quota on the baby front. One of our mature students was threatened with the sack when she became pregnant with a second child. The school she worked for tried to persuade her to have an abortion, but she refused.

'No, you see, we have permission from the government to have a second child.'

'Is that easy to get?'

Song Jiang gave a quick laugh, almost like a cough. 'No. Not easy. You must fill out a form to have a second child. You give this to your work unit, and wait.'

'So how did you get permission?'

'There are a number of ways that you can have a second child. If your first child is diseased; if you are a farmer and you have a daughter, then you can try again for a son, because farmers need sons to do the heavy farm work as very few have any machinery at all, and many have no animals; and if you are the only son of an only son, and you have a daughter, you can try again for a son to continue your family line. It was found that my son was diseased when he was two years old –

that he had epilepsy. It troubles him, and we still don't know what effect it will have on him in future life.

'We had to take him to be examined, and then we talked to the college leaders, eventually we were given a one-year certificate – a *ZhunShengZhen* – for a baby. My wife and I – we had to make a baby within one year! You see, the government tries to control the number of babies born each year so each is well balanced. Even for a first child you must have permission. Sometimes people are told to wait until next year to have a child, as this year's quota has run out.'

'Did you need a lot of *guanxi* to get permission?' I asked.

'*Guanxi* is very important. Especially with officials. Even if you have a good reason, you must go and see people if you want to get a quick answer. Many people apply, you see. The officials decide who should have a child first. You're only allowed a second child normally after your first child is more than five years old.'

'Aren't there fines for having a second child illegally?'

'It's not expensive if you have permission. If you don't have permission then you are fined 3,000 *yuan* until the second child is seven years old, then you must pay a yearly fine. But many people think this money is worth losing for an extra child. They say to themselves, "One child may be lost through disease or accident. Then who will look after us when we are old?" They are very worried. After the first has died, then it may be too late to have another child.'

'What about if you have a child, and then get divorced, then marry a childless woman? What happens there?'

'You are only allowed a child if the child doesn't live with you.'

'So what percentage of people in China have a second child, would you say?'

'In the college, less than ten per cent, much less I think. In the cities the number is about five per cent. In the countryside I think more than sixty per cent have another child. They don't have a boy first time, think a girl is no use. Maybe they will give the first child away, or kill it. That is why the government is more tolerant of peasants having two babies.

'Now more and more people are thinking that one child is OK. More than one increases the difficulties and becomes more difficult to support. Now both husband and wife will work, then fewer couples have the time for large families.

'My younger sister, for example, she doesn't want children. She's thirty years old, she thinks a child would be a burden. She wants to work first, and then maybe someday have a child. My family accepts this.

'In the countryside, if they don't get any children after two or three years then they are eager to adopt – to have their own. After that they relax. You see, when they are old then they must depend on their children for support. But even with the One-Child Policy there are too many children, and so fewer opportunities. Education is very important, it is important to go to university. In most schools only very few pupils reach college or university. The teachers prepare the children for education, and marriage, and work. They are not highly paid, and are badly motivated.'

CHAPTER FOURTEEN

Zaijian: Goodbyes

再 見

The phone rang.

'Are you ready?' asked Mr Cao, then put the phone down before I could answer.

Yes, I thought, I was ready.

He must have telephoned from a downstairs flat because I could already hear footsteps and voices echoing up the narrow concrete staircase coming up to our flat.

A quick look into my room, to check everything was in order. I had been preoccupied over the last few weeks with sending boxloads of things home. Two of books, one of videos, clothes, shoes, and all kinds of miscellaneous objects: scrolls, medicine balls, carved chopsticks, opera masks, a Tibetan robe, a sword for my *taiqi* – I had picked up so much in the last two and a half years. Everything I'd bought, bargained for or been given had been posted off to England and awaited me there.

Posting things home, I'd whittled away at all my belongings and acquisitions till all that was left fitted inside my rucksack and a shoulder bag. They sat on top of one another alone in the peculiar emptiness of my bedroom.

It had been a difficult decision about whether to extend my contract here or not. Yuncheng was home to me, but I was missing England and friends so much now that I dreamed only of getting slowly drunk in a pub somewhere over a long conversation.

When it became known that I would be leaving at the end of term, then everyone seemed to open up a bit, and I began to feel that at last I was beginning to get under the shell of Chinese life. But it is easier to say things to people when they're leaving. However long I stayed, I think that I would always be at that point – just about to get there, but never making it.

One regret for me was that I didn't think I had made a life-long friend here. I had been the recipient of a lot of kindness, and given a lot to the people I had met, but I didn't feel I'd made a really close friend. Maybe if I'd stayed longer ... No – I really didn't think I could stay any longer.

Now, just as when I left England so long ago, I was at a bit of a loss. The thought that tomorrow I would be far away from Yuncheng – perhaps never to return – didn't feel real.

Cao and Wu came in and both poked their heads into all the rooms, checking what I'd left. In ten minutes, when I would be on a bus to my train, all my neighbours would be in, ransacking the flat for anything that they thought would be of some use to them. Mrs Bao had already been round for a preview, asking for our oven and washing machine, which I was happy to tell her belonged to the college.

Teaching aids and a library of books for the students had been left for whoever might follow us, and these had been safely locked up.

'Are these all your bags?' Cao asked. He picked one up and I fought Dean Wu for the second one. He seemed strangely subdued today as he smoked his cigarette, and for the first and last time in China I actually won this tussle and remained in possession of the bag. We all followed Cao down the stairs, and I tried to imagine life away from here, back in England – but couldn't.

At the front of the college we were joined by a few students. I thought they'd been appointed by someone in the department to say goodbye, as they weren't really my favourites, and some I wasn't very familiar with at all, but we had in common the fact that we were all leaving Yuncheng: I was bound for England, they back to their villages to seek work, or to take up their appointed teaching posts. I had said goodbye to all my students many times, in an effort to make my leaving seem real.

The drive to the station passed much more quickly than when we'd arrived that first time, the familiar streets passing like a dream as I thought about what was in store for me at home. I'd been like this for weeks: mentally I'd left Yuncheng a long time ago, and now my mind was waiting for my body to follow.

Ling Zhen joined our little gathering on the station platform. Mario and I'd been around to his bar last night for a goodbye drink or two – watching the prostitutes going in and out of the closed doors of the high-class nightclub.

'How's your stomach?' Ling Zhen asked now, grimacing. 'Last night's beer was off – it's given me the shits.'

'Shits?' Me too.

A few group photos, and then the train arrived. Some mature students came dashing up at the last minute, crying, happy to have caught me before the train left – but with tears in their eyes at this overwhelmingly sad moment. They were so emotional at my departure that I wished I could feel the same, but I was just beginning to feel relived that it was almost over. I could see the frustration they felt as their English failed them at this of all moments and I switched to Chinese to say goodbye. They pressed their addresses into my hand and I promised to write. I hugged Mario who was leaving later to return to Spain. There was a sudden flurry of people pushing at the wrong doors to get on, and I struggled through them onto my carriage.

We continued waving as the train moved off unbearably slowly, then picked up speed. Then they were gone. I was suddenly aware of a carriage-load of Chinese peasants staring at me – and sat down quickly.

For a while I was a bit put out that more students hadn't come to say goodbye. Maybe the college asked them not to come – there certainly wouldn't have been room for all two hundred and fifty of them – but I would have liked more of the students I liked to come along. But then I told myself it was time to forget my star-ranking.

Six hours later I was in Xian, a racy modern city compared to Yuncheng. The Bell Tower Hotel had its usual adornment of mis-shapen Western tourists and accompanying beggars, who pleaded and whined and grinned as they waved their stumps in the air. I found myself looking at the French and German OAPs with the critical eye of a Chinese person. To me they all looked too tall, fat, big-nosed, hairy – just like me.

Buying a ticket to GuanZhou was not too much of a problem, and by the afternoon of the next day I was setting out on the forty-six-hour train ride. I was travelling first class – an expensive luxury for my last trip in China – and shared my cabin with three affluent Chinese people. They mistook me for another Western backpacker, and presumed I couldn't speak Chinese, so they didn't even attempt to talk to me, which was rare but nice, as I didn't feel like chatting. One was a Communist Party official; another the wife of one; and the third a stunning lady of thirty-two who was from Xian, but who now worked for a business in Hong Kong. She had just been visiting her husband, a businessman in Xian.

They were a world away from the Chinese people I knew, and spent the day-and-a-half's journey talking about Hong Kong: the people there, the money, the business opportunities, the run-up to 1997. These were the people who would probably make their millions out of Hong Kong, if they hadn't already. Loaded with connections, money, confidence and *guanxi*, they looked like they were from a different country – and were very unfazed at sharing a cabin with a foreigner. They didn't even talk about me, so I couldn't embarrass them by suddenly talking Chinese – and to my surprise I found that I resented this.

The train rumbled slowly through terraced fields dotted with trees, away from the dusty loess plateau into an entirely different China. Over the Yangtse River, through huge grey and polluted cities; along muddy paddyfields with water buffaloes and peasants wearing straw hats, knee deep in mud, and strange domed hills fading into the distance. This was a China that had been familiar to me before I ever set foot in the country, the China of the Westerner's imagination, but a very different China to the one I had lived in.

We arrived in Canton five hours late, and with the shrill of cicadas all around I pushed through the crushing crowds to the exit.

I saw the JUSTIN HILL sign before I saw DaiYu, and she ran up, hugged me and gave me a kiss on the cheek. I had not seen her since she'd left Yuncheng, and she was as I had expected – more modern.

'I thought you'd never come! Luckily I had these nice men to talk to – they were also waiting for a friend, so we waited together.'

She hailed a taxi, and we started driving through Canton – under fly-overs, down five-lane roads, all full of traffic and fumes and the blare of irritated horns. I was speechless as DaiYu talked on and on, until at last we arrived at her road. She paid the driver – she earned more than me now! – and then we walked down a mud road towards some white-tiled flats, while choirs of bullfrogs belched forth from all around.

'The villagers built these flats to rent out. Can you see the old buildings?' I could, tile-roofed compound houses, not unlike those up north, except that the mud here was red, not yellow. 'They still live in those. They have built the flats to rent out.'

'Isn't there any problem with having me stay in your flat?'

'Oh no! There are many foreigners living in the same building too. They're students at the Foreign Language Institute.'

I got quite excited at the prospect of 'foreigners', but these were all Koreans and Japanese, and for me at the moment that didn't fit the bill.

That evening we sat on top of the flats with a damp warm breeze blowing up from the sea while DaiYu told me her plans.

'You know, the people here, they are only interested in money. They have no artistic soul, not like the people back home. They are so rich, but they are not happy. If you see the students in the university – they all have mobile phones and they spend all their time doing business. I want to open up an art nightclub, for foreigners and Chinese. I would put pictures on all the walls – and sell them during the day. Art is so important in life.

'There was a Frenchman, we spent a night together – it was very good! It was just the right thing for us, and in the morning we said goodbye, and that was it. I see him sometimes, he has some very interesting ideas. You should meet him.'

Next morning DaiYu and I set off into the centre of Canton and bought a one-way ticket to Hong Kong.

'See if any of your friends want to open a nightclub in Canton,' DaiYu said as a parting shot.

We hugged again, waved, and then I headed in through the 'Customs' channel.

It was only one hour from GuanZhou to Hong Kong by train; a train full of executive Chinese people and very few Westerners. During my time in Yuncheng, I'd imagined Hong Kong to be a kind of Little England, but speeding through the New Territories it was obvious that it was nothing of the kind; more like the Future China; and someday, maybe even the Future Yuncheng.

All Orion/Phoenix titles are available at your local bookshop or from the following address:

Littlehampton Book Services
Cash Sales Department L
14 Eldon Way, Lineside Industrial Estate
Littlehampton
West Sussex BN17 7HE
telephone 01903 721596, *facsimile* 01903 730914

Payment can either be made by credit card (Visa and Mastercard accepted) or by sending a cheque or postal order made payable to *Littlehampton Book Services.*
DO NOT SEND CASH OR CURRENCY.

Please add the following to cover postage and packing

UK and BFPO:
£1.50 for the first book, and 50P for each additional book to a maximum of £3.50

Overseas and Eire:
£2.50 for the first book plus £1.00 for the second book and 50p for each additional book ordered

---

BLOCK CAPITALS PLEASE

name of cardholder ....

address of cardholder ....

....

....

postcode ....

delivery address
(if different from cardholder)

....

....

....

postcode ....

☐ I enclose my remittance for £.............................

☐ please debit my Mastercard/Visa (delete as appropriate)

card number ⬚⬚⬚⬚⬚⬚⬚⬚⬚⬚⬚⬚⬚⬚⬚⬚

expiry date ⬚⬚⬚⬚

signature ....

prices and availability are subject to change without notice